Discovering the Americas

Over much of this century Canada played only a minor role in hemispheric affairs. In recent years, dramatic changes have occurred which have catapulted Canada to the role of full partner in the Americas. These include Canada's decision to enter the Organization of American States as a full member, its involvement in the NAFTA negotiations, its peacekeeping role in Central America, and its support for a process of hemispheric integration.

Discovering the Americas provides a systematic analysis of the evolution of Canadian foreign policy towards Latin America. The central thesis of the book is that changing hegemonic structures represent the most significant factor shaping Canadian policy in the region. Rochlin argues that the emergence, in the late 1980s and 1990s, of global trading blocs and the trend towards ideological convergence have opened up new opportunities for Canada in the hemisphere. Although Canadian interest in Latin America has waxed and waned over the century, Canada's role in inter-American affairs has become increasingly entrenched and is unlikely to recede.

James Rochlin is Research Fellow at the Centre for Latin American and Caribbean Studies at York University and Professor in the Department of Political Science at Okanagan University College, Kelowna, BC.

Canada and International Relations

James Rochlin

Discovering the Americas: The Evolution of Canadian Foreign Policy Towards Latin America

UBCPress / Vancouver

© UBC Press 1994
All rights reserved

ISBN 0-7748-0476-9 (hardcover)
ISBN 0-7748-0477-7 (paperback)

Canadian Cataloguing in Publication Data

Rochlin, James Francis, 1956-
  Discovering the Americas

  (Canada and international relations, ISSN 0847-0510; 8)
  Includes bibliographical references and index.
  ISBN 0-7748-0476-9 (bound). – ISBN 0-7748-0477-7 (pbk.)

1. Canada – Foreign relations – Latin America. 2. Latin
America – Foreign relations – Canada. I. Title. II. Series.
FC244.L3R63 1993   327.7108   C93-091601-8   F1029.5.L29R63 1993

Publication of this book was made possible by ongoing support from the Canada
Council, the Province of British Columbia Cultural Services Branch, and the
Department of Communications of the Government of Canada.

Set in Stone by Vancouver Desktop Publishing Centre
Printed and bound in Canada by D.W. Friesen & Sons Ltd.

UBC Press
6344 Memorial Rd
Vancouver, BC V6T 1Z2
(604) 822-3259
Fax: (604) 822-6083

To all those who have struggled for social justice in the Americas

Contents

Acknowledgments

I am indebted to a number of people who helped during the preparation of this work. Professor Liisa North provided lucid observations regarding a previous draft. I am grateful to Professor Larry Pratt for his inspiration and remarkable savvy. I am also very thankful to Peter Milroy and Jean Wilson of UBC Press for their warm encouragement and astute professionalism.

Edgar Dosman helped facilitate some of the research. Kelly Beardmore did a truly superb job as research assistant. I am grateful to the library staff at Okanagan University College, especially Anne Cossentine, Garth Homer, Faith Peyton, and Gwen Zilm. Carla Lundy provided crucial administrative assistance.

Needed support and helpful diversion came by way of Ruth, Woody, Nicky, Minnie, and Balloo. And a special thanks goes to Janice and Alan.

Research was conducted with the assistance of the Academic Relations Division of External Affairs and International Trade Canada. Generous funding was provided by the Social Sciences and Humanities Research Council of Canada, the Canadian Institute for International Peace and Security, and the Cooperative Security Competition Program.

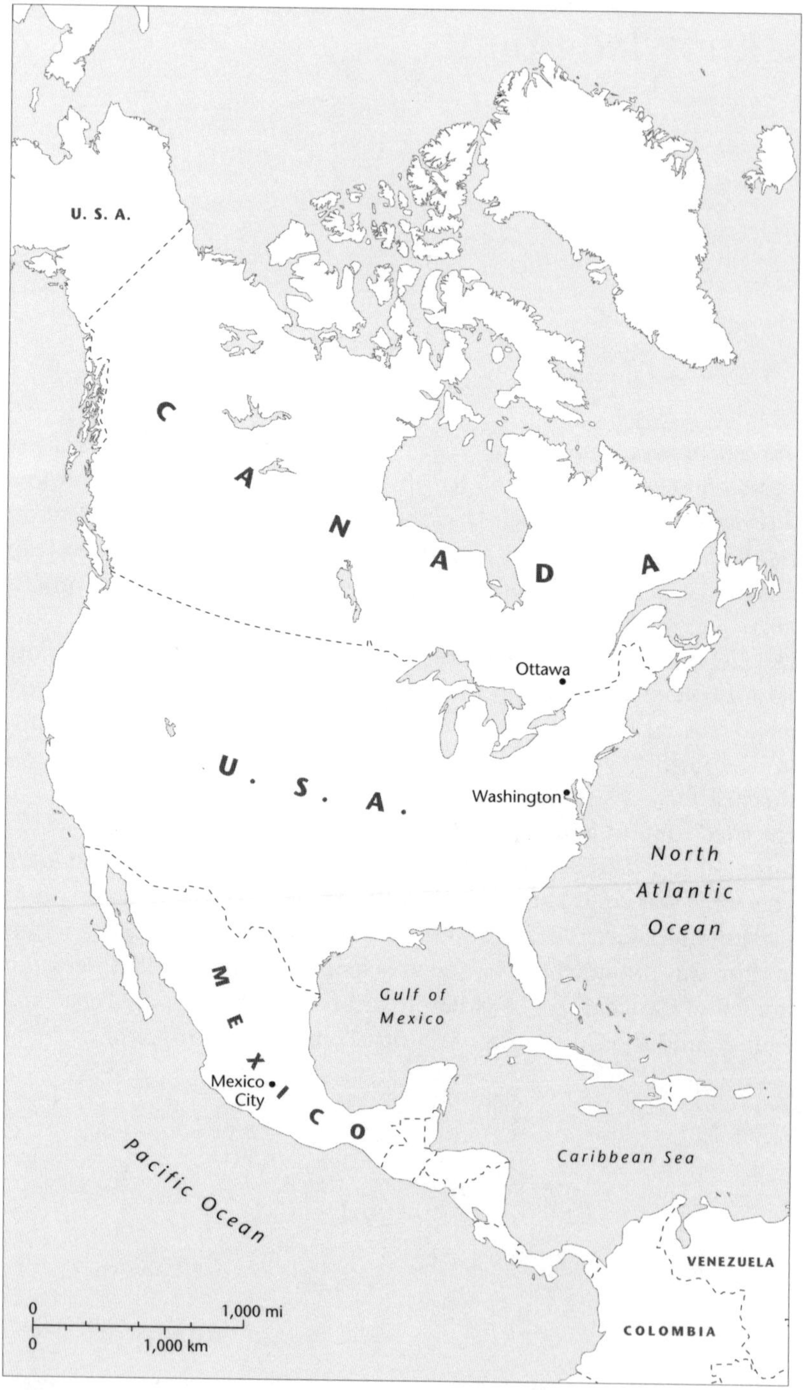
U. S. A.
CANADA
Ottawa
U. S. A.
Washington
North Atlantic Ocean
Gulf of Mexico
MEXICO
Mexico City
Caribbean Sea
Pacific Ocean
VENEZUELA
COLOMBIA
0
1,000 mi
0
1,000 km

North America

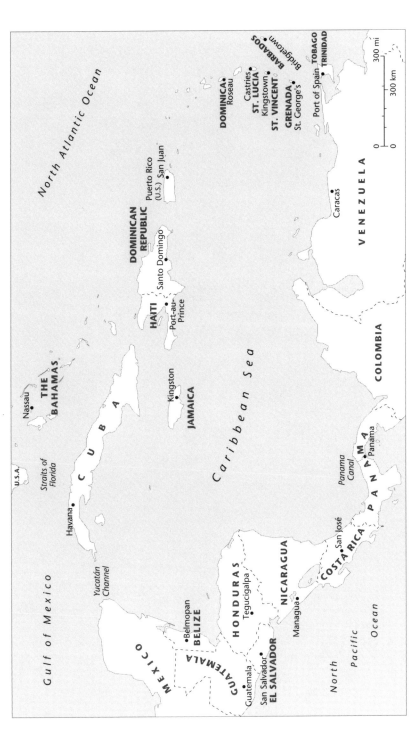

Central America

Caribbean Sea

North Atlantic Ocean

Caracas

VENEZUELA

Georgetown

Medellín

GUYANA

Paramaribo

Bogotá

SURINAME

Cayenne

COLOMBIA

FRENCH GUIANA

Quito

ECUADOR

P E R U

B R A Z I L

Lima

B O L I V I A

Brasilia

La Paz

PARAGUAY

Rio de
Janeiro

São Paulo

Asunçíon

C H I L E

A R G E N T I N A

URUGUAY

South Pacific Ocean

Santiago

Buenos
Aires

Montevideo

South Atlantic Ocean

Falkland/
Malvinas
Islands

0   1,000 mi

0   1,000 km

South America

Discovering the Americas

Introduction: Canada and Latin America

Canada is on the threshold of a new partnership with Latin America. The evolution of its new role has been fascinating, and perhaps even more interesting are the implications for future directions. Certainly the policy environment is extraordinary. Beginning in 1988-9, when research for this book commenced, it was clear that the Western Hemisphere, and the international scene generally, were witnessing something new. Drastic and incredibly rapid changes in the global arena promoted the entrenchment of Canadian interests in Latin America.

While there have been times when Canada seemed finally to discover Latin America, these episodes have usually been followed by this country's abrupt and unanticipated withdrawal. If one were to graph Canada's position in Latin America, one would behold a scribble of peaks and valleys. It now appears, however, that we have reached a high plateau, as Canada's increasingly profound role in the region seems permanent. The following pages document the evolution of this new orientation of Canada's foreign policy and examine the often controversial implications for its future development.

When presented with an overview of Canada's involvement in Latin America, one is struck by its peculiarity. In the first few decades of this century, while Canada had significant economic relations with Latin America, attempts to foster a greater political presence in the Western Hemisphere were thwarted by complications surrounding Canadian ties to both the United Kingdom and the United States. More recently, in the 1980s, Latin America received less priority in Canadian foreign policy than did Africa. And the policy which did exist during that decade was almost exclusively focused upon Central America, largely ignoring Mexico and South America.

Dramatic changes have occurred since 1988, however, and have catapulted Canada to the role of full partner in the Americas. Canada's decision to enter the Organization of American States (OAS) as a full member, its involvement in the North American Free Trade Agreement (NAFTA) negotiations, its support for a hemispheric integration process, and its important peacekeeping role in Central America, all signify an unprecedented interest in the Americas.

This book is divided into three parts, each reflecting a distinct phase of Canada's relations with Latin America. Part One traces Canadian interest in the region from the beginning of the century until the Trudeau years. It starts with a discussion of Canada's relationship with the Pan American Union (PAU), the precursor of the OAS. While the PAU itself was not particularly significant, Canada's relationship to it was a microcosm of Canadian political interests in Latin America. Canada's loyalty to the falling empire of Great Britain and Ottawa's simultaneously growing links with the U.S. set the stage for considerable complications, which, in some respects, retarded Canadian policy towards Latin America.

In retrospect, the Second World War had a profound effect on the global positioning of both Canada and Latin America. Before 1939, for example, Canada and Argentina were not dissimilar in wealth per capita, though Argentina weathered the Great Depression more successfully than its northern counterpart. In comparison to the spectacular urban and cultural environment of Buenos Aires, the Canadian cities of Toronto and Montreal, not to mention the capital city of Ottawa, were bleak provincial outposts. Argentina was also privileged by the quality of its public administration (though blighted by corruption), its position as de facto member of the British Commonwealth via its privileged trade links, and so forth.

Following the Second World War, however, Canada began a spectacular upwards curve; Argentina, in contrast, stagnated and declined. Canada became a 'minor great power' in the war and a major player in the northern associations. Latin America grew quite rapidly, but within the context of Pax Americana on the one hand and its own import substitution strategy mixed with dictatorship on the other. Then, as today, Latin America was not really a homogeneous region, though it does share some broad characteristics. For our purposes, Latin America consists of Mexico, Central America, South America, Cuba, Haiti, and the Dominican Republic. A new hegemonic era arose in the aftermath of the Second World War, a period characterized by the so-called 'Great Contest' between the U.S. and the USSR. Despite Canada's deepening economic ties with Latin America over the war years, Ottawa avoided a more profound relationship with the Americas because of its dislike of Washington's hemispheric Cold War agenda and because of the predominance of military dictatorships in the region. Despite the general shallowness of Canada's relations with Latin America in this era, there were some significant developments. For example, Ottawa formulated a view of regional development and stability that was quite distinct from Washington – one which was to guide Canadian policy for decades. This period also witnessed the beginning of Canada's important and unique relationship with Fidel Castro's Cuba.

A major watershed with respect to Canadian foreign policy occurred in the Trudeau years, and this is the subject of Part Two. Shortly after taking office in 1968, the Liberals embarked upon a major foreign policy review, which highlighted the development of a new international distribution of power. The Trudeau government observed the decline of U.S. hegemony and the development of a more multipolar world. Within this scenario, Canada formed deeper relations with Latin America in an attempt to diversify Canadian trade away from the U.S. through Trudeau's 'Third Option' formula. To some extent, nationalism in Canada and Latin America united them. Not only was there significant progress on the economic front, but there was a focus upon establishing important bilateral relations with key Latin American powers. As well, Canada's multilateral presence was advanced by its decision to join the OAS as a permanent observer.

Part Three addresses the reorientation of Canadian foreign policy, beginning with the election of Brian Mulroney in 1984. From the late 1970s to the early 1980s, it seemed as if Canada and Latin America were well on their way to establishing a more intense relationship. But the momentum quickly dissipated in the mid-1980s, halting progress that had been made economically, bilaterally, and multilaterally. The Latin American debt crisis, which emerged in 1982, as well as the recession in Canada, largely destroyed earlier commercial progress. Further, preoccupation with the important Central American crisis during the 1980s eclipsed the pursuit of what could have been equally significant bilateral relations with other states in Latin America. On the multilateral stage, Canada grew increasingly disinterested in the OAS as a result of the institution's failure to deal effectively with the profound problems facing the Americas.

By the end of this period, however, some remarkable changes had occurred. Along with the implementation of the Canada-U.S. Free Trade

Agreement in 1989 (CUSFTA), a global movement towards the creation of regional trade areas contributed to the notion of North American free trade and even a hemispheric common market. Paralleling the drift towards economic integration was Canada's decision to join the OAS as a full member, symbolizing a deeper Canadian political commitment to the rest of the Americas.

The remainder of this book discusses Canada and inter-American affairs in the 1990s. Considerable attention is devoted to hotly contested debates surrounding the NAFTA negotiations as well as to the possible establishment of a hemispheric common market. With the collapse of the Soviet Union and the end of the Cold War, the strategic agenda in Latin America is also being redefined. In the post-Cold War era, the crucial question emerges: who or what is the enemy of the inter-American system?

To tell the story of this metamorphosis of Canada's position with respect to inter-American affairs, it is useful to examine the shifting hegemonic structures and international distributions of power which have conditioned Ottawa's hemispheric policy. The term 'hegemony' is used here in the context of critical theory. The realist tradition views 'hegemony' as denoting dominance based largely upon the potential to use coercive force. By contrast, a critical-theory perspective views hegemony as a situation whereby the dominant power (which may represent an alliance including both state and non-state actors, such as transnational corporations) creates an international order based, to a large extent, upon ideological consent.[1] Furthermore, hegemony is constituted as a fit between material power (both productive and destructive), ideas, and institutions.[2]

Within this context, power arrangements associated with changing production relations are key. For example, the 'Great Contest' between the U.S. and the USSR can be viewed, at least on one level, as a contest between two productive systems: capitalism and socialism. This contest was particularly significant in Latin America and other developing regions. Furthermore, Canada's new role in hemispheric affairs in the post-Cold War era is closely related to new production arrangements. The emergence of global trade areas, the predominance of globalized production, and the concomitant rise in power of transnational capital are important in this regard.

Changing hegemonic structures may represent the most significant factor in the evolution of Canadian policy in Latin America. Canada's growing relations with the region have corresponded with shifts in the capabilities of states and blocs, with changes in ideological structures, and with the evolution of political institutions. This book will also explore how Ottawa's hemispheric policy has paralleled alterations in the world order which have corresponded to changes in state structure as well as state-society relations. All this is to say that the evolution of Canada's new role in inter-American affairs must be placed in the context of general shifts in Canadian foreign policy within a dynamic international situation. The approach adopted here fits largely within the rubric of international political economy. While international determinants of Canadian policy are crucial, there will be considerable discussion of the important role assumed by key decisionmakers in shaping Canadian relations with Latin America amidst an ever-changing global environment. As always, the issue of government leadership remains crucial.

Finally, it is worth emphasizing the complexity of the task at hand. As noted above, Latin America is extraordinarily heterogeneous, and this poses obvious limitations regarding analytical generalizations. Because this work provides an overview of Canadian policy regarding inter-American affairs, some issues are treated fleetingly (although it is hoped that the notes provide assistance for those wishing to investigate particular topics more thoroughly). And, while much of the research here has relied upon Canadian government archives, a future project might entail an investigation of Latin American, U.S., and British archives vis-à-vis the role of Canada in the inter-American system. Despite the innumerable complexities, the simple fact is that Canada is poised for a new and important orientation in hemispheric affairs. We are currently at a crucial juncture in international history, witnessing a change in global hegemonic structure. The time is ripe to reconceptualize Canada's role in Latin America, as well as the country's position in global affairs.

Part One:
Distant Neighbours

1

First Encounters

Canada's involvement in Latin America is, it might be assumed, of recent vintage. But the reverse is true. Even before the turn of the century, Canadian enterprises had established lucrative ventures in the region.[1] As Nelles and Armstrong describe it, 'Bursting with energy, capital, and confidence, Canada found itself strategically located between the technological dynamism of the United States on the one hand and the capital surplus of Great Britain on the other.'[2] Canadian companies (i.e., corporate interests) vigorously exploited those advantages, especially in finance and the operation of utilities companies in Latin America – systems for tramways, telephones, light, power, gas, and hydroelectricity (particularly in Mexico and Brazil).

Fortified by an active trade commissioners service, this commercial contact introduced Canada to a number of countries in Latin America. At this time, Canadian foreign policy was handled by the British, with Canada still being burdened by some of the state structures associated with its previous colonial status. Economic endeavours, then, preceded the development of Ottawa's political contact with Latin America.

In addition to Canada's economic interests in the region, the presence of Quebec missionaries in the region was significant. Quebec had a surplus of priests; Latin America faced an acute shortage. Thus, there was a bond between Roman Catholic Quebec and Roman Catholic Latin America. Along with formal political ties, the missionaries provided a grass-roots connection between Latin America and Canada. Furthermore, Quebec, as the principal political base for projecting the French reality in the Americas, saw the movement of priests as a reinforcement of its 'special status' as a 'Latin' region of North America. This image of a privileged cultural relationship between Quebec and Latin America became an integral and permanent feature of Canadian foreign policy.

Nevertheless, Canada's political relationship with the countries of Latin America and the Pan American Union (PAU) lacked cohesion and depth. At the bilateral level, Canada's foreign policy was officially handled by Britain a century after the Latin American countries had won their independence from Spain. While the trade connections of the British Empire undoubtedly assisted Canadian interests in certain Latin American countries, the diplomatic link was weak. Not until 1931, with the Statute of Westminster, did Canada officially gain independence in foreign policy. Ground down by the Great Depression, aggravated by serious droughts in the West, Ottawa remained passive in hemispheric relations. That scenario changed with the outbreak of the Second World War on 3 September 1939 – an event which fundamentally altered Canada by enabling it to become a significant power and which reshaped the structure of U.S.-Latin American relations.

Canada and the Pan American Union

The protracted debate over Canadian membership in the PAU serves as a helpful illustration of Canada's ambivalence towards Latin America, and as a useful tool for assessing the nature of Canadian interest in the region. Canada's commercial intercourse with the Latin American states prompted them to encourage greater Canadian participation in the inter-American system. Since 1909, for example, Latin America had urged Canada to join the PAU (one year prior to the official establishment of that institution).[3] The new hemispheric organization constructed a chair with Canada's name inscribed upon it, but it gathered dust in the basements of both the PAU and the OAS headquarters until Canada finally became active in the latter. Latin American interest in Canadian political participation in the hemisphere intensified, especially regarding the issue of membership in the PAU. Essentially, during the first four decades of the century, certain Latin American countries hoped that Canada, through its association with Britain, could help balance growing U.S. power. A list of nations formally urging Canada to join included Chile (1923), Brazil (1925 and 1941), Mexico (1928 and 1931), Argentina (1929 and 1941), and the Dominican Republic (1941) as well as a host of others.[4]

Beginning in 1925, amidst a chorus of Latin American powers which were obviously keen on Canadian membership, the U.S. attempted to investigate whether or not Canada wished to join the PAU. By 1928, it was clear that Washington opposed any attempt by Ottawa to take a seat in the organization. A memorandum by the Department of External Affairs (DEA) reveals that 'it appears that the United States delegation was instructed to oppose Canada's admission to the Pan American Union on the ground that the foreign relations of Canada were controlled by a European power, Great Britain.'[5] Supporting this view is a copy of a text of instructions to the U.S. secretary of state for the Pan American Conference of 1928, entitled 'Canada.' It read, in part: 'If colonies, possessions or dominions, whose foreign relations are controlled by European States, were represented in these conferences, the influence and policies of European powers would be injected into the discussion and disposition of questions affecting the political entities of this hemisphere.'[6] One is immediately reminded of the Monroe Doctrine, in which, as early as 1823, Washington expressed its dream of exercising hegemony over the rest of the hemisphere and its distaste for intervention by European powers in what would eventually become the so-called 'backyard' of the U.S. Despite these rather interesting manoeuvres regarding the triangle of Canada, the U.S., and the PAU, there was very little Canadian press coverage,[7] reflecting the media's lack of interest and resulting in an uninformed public.

It is striking that the U.S. assessment noted above came after the Balfour Agreement of 1926, which provided de facto autonomy for Canada in foreign policy and which would be formalized in the Statute of Westminster in 1931.[8] Furthermore, U.S. Secretary of State Kellogg indicated that President Coolidge still opposed Canadian membership in the PAU because he did 'not like the idea of the British Empire being indirectly admitted.'[9] Ambiguously, the U.S. suggested, in 1936 and again in 1938, that it was not opposed to (although not encouraging) Canadian participation in the PAU.[10]

During the mid-1930s, leaders in Quebec campaigned for closer Canadian relations with Latin America. Among them was the publisher of *Le Devoir*, Henri Bourassa, who espoused the virtues of Canadian membership in the PAU. For decades, beginning in 1915, the nationalist leader Bourassa encouraged contact between Quebec and Latin America and argued that Canada in general could benefit from closer association with its sister states in the region, as together they could attempt to neutralize any imperialist designs by the U.S.[11] In addition to Bourassa, an assortment of his Anglo compatriots in the 1930s, including Paul Martin, Agnes Macphail, and J.S. Woodsworth, also went on record favouring Canadian membership in the PAU.[12]

Latin America was simply not a major issue in Canada during most of the 1930s. Commercial interests were entrenched in well-defined areas, such as insurance and infrastructure development, but were not very significant in overall trade and investment. Nor did Latin American countries identify Canada as a major economic or diplomatic partner, despite their interest in having it in the PAU. Even for Argentina, the most powerful and advanced Latin American country at the time, Canada was principally a competitor in world markets (particularly in cereals). Government officials in Buenos Aires admired the equitable social structure of Canada, which permitted innovative agricultural and farm marketing methods, and they were impressed with the quality of Canadian public and statistical services. These were, in fact, the bases for Canada's remarkable future growth.

The Second World War Era
When the Second World War erupted in 1939, Canada was the only country in the Americas to become a belligerent. This resulted in a sense of isolation by Ottawa, which was exacerbated in September of that year when the Pan American Conference established an agreement to set a 300-mile neutrality zone around the Americas.[13] At this time, Canada's trade with Latin America was relatively small, 2 to 3 per cent of Canada's total world trade, though it had six trade missions in the region. While Canada was officially independent, all Canadian diplomatic relations in Latin America were still handled by Great Britain (outside of London and the League of Nations, Canada had only five legations worldwide in 1939). This demonstrated Canada's immaturity as an independent power and also explains, in part, the loyalty Canada felt towards the U.K. when contentious issues arose in Latin America, a point to which we shall return later.

By 1940 Ottawa had identified some clear interests in Latin America which would later encourage Canada to join the PAU. These interests were principally in the realms of security and commerce. With respect to security, in the summer of 1940 the German successes in the Low Countries and the capitulation of France prompted Ottawa to consider the possibility of a Nazi threat to the Americas. Consequently, in 1940 Canada entered into the Ogdensburg Agreement[14] with the U.S., which stipulated that Canada would assist in the defence of the northern half of the hemisphere (above the equator). The fall of France also had other implications for Canada. For example, Quebec's belief that it was responsible for exerting French cultural leadership in the

Western Hemisphere assisted in intensifying Canadian interest in Latin America.[15]

While a solid Latin American foreign policy had not yet materialized, in the 1940s Ottawa had established a clear hierarchy of regional powers deemed to be the most significant to Canada, especially economically. The top of the list was occupied by Argentina and Brazil, with Chile, Mexico, and Cuba holding positions on the second tier.[16] In 1940, Brazil and Argentina pressed for an exchange of diplomatic representation with Canada. Rio de Janeiro used the Canadian-owned Brazil Traction, Light and Power Company[17] to persuade Ottawa to open a diplomatic mission in Brazil, which it hoped would result in further investment. Argentina, with Canada ranking as its third largest trading partner at the time, also pressed for an exchange of diplomatic representation. On Ottawa's side, there were hopes that Canada's trade deficit with the U.S. and the subsequent shortage of U.S. dollars could perhaps be alleviated by closer economic and political relations with Latin America.

There were also proposals to form an inter-American economic cartel led by the U.S. and designed to absorb surplus products, which could not be purchased by a war-torn Europe. Hence, economic, strategic, and ideological concerns motivated the argument for the establishment of Canadian diplomatic representation in Latin America. It was also felt that a greater Canadian role in the region could help forestall any proclivity towards totalitarianism – a feeling that grew as the war developed.[18]

Thus, amidst other developments, in 1940 Canada began to appreciate the potential economic significance of Latin America. The region offered new sources of strategic minerals, and, equally important, it offered an alternative market for Canadian products. As a result of these potentialities, the Canadian minister of trade and commerce organized a trade mission to tour Latin America. That mission was ill-fated, however, as a result of the illness of the minister at Cristobal, and it was subsequently postponed.[19]

The trade mission resumed in 1941, led by Minister of Trade and Commerce James MacKinnon, and succeeded in fostering commercial opportunities and promoting increased contact between Canada and Latin America. Trade agreements were reached with Chile, Argentina, Brazil, Uruguay, and Ecuador. These accomplishments were accompanied by other attempts to establish broader relations between Canada and its Latin American counterparts. The Canadian Broadcasting Corporation, the National Film Board of Canada, and the Canadian Information

Service launched efforts to facilitate Canadian-Latin American contact.[20] The trip also coincided with the opening of Canadian legations in Brazil, Argentina, and, in the following year, Chile.[21] Also, it was during this period that President Roosevelt urged Canada to extend its diplomatic representation in Latin America as part of the 'struggle between the forces of totalitarianism and the forces of democracy.'[22]

It is significant that the trade mission, in a memorandum to the prime minister, argued that 'the important and useful role which Canada can play in the international politics of this hemisphere is as interpreter and mediator between the United States and Latin America and between the United States and Great Britain in Latin America.'[23] Throughout this century, in discussions of Ottawa's potential contribution to conflict resolution in the Western Hemisphere, the notion of Canada as a mediator has been a recurrent theme.[24]

In 1941, the Canadian trade mission recommended that Canada join the PAU 'immediately.'[25] But it also identified a related issue which would haunt Ottawa when the topic of the PAU, and then the OAS, arose. 'If Canada joined the Pan American Union a solid or almost solid bloc of Latin American states would attempt to use Canada as a makeweight against the United States.'[26] Thus, there were early hints that, while there might be certain benefits derived from Canadian participation in hemispheric international organizations, there would also be costs. Not the least of these would be the likelihood of Ottawa being caught in the crossfire between the U.S. and Latin America.[27]

Overall, commercial opportunities and security concerns quickly led to greater Canadian awareness and appreciation of Latin America after 1939. By 1941 – with the Ogdensburg Agreement signed, new diplomatic relations in Latin America established, regional trade agreements reached, and cultural contacts made – the DEA declared that 'the people of Canada were, with few exceptions, ready to approve any action that would lead to closer relations between this country and the Latin American states.'[28] One prominent manifestation of these 'closer relations' was to be Canada's attempt to join the PAU.

By this point, Canada had balanced the arguments for and against joining the institution. On the negative side, staunch loyalists to the U.K. worried that, by pursuing options which drew it more tightly into the Americas, Canada would find itself dangerously integrated with the U.S. Others argued that Canada should focus upon its membership in the Commonwealth, where it and other members enjoyed protective tariffs. And there was the enduring fear that joining the PAU would mean Canada would find itself unhappily caught up in battles involving the U.S. and Latin America. On the other hand, membership in the PAU would help muster Latin American resistance to Axis powers, could augment economic opportunities in the region,[29] and might even enhance the friendship between Canada and the U.S.[30] (the latter, as it turned out, was a misplaced hope).

DEA documents reveal that in 1941 'Canada [would be] prepared to accept an invitation to join the Pan American Union [as a full member]'[31] and would be sponsored by Brazil. But suddenly and, at first, inexplicably, the U.S. voiced its discontent with Ottawa's apparent intention to join the organization. In a preliminary step, in 1941, Washington opposed Canadian participation at a meeting of the foreign ministers of the PAU. The DEA observed that

> it was immediately ascertained that the Government of the United States ... had completely reversed the attitude that had previously been adopted by the United States in relation to the proposal that Canada should seek membership in the Pan American Union. This reversal was as complete as it was unexpected, and it was not accompanied by any explanation that could be seriously accepted.[32]

The U.S. had claimed that if the matter were to come to a vote, foreign ministers from the PAU would oppose Canadian participation. That excuse appeared to have little factual basis, however. By 1941, supporters of Canadian membership in the PAU included Argentina, Brazil, Chile, Colombia, Bolivia, Ecuador, Peru, Honduras, the Dominican Republic, Nicaragua, Panama, Haiti, Paraguay, Uruguay, Guatemala, and Mexico.[33] Only three states appeared 'uncertain' about Canadian membership – Costa Rica, Cuba, and El Salvador.[34]

What, then, was the real motivation behind Washington's opposition to Canadian participation in the PAU? The Brazilian foreign minister revealed to Canadian officials that the U.S. acting secretary of state, Sumner Welles, had indicated that Washington opposed Canadian membership in the PAU on three grounds: (1) Canada represented a mouthpiece for British interests; (2) Canada was viewed as a potentially dangerous competitor for markets in Latin America; and (3) the U.S. did not want Canada to claim the same concessions that were offered to South American countries.[35] Regarding the first point, according to the Brazilian foreign minister, an 'important official of the U.S. Government' told the Brazilian minister of finance: 'We in the United

States will not permit Canada to enter the Union as long as she remains the straw man of England.'[36]

It was obvious that, although Latin America welcomed an increased role by Canada in the inter-American system, the impact of war had vastly extended U.S. powers in the Western Hemisphere – Pax Americana was on the horizon. American opposition to Canadian involvement in the PAU appeared to sour Canadian-U.S. relations, especially with respect to inter-American organizations.[37] From Ottawa's perspective, it exemplified Washington's descent into 'secret and dishonest diplomacy.'[38] This blunt evaluation was not made public at the time. Prime Minister King told the House of Commons that 'there have been times quite recently when we might have expected invitations [to join the PAU] but were given reasons why it would not be advisable to have an invitation extended. That position still exists to a certain extent, for reasons which I cannot explain publicly.'[39]

It is ironic that, despite U.S. opposition to Canada joining the PAU, Washington viewed Ottawa as increasingly converging with its political agenda in Latin America. Indicative of this, the U.S. secretary of state, Dean Acheson, pointed to 'the similarity of interests between the two Governments in post-war economic policy and ... their collaboration for mutual aid in defense and economic matters.'[40] On the other hand, it appears that there was some basis for U.S. fears regarding Canadian support for the U.K. in Latin America, which was the main source of U.S. concern about Canada joining the PAU. Throughout the 1940s, Vincent Massey (of the Office for the High Commission of Canada in London) was critical of the U.S. and argued for a renewed focus upon Canadian ties with Britain. While Massey may not have represented a majority view, his voice was important. Regarding the balance of power in the Americas, he wrote:

> It would not be in the interests of Canada that British political and economic influence in Latin America should be eliminated or even weakened, and that the United States should be without rival in that part of the world. On the contrary, it appears desirable that British influence should remain relatively strong in Latin America as a makeweight to what promises to be an overwhelming United States preponderance, so that if at any time United States commercial policy should assume an exclusive character, Canada would be able to count on the support of the United Kingdom in defending her own position.[41]

Not only did highly placed components of the Canadian political bureaucracy prefer a balance between the U.K. and the U.S. in Latin America, Canada believed that Latin Americans did as well. 'The countries of Latin America fear too complete economic and political domination by the United States. They therefore show, in varying degrees, a desire to use Great Britain, and to a lesser extent Canada, as counterweights to the United States.'[42] This is an obvious example of balance of power theory.

It is also apparent that certain Canadian analyses of the determinants of U.S. policy in Latin America would not have pleased Washington. Vincent Massey argued, for example, that there existed

> a tendency of the United States Government to give way to pressure from business interests in their policy in South America. Can we, in fact, be altogether sure, particularly in view of powerful forces in the United States which lean towards imperialism, that United States policy in Latin America will always give full consideration to the legitimate interests of other countries, including our own?[43]

The tone of this analysis surely would have set alarm bells ringing in Washington.

Compounding those worries, Massey seemed to be echoing what the British themselves had thought of U.S. policy in the Americas, as the following excerpt from an official memorandum from the British Foreign Office demonstrates.

> Relations with the United States constitute the biggest long-term problem facing us in Latin America. Whether or not there is in theory room for the two Powers in the sub-continent, the imperialistic pressure of big business, if not of the United States Government, will inevitably place us on the defensive and force us to defend our position in so far as is consistent with maintaining those general relations with the United States which the war and post-war situations dictate. In the main the problem is a post-war one.[44]

London expected that Canada would do its bidding in the Western Hemisphere on both bilateral and multilateral levels. Bilaterally, Ottawa could come in handy, in Cuba for example, by establishing closer relations with the island. This would neutralize the U.S.'s 'rapidly increasing control ... of Cuba's foreign trade, regarding which there [were] signs of resentment.'[45] British officials also encouraged Canadian diplomats to pressure Ottawa into joining the PAU, since Canada could then represent U.K. interests in the Americas.[46] But London's plans were thwarted by Washington's opposition to Canadian membership for the usual reasons.[47] Thus, Canada seemed to find itself in the rather difficult position of being caught between its alliance to a declining power and its growing attachment to a rising hegemon.

Much of the conflict between the U.S. and the U.K. during the early 1940s seemed to centre around Argentina, Brazil, and the alleged U.S. domination of these markets. The conflict between the two powers in Brazil (considered the jewel of the region) was described as 'grave' in what was then a secret memorandum from a Canadian diplomat.[48] Washington and London also quarrelled over the appropriate way to handle the fascist government in Argentina.[49] Canada, too, was worried about Argentine nationalism, its anti-U.S. spirit, and its proclivity towards the Axis powers.[50] What was Canada to do regarding concerns it shared with both the U.K. and the U.S., but on which those powers could not see eye to eye? Influenced by the warfare which tarnished the period, Canadian diplomats borrowed strategic terminology to analyze their dilemma.

> Canadian policy can also be expressed in military terms: it is to try to keep out of the line of fire. There is no reason why Canada, an innocent bystander, should deliberately run the danger of getting hurt in Anglo-American skirmishes or battles in Latin America. But if firing breaks out between the British and the Americans in Latin America there is grave danger that Canada may get hit by a stray shot. Canada, therefore, has a direct interest in trying to reduce to a minimum the chances of firing breaking out.[51]

With respect to the Brazilian problem, the rational solution, according to Canada, was for the U.K. to retain its absolute share of prewar Brazilian business and for the U.S. to absorb the spoils of Brazil's economic growth. Thus, 'United Kingdom economic interests in Latin America would dwindle relatively but not absolutely.'[52]

Implicit in this solution is Canadian acceptance of U.S. dominance, both economically and politically, in Latin America. This was largely because, with Britain and other European powers devastated by the

Second World War, the U.S. was the only power capable of exporting badly needed capital to the region while at the same time remaining militarily strong.[53] The U.S. could also build upon its established momentum in Latin America, which had begun in the previous century. Ottawa seemed intent upon establishing a soft landing for the British, while recognizing that the wind was clearly blowing towards U.S. hegemony in the Americas.

With the Japanese attack at Pearl Harbor on 7 December 1941, geopolitical rivalry in Latin America was redefined. Now that the U.S. was formally at war, its crusading zeal quickly became Napoleonic. Having sat back and watched comfortably from the sidelines as Canada and Britain fought Nazi Germany virtually alone, Washington suddenly demanded knee-jerk Latin American obedience to its self-proclaimed role as 'leader of the free world.' Brazil's foreign minister, Itamaraty, immediately saw the inevitability of a Pax Americana in the postwar era. Not only did Brazil quickly declare war on Germany, it also committed land forces in Italy. Brazil was rewarded for its loyalty by U.S. recognition and by massive wartime and postwar financial assistance.

In contrast, Argentina diverged from U.S. wishes and, with the support of the British (who feared a disruption of beef shipments), maintained neutrality. Enraged by its stubbornness, the U.S. waged economic warfare upon Argentina, isolating it both globally and regionally. Indeed, this latter dimension – particularly the termination of the October 1940 Brazil-Argentina Free Trade Agreement (which presaged a similar accord forty-six years later) – was a particularly serious blow to future cooperation between these Latin American countries. The British link with Argentina and Brazil was no longer a viable counterweight to U.S. power and influence.

Canada had now to clarify its own future in the Americas. One result was a 1942 review of the national interest in Latin America – the first of many similar postwar exercises. Canada's objectives were identified as: (1) the establishment and maintenance of cordial relations with Latin American countries; (2) an effort to foster harmonious relations between the U.K. and the U.S. in the midst of the 'grave' conflicts between them; (3) an attempt to rally countries of Latin America to defeat the Axis powers during the war; (4) support for U.S. efforts to bring economic prosperity to Latin America, largely as a result of strategic considerations; and (5) the protection and the increase of Canadian investment and commercial interests in Latin America.[54] While some of these interests naturally changed over time, they are important in that they represent an initial attempt by Ottawa to define Canadian objectives in the Americas.

Also with regard to national interests, especially in the long term, some Canadians were concerned about the development of regionalism in Latin America and argued that Ottawa should do its utmost to prevent it. Paul Martin, minister of national health and welfare, opposed the position of Latin Americans who wished to establish the Economic Commission for Latin America (ECLA) to operate in a parallel fashion with the United Nations (U.N.).

> We are concerned lest in the future regionalism and regional autarchy play the dangerous role which nationalism and national autarchy have played in recent years. A wall that is built around a number of countries in a single area of the world can constitute no less a barrier to the well-being and prosperity of the world at large than a wall built around the boundaries of a single state.[55]

Overall, in terms of Ottawa's priorities, Latin America still ranked considerably below Europe. There were a number of reasons for this. First, Canada looked forward to the economic opportunities associated with rebuilding postwar Europe, an area in which it had deep historical ties. As well, Ottawa felt it knew little about the Latin Americans, and, coupled with this sense of strangeness, Canada harboured no illusions about competing economically with the U.S. in 'its' region.[56]

By 1943, Ottawa was committed to the development of an independent hemispheric foreign policy, that is, one that would not be viewed as mimicking that of the U.S. or the U.K..[57] Beyond that, and the establishment of general interests noted above, Canada still lacked concrete, coherent plans for Latin America in the imminent postwar era. A Canadian diplomatic representative in Brazil lamented the absence of a postwar foreign policy for what had been deemed the second greatest power in the Western Hemisphere.[58] The diplomat was concerned that when and if plans were finally formulated, Canada would be disadvantaged by having to contend with the enormous and growing influence of the U.S. in Brazil (similar concerns were raised by Canada's ambassador to Mexico during this period). From the Canadian perspective, growing American power in Brazil was a product of such factors as significant amounts of U.S. developmental assistance, U.S. strategic connections (including the establishment of a military base), and the effects of a $10 million per year U.S. propaganda machine.[59] The presence of Brazilian monetary debts also provided the U.S. with mounting influence.[60] Facilitating all this was the fact that it was the world's leading capital exporter. These elements foreshadowed the array of mechanisms whereby the U.S. would attempt to exert its power in the region over the next decades.[61]

Ironically, the same elements which were viewed as a source of American strength also served as a source of weakness, at least in the eyes of Canadian diplomats in Rio de Janeiro. Brazilians allegedly resented the U.S. for its brash manifestations of power. The typically understated Canadians, therefore, could benefit from Canada's role as an alternative industrialized country, which the Brazilians could tap into – if only it would develop a coherent and inviting foreign policy. American policy could also backfire in other ways, according to a Canadian diplomat in Brazil.

> The animosity which is being engendered in his [Brazilian] mind towards the United States throws into sharp relief his recollection of the pleasant relations he used to have with German and Italian exporters and he looks forward to a resumption of these relationships. Galling, as it may sometimes be, I can only feel that we are fortunate that the United States insisted on taking the lead here, but it appears that their tastelessness and bullying may drive Brazil back to Germany and Italy after the War.[62]

Obviously, there existed important distinctions between American and Canadian points of view.

The seemingly undying issue of whether or not Canada should join the PAU arose again in 1943, at least at the level of political elites. In that year and stretching into the following one, among those favouring membership were Quebec nationalists and the Co-operative Commonwealth Federation (CCF). The Liberals were split, with the Progressive Conservatives being generally opposed. Those who did not support Canadian membership tended to distrust U.S. imperial ambitions in the hemisphere.[63] Ottawa also fretted over what it regarded as a tendency by the U.S. to overlook collective decisions reached by international organizations.[64] Beyond that, a poll taken in 1944 indicated that 72 per cent of Canadians had never heard of the PAU, and so the issue was not exactly a burning one in the domestic Canadian political scene.[65]

But now, internationally, the tables began to turn. Although Ottawa was generally dubious about the PAU, Washington at last warmed up to the idea of Canadian membership. In 1944, with the U.K. in ruins, the U.S. finally became comfortable with the idea of Canada joining the PAU – that is, the possibility of Canada representing British interests no longer appeared threatening. In October of that year, the State Department offered a policy recommendation in support of Canadian membership in the hemispheric organization.[66]

The year 1944 witnessed significant improvement in Canadian diplomatic representation in Latin America. While in 1941 legations were opened in key countries, in 1944 some of these were elevated to the status of embassy. Canadian ambassadors were appointed to Brazil and Mexico, and diplomatic relations were established with Peru. The DEA noted that this was 'part of a general expansion of Canadian representation in Latin America during the turbulent war years and was based not only on the development of Inter-American trade but also on the conviction that a closer understanding between hemispheric neighbours was necessary to the solution of common problems during the war.'[67] Regarding the Canadian-Mexican relationship, it was primarily motivated by trade and strategic considerations. Canada particularly appreciated Mexico's cooperation in war efforts. Such considerations were underscored when 'Marshall Stalin acknowledged the strategic geographical and political position of Mexico,' and when Ottawa considered the consequences of a hypothetical situation whereby 'the Mexican government [became] sympathetic to adverse influences such as the Argentine.'[68] With the Axis powers representing the major adversary in the early and mid-1940s, and with the USSR emerging as the enemy superpower after 1945, Canada began to ponder the consequences of the region south of the Rio Grande falling into hostile hands. It was communism that perhaps represented the greatest threat, as a result of Mexico's inequitable division of wealth, with the majority of the population having insufficient access to food, shelter, education, health care, etc.[69]

In contrast to fortified relations with Mexico and Brazil, Canada's relations with Argentina remained turbulent in 1944. According to the Canadian prime minister, Argentina's alleged sympathy towards Axis powers in 1943 and early 1944 has 'caused considerable anxiety, both to her neighbours in the Western Hemisphere and to the United Nations ... This concern [was] provoked by the need for solidarity in the Western Hemisphere against Axis intrigues and by the importance of Argentina as a source of foodstuffs and important raw materials for the United Nations.'[70] Canada and other Allied nations viewed the official rupture between Argentina and the Axis powers in January 1944 as a positive development. But shifts within the Argentine government in February of that year, which resulted in the installation of officials sympathetic to Axis powers, again alienated both the U.S. and later Canada.[71] This prompted Ottawa to place relations with Argentina on hold and retarded plans for the opening of a Canadian embassy, which originally was to parallel the opening of the Brazilian one in 1944.

With the crushing defeat of the Axis powers, a new world order emerged – one with military, economic, and ideological implications. With fascism no longer representing a threat, Canada now felt comfortable boosting its legation in Buenos Aires to embassy status. Argentina, according to the DEA, was now to be 'judged by her current conduct' rather than by dredging up unpleasant aspects of the past.[72]

Although the fascist threat dissipated, a new ideological contest was to emerge in the form of Western competition with the other emergent superpower, the USSR. The global political arena would be dominated for the next four decades by the 'Great Contest' between capitalism and communism, with the U.S. and the USSR representing poles around which subordinate states would orient themselves.[73] This contest was amplified in developing countries, such as those in Latin America, whose societies were often rife with social inequities, and which were characteristically divided as to the most appropriate path to politico-economic development. Thus, it was necessary for Canada to concoct its own policy regarding Third World development as well as towards the conflict between capitalism and communism in Latin America.

Canada's chargé d'affaires in Chile offered a lucid analysis of the forces that would promote communism in Latin America during the postwar era.

Semi-feudal countries are an easy prey for Communist infiltration through the awakening of the masses to political life. While it would be difficult to envisage the spreading of Communism on a large scale in countries like the United States and Canada, where the majority consists of middle class people and the wealth is more or less evenly distributed, the picture is entirely different when we are faced with a country where the wealth is accumulated in very few hands, and the great majority has little or nothing to live on. Such a state of affairs lasts as long as the majority has no way of expressing itself, but has to change, sometimes by revolution, when the lower classes become politically conscious.[74]

Thus, the prospects for communism in Latin America, from the Canadian perspective, were primarily dependent upon indigenous inequities rather than on foreign (i.e., Soviet) adventurism. Similarly, in 1944 the Canadian ambassador to Moscow noted: 'I should be surprised to find that the Soviet Government would consider the present or the immediate post-war period suitable for exerting that influence they are in a position to exercise on developments in those Latin American countries ripe for political change.'[75] This contrasts sharply with some American analyses, which point to the intervention of the USSR as the primary instigator of socialist or communist uprisings.[76]

Canadian analyses suggested that if Moscow did indeed enjoy close relations with Latin American countries, it would not be the Soviets who served as the catalyst for such a phenomenon, but instead would be a product of the manoeuvring of the indigenous 'lower classes to associate themselves with the more advanced political forces, wherever they may be and under whatever name they may be known, to combat their political opponents.'[77] Furthermore, Canadian diplomats suggested that the U.S. itself might be partly responsible for Latin America's drift towards the Left, due to Washington's failure to draw proper distinctions between 'communism, nationalism, and avoidance [by Latins] of economic penetration by the United States.'[78]

Although there were salient strategic and ideological concerns, it was clearly commercial interests which dominated the early postwar years. Canada had to choose which global areas to focus upon during this period. Although it could rely upon its traditional North Atlantic market, with opportunities emerging from the reconstruction of Europe, Canadian diplomatic personnel argued that this might prove to be short-sighted. In a prophetic analysis written at the end of 1945, which correctly predicted trends that would animate Canadian policy half a century later, Canada's ambassador to Mexico, H.L. Keenleyside, arrived at the following conclusions:

Traditional markets [in Europe] will not meet Canadian export needs in the future and must be supplemented by the development of new outlets. New markets like Mexico can be developed today with a fraction of the effort that will be needed to switch them to Canadian goods later if we leave them to the Americans now. If we don't take advantage of these opportunities now we can whistle for the Mexican market when competition becomes stronger or a new depression hits the trading world.[79]

Thus, the traditional North Atlantic market might eventually fade, and Canada was now well placed to take advantage of the glimmering opportunities foreseen in Latin America. This could be accomplished by 'a relatively small deduction' from Canadian exports to the U.S., the U.K., and other traditional markets.[80] Tremendous growth in the Mexican market was forecast over the next twenty-five years, and Canada's ambassador to Mexico argued that if Ottawa did not vigorously promote commercial activity the U.S. would entrench itself and make it difficult for Canadians to compete.[81] One senses the Canadian ambassador's frustration, which was directed principally at Ottawa but also at Canadian business, which was often too conservative to veer away from the traditional markets of yesteryear.

In 1946 Canada's trade minister, James MacKinnon, launched an ambitious trade mission to Latin America – a mission which aimed to increase Canadian exports to the region to ten times their 1939 levels.[82] A first-ever trade agreement with Mexico,[83] which initiated reciprocal most-favoured-nation (MFN) status and which reduced tariffs, was expected to increase Canadian exports to that country twentyfold in the short term, from $3 million in 1939 to $60 million by 1949.[84] If that could be achieved, it would spell intensified competition among Canada, the U.K., and, especially, the U.S. for the Mexican market and, perhaps, for Latin American markets in general.[85] Between 1939 and 1945, Canadian exports doubled from about $20 million to $40 million, while imports more than quadrupled from $16 million to $67 million (much of this being made up of wartime oil imports).[86]

In 1947 the issue of the PAU again became prominent, this time against the backdrop of the question of how deeply Canada would attempt to integrate itself in inter-American affairs. In that year and beyond, the weightiest elements of the Canadian government and the business community opposed membership in the PAU, as well as the Organization of American States (formed in 1948). Arguments were launched that these institutions were limited as meaningful international organizations due to the overwhelming influence of the U.S.[87] Ottawa wondered what could be gained by joining a political body apparently dominated by one power. And surely, the allegedly dishonest manner in which the U.S. had handled Canada during earlier attempts to join the PAU must have added to Ottawa's hesitation.

In 1947 Lester Pearson argued against Canada joining the PAU, basing his argument on a rationale that would also be applicable to Canadian membership in the soon-to-be-formed OAS.

> I think myself that the most important argument against joining the Pan American Union is that air transport has completely altered Canada's geographic position vis-à-vis other countries. We are now, of course, closer to Holland and Denmark and Norway than we are to Chile and the Argentine, and our political affinity is certainly as great with those countries as with Latin American dictatorships. It might well, therefore, be argued that for Canada a northern union of democratic states would be of greater value and interest than association with Ecuador, Bolivia, Venezuela, etc.[88]

Two significant points emerge here with respect to Canada's relations with Latin America in the immediate postwar period. First, Canada primarily embarked upon a North Atlantic orientation. Economic, cultural, and political similarities between Canada and Europe, and all the prospects associated with reconstructing that continent, led Ottawa to concentrate on it at the expense of other parts of the globe. Second, the dictatorial nature of some Latin American states, in conjunction with a 'strangeness' assigned to, and a general Canadian ignorance of, the region contributed to Ottawa's focus away from Latin America.

While Canada's diplomatic corps could not agree on the matter of the PAU,[89] the majority seemed to disfavour association with the body. In addition to points mentioned above, there were other reasons for Canada to avoid membership in the organization. Since the U.S. was obviously the dominant player in the region and in the PAU, Ottawa was concerned about what it considered to be a U.S. tendency to equate Latin American nationalism with Soviet-led communism.[90] Thus, with escalating tension between Washington and Moscow, Canada feared being immersed in a cold war contest in Latin America. These Canadian fears were heightened, as Ottawa detected rising anti-American sentiment in Latin America, in Argentina, for example.[91]

There were other reasons why Canada no longer wanted to join a postwar hemispheric organization, especially the OAS, which was established on 2 May 1948. Given that the OAS represented a regional U.S. bulwark against the Soviet Union in the nascent Cold War,[92] Canada was concerned that joining it would also require signing the Rio Treaty, which could potentially involve Canadians in active hemispheric defence.[93] At the inception of the OAS, it was more or less expected that organization members also sign the treaty. It was not until much later that OAS membership would be possible without entailing the signing of this treaty. At any rate, through a unilateral move by the Inter-American Conference for the Maintenance of Continental Peace and Security held in 1947, Canada was included in the territory to be defended by the Rio Treaty.[94]

Perhaps the most eloquent argument against Canada joining the OAS came in the form of a lengthy article by Vincent Massey. For him, Canada shared a cultural and political disposition with Europe, in contrast to the non-democratic region of Latin America.[95] He criticized the tendency throughout the Americas to remain neutral at the beginning of the Second World War, in contrast to Canada's position as a belligerent.[96] Furthermore, Canada could more fruitfully pursue trade through bilateral relations with Latin American states, rather than through the OAS. Canada's defence commitment in the region was initiated by the Ogdensburg Agreement of 1940, which, on 12 February 1947, was extended into the postwar period.[97] Thus, Canada already had a commitment to hemispheric defence, at least as far south as the equator. Therefore, alienated from Latin America, culturally and politically, with Canada's real interests defined in Western Europe and in the U.S., and with prominent interests in Latin America which could be cultivated bilaterally, Massey arrived at the conclusion that it was wise to steer clear of the OAS and to avoid immersing Canada in what he viewed to be irrelevant problems.[98]

In 1948, Canada continued to avoid membership in ECLA. Canadians viewed it as a duplication of the OAS, which promoted regionalism at the expense of globalism. Besides, it would have been awkward for Canada to join ECLA without joining the OAS, and Ottawa felt it was prudent to avoid membership in both.[99]

Conclusion

These early years may be deemed the 'wonder years' of Canadian foreign policy, as they witnessed Canada's evolution from having its foreign policy controlled by Britain to charting its own course in world affairs. Certainly, this metamorphosis found expression in Canadian relations with Latin America, as Ottawa began to appreciate its interest in the region as well as the complications entailed in concocting a coherent foreign policy south of the Rio Grande.

Canada officially received its autonomy from the U.K., with respect to foreign policy, in 1931, and, as it developed a maturing diplomatic corps and created its own embassies, it found this new independence to be, at times, rather confusing. With respect to Latin America in particular, Ottawa would now have to weigh competing domestic aspirations vis-à-vis the global arena. French Canadians were generally much more ambitious than were English Canadians in their efforts to foster closer ties with Latin America. There were also splits among the country's federal parties. As well, Ottawa would have to contend with a diplomatic assembly which did not converge on the issue of how to handle Latin America, especially in terms of economic policy and the question of the PAU. All of this must be placed within the context of Latin America demanding closer Canadian attention. Shifts in the structure of the Canadian state, which presided over divergent domestic forces, then, represent an important analytical consideration here.

At this time, Canada was undergoing important changes in its industrial structure and global economic status. Since 1939, Canada had become one of the world's leading industrial producers. This translated into a search for new markets and new economic relationships, which found an outlet in Latin America. With Europe increasingly devastated by war, Canada required fresh targets for its bloated productive capacity. The post-1939 period also challenged Ottawa to define a new economic relationship with the region once the war was over. Would Canada cling to its traditional markets in Europe and the U.S., or would it follow the advice of its diplomats in Mexico, Brazil, and elsewhere, who argued that the time was ripe to seize the Latin American market before the U.S. completely dominated it?

While changes in state structure and production capabilities affected Canadian interests in Latin America, it was obvious that upheavals in the world order were also important. The decline of the U.K. as a global leader ultimately meant a new set of allegiances for Canada. In particular, it meant a stronger relationship to the emerging hegemony of the U.S. Canada, still loyal to Britain and the Commonwealth, endeavoured to cushion the U.K.'s fall in Latin America, but would be increasingly affected by U.S. interests.

Canada fought the fascist challenge in Europe earlier than its counterparts in the Western Hemisphere, and it also took exception to Axis leanings on the part of Latin America, particularly Argentina. In efforts to ward off the Axis threat, Ottawa signed the Ogdensburg Agreement, a defence arrangement covering the Americas down to the equator. But with the defeat of Germany and its associates came the ascendance of a great power other than the U.S. In the postwar period, Canada now found its global and hemispheric enemy to be the Soviet Union, although it viewed this adversary with less enmity than did the U.S.

Shifts in the world order correlated with new patterns of ideological concerns. While Canada's commitment to liberal democracy and capitalism remained consistent, global ideological challenges changed from fascism/corporatism associated with Germany's hegemonic bid to the forces of communism associated with the emergence of the USSR after 1945. Hence, while fascism initially represented the ideological enemy for Canada in Latin America, especially in Argentina, the next enemy would be Soviet-style communism. This challenge represented a great threat, from the Canadian perspective, since diplomats and analysts seem to have believed that the social and economic inequities rampant in the region rendered the communist ideal appealing in many quarters of Latin America. Hence, this period marked the beginning of the Great Contest between the global forces of capitalism and communism. While Canada's commitment to capitalism remained unquestioned, even in this early period Canada distinguished itself ideologically from the U.S., since it believed that Washington too often mistakenly associated nationalism, socialism, and anti-Americanism with allegiance to Soviet communism. This distinction would intensify as the Cold War period progressed.

Canada's relationship with the PAU epitomized Canadian interests and dilemmas in Latin America. Latin American powers took the lead in requesting and establishing political and diplomatic relations with Canada, dating back to the year prior to the formation of the PAU. While Canada benefited from economic relations with the region, it was hesitant to develop political contacts. At first, Canada was not functionally independent and, therefore, could not accept overtures to join the PAU in the 1920s and earlier. Once independent, however, the U.S. was fearful of Canada's capacity for representing British interests in Washington's 'backyard' and, therefore, blocked its membership in the institution.

It was only after the British collapse during the Second World War that the U.S. was comfortable with Canada's presence at the PAU. By this time, however, Canada doubted the value of an organization which it viewed as unacceptably dominated by the U.S. Canada subscribed to traditional balance-of-power theory and worried about the flagrant imbalance apparent in the organization. Canada was also concerned with the regional focus of the PAU, at a time when Ottawa believed that globalism was the correct path to international peace and security. A more appealing global institution was the United Nations, and this was the focus of Canadian policy in the immediate postwar period.

The first four decades of this century marked the beginning of Canadian political relations with Latin America, relations which often coincided with existing economic interests in the region. While Latin America was never accorded the status that Europe possessed in terms of Canadian foreign policy interests, this period nevertheless would lead to an appreciation of hemispheric affairs that would heighten decades later in the Trudeau era, and even more so in the 1980s and 1990s.

2

The Cold War: Diverging Paths

The Cold War laid the foundations for Canadian relations with Latin America. Despite contradictions and differences among policymakers and diplomats, throughout the 1945-67 period successive governments in Ottawa established an overall policy framework incorporating both security and developmental dimensions. It has proven surprisingly resilient and has carved out a position quite distinct from that in Washington. This chapter focuses on the 1945-58 period.

Although Ottawa and Washington shared many major political goals in the Western Hemisphere, they often disagreed as to the appropriate means to achieve them, thus precipitating a major distinction between U.S. and Canadian policy. Canada often had analyses of Latin American political turmoil and revolution which were clearly independent of those emanating from Washington. It is important to emphasize, however, that Ottawa's primary foreign policy focus during this time remained the North Atlantic generally, and in the realm of international organizations, the North Atlantic Treaty Organization (NATO) and the U.N.

Perhaps of greater importance, the Cold War epoch defined Canada as a charter member of the 'northern club,' while Latin America, including the advanced Southern Cone countries, became defined as members of the 'Third World.' Canada emerged from the Second World War as a privileged haven for investors. If, before 1939, Canada and the major Latin American countries attracted similar amounts of capital, by 1965 Canada was the site of considerably more foreign investment than its Latin American counterparts. While growth in Latin America was strong (except in Argentina, which experienced persistent economic and political decline), Canada's development was spectacular on into the 1960s. This divergence into different worlds aggravated the ideological factor, and limited the scope of cooperation in the first postwar era.

Dawning of the Cold War

The hallmarks of Canadian foreign relations during the early postwar years can perhaps best be epitomized by Prime Minister Louis St. Laurent's 'Gray Lecture,' which was delivered at the University of Toronto in 1947. Clearly, at the centre of foreign policy during his tenure was the contention that 'the security of this country lies in the development of a firm structure of international organization.'[1] Global peace and security, to be facilitated by the painstaking development of international law and by the construction of formidable international organizations, would be the key to Canadian prosperity and well-being in the wake of the most devastating war the world had yet witnessed.[2]

During this period, Canada was instrumental in the formation of the U.N. The world's former great power, the U.K., and the globe's new superpower, the U.S., would be the central objects of Ottawa's policy.[3] And it would be incumbent upon Canada to strike a balance between the two. Outside of its preoccupation with the Anglo-American powers, and to a lesser extent with Europe, St. Laurent's government would also foster ties with the Commonwealth – especially with India. While trade with Latin America grew during this period, and some important diplomatic relations were established, it was clearly not high on Canada's foreign policy priority list.

While the Cold War era ushered in a new agenda for Canada in the hemisphere, some prominent themes from the past were still present. Ottawa, for example, maintained its resolve to buffer the fall of the U.K.'s power in the Western Hemisphere, although with diminished fervour than had been the case prior to 1945. In 1950, for example, this was expressed by Canadian concern over Latin American opposition to British claims in the Falklands, Antarctica, and what is now Belize.[4]

This was a time of incongruity between various Canadian diplomats and policymakers regarding both analyses of Latin American politics and the appropriate means of dealing with some pressing problems. Illustrative of this is the apparent discord among Canadian diplomats and policymakers with respect to perceived threats from leftist movements and leaders in Latin America. There was indisputable Canadian support for Peru's leftist reformer Haya de la Torre and his APRA (American Popular Revolutionary Alliance) party, as shall be seen shortly. In sharp contrast was a decidedly negative analysis, by a Canadian trade commissioner in Bogotá, of Colombia's enormously popular left-of-centre liberal, Jorge Eliécier Gaitán,[5] which portrayed him as an 'extreme leftist leader'[6] who threatened both democracy and capitalism – a misinformed view that demonstrated a pronounced hostility to socialism.

More extreme was a study by the Canadian trade commissioner in Guatemala regarding the possibility of Jacobo Arbenz Guzmán becoming president of the country.

> Businessmen and landowners do not have any cause to view the prospect of Arbenz as future president with any optimism. He is unscrupulous, daring and ruthless, and not one to be allayed in his aims by bloodshed or killing. He is a drug addict and is especially egotistical and sadistic when under the influence of drugs or alcohol.[7]

That characterization of Arbenz, who assumed the presidency through a peaceful transition in 1951, deviates from the view of mainstream historians, who regard him as a rather benevolent social democrat who attempted to represent the interests of the majority.[8] Furthermore, the same Canadian analysis sides with the United Fruit Company, which is notorious for its exploitation of Central America.[9] 'Unionism has been encouraged and no effort made to discourage labour leaders from bedeviling the United Fruit Company, foreign coffee interests and the foreign owned railway which crosses the country.'[10] I shall soon show that the general tone of this analysis differs noticeably from the majority of other government reports, which are supportive of greater social and economic equity in Latin America. Naturally, there was considerable ideological variation among Canadian officials concerned with Latin America during the Cold War. But the pronounced extent of it here may display an element of incoherence on the part of the Canadian government, which exemplifies its immaturity in dealing with Latin American affairs during the early years of the period.

In 1950 the DEA prepared a report that probed the causes and implications of communist activity in Latin America – probably the most extensive and insightful study of the early Cold War period and, therefore, deserving of considerable attention. It emphasized the prestige of the Soviet Union in Latin America during the Second World War and its immediate aftermath, as well as the precipitous decline of Moscow's popularity once it became obvious that the U.S. and the USSR would be superpower adversaries peddling competing models of political economy.[11] The report cited widespread poverty, illiteracy, disease, and an inequitable division of wealth as the chief catalysts for leftist support in the region – a view consistent with analyses from previous years.

Labour unions, according to this DEA study, were favourite venues for communist infiltration, since they could be utilized as convenient fronts, especially in the likely event of communist parties being declared illegal.[12] Hence, there existed the worry of labour movements being manipulated by communists who took orders from Moscow, a predicament which the Canadian consul general in Venezuela assumed to be the case in that country.[13] The grand design of the Left, this DEA report argued, would be to control labour unions in transportation, energy, and strategic industries, which could disrupt the flow of crucial raw materials to NATO allies in the event of a war with the Soviet Union.[14] As was noted, NATO and the U.N. were the primary objects of Canadian foreign policy during this period, and so it is not surprising that they influenced Ottawa's view of inter-American politics. However, Ottawa seemed to hope that Canadian labour movements could wield a positive impact upon Latin American labour movements by providing 'more constructive views to the non-communist movement.'[15]

What would prevent communist proliferation in Latin America? Interestingly, the 1950 DEA analysis suggests that social reform movements, even socialist ones which steered clear of Soviet-style communism, could assist in alleviating the dangerous social and economic inequities which Canadian officials worried would breed support for communist parties. To reiterate, socialism per se was not a problem if it avoided an alignment with Moscow and if it did not threaten Canadian capital. Thus, for example, Canada supported Peru's APRA movement and its founder Haya de la Torre,[16] who advocated democratic socialism and who criticized certain aspects of Castro's Cuba. 'The Aprista movement has served as the most important counter-force to Peruvian communism.'[17]

Also in this vein, Canadian officials appreciated the way in which the Peronista movement in Argentina functioned to block communism. Until 1945, Ottawa resented what it perceived to be the fascist nature of the Perón government, but in the new context of the Cold War the Argentine regime served Canadian and Western purposes.

> The Communists have been severely hampered in their appeal by the pro-labour policies of President Peron, which force them to adopt a sadly negative position of carping criticism toward the Administration

... There are indications, however, that mounting inflation is straining the close association of government and labour ... This, as well as the international aspects of the Cold War, is probably responsible for the recent hardening of Peron's attitude toward the Communist Party.[18]

In the great global contest between the blocs of the U.S. and the USSR, Canada believed that movements spanning the ideological spectrum from socialism to fascism could serve as useful strategic allies for the Western camp in Latin America.

Other forces which could assist in the battle against communism included the Roman Catholic Church and the armed forces. But these were troublesome allies. The 'Church has been hampered by close association with the landed and ruling interests,' while the military represented a force unto itself and could threaten democratic development.[19] Thus, social reform was considered to be the most reliable foe of Soviet-led communism.

Prophetically, the 1950 DEA report located the weightiest communist threat in Cuba. This was because the 'Cuban Communist Party [was] probably the strongest and best-organized in Latin America.'[20] Why so?

The Communist Party of Cuba has been allowed a much freer line than most others, and this undoubtedly accounts for a considerable part of its success ... Its platform is the usual popular one of nationalism, nationalization and industrialization, involving even co-operation with native capitalists to overcome United States imperialism.[21]

A number of contradictions regarding Canadian interests and policy in Latin America became apparent during the Cold War. The first of these involved democracy. Democratic development in Latin America was a long-standing Canadian objective.[22] But this objective was tempered during the Cold War by an overriding strategic imperative to retard the prospects of Soviet-style communism in the Western Hemisphere, as well as by the perceived threat to Canadian capital that Soviet-inspired regimes might create. Canadian policymakers believed that the Communist party in Cuba was afforded a perilous degree of freedom which allowed it to flourish, and which finally resulted in the overthrow of the Batista regime. This was not thought to be in the Canadian national interest. Hence, there was a contradiction between Canada's support for democratic development and free political participation on the one hand, and the potential for negative consequences such a scenario could generate in the context of the Cold War on the other.

A second contradiction involved tension between military spending by First World countries and developmental assistance programs for the Third World. As was noted earlier, Canada's support for the U.N. and for NATO represented the cornerstone of Canadian foreign policy during this era. Courting Latin American votes at the U.N., and ensuring that supply lines remained open for raw materials to reach NATO allies, were central strategic objectives in the bipolar global contest. But those interests did not necessarily mesh with those of Latin Americans. As the Canadian secretary of state for external affairs noted in 1952, in what was then a secret document:

> There is also a tendency on the part of the non-NATO Western nations to criticize what might be described as the exclusiveness of the NATO Club. This criticism, although not so worded, is focussed mainly on defence expenditures necessitated by the Communist menace as compared to the amounts devoted to assist economically under-developed nations.[23]

A third contradiction, then, may have been Canada's expressed concern for alleviating economic inequity in Latin America on the one hand, especially given that such inequity invited communist inroads. And, on the other hand, there existed what Latin Americans considered to be insufficient developmental assistance programs – either through multilateral agencies or bilaterally to forestall communist threats (Canada had no bilateral programs at this time).

A fourth contradiction entailed a clash between the ideal of economic equity and the reality of exploitation, as the predicament of Canadian investment in Nicaragua demonstrates. While major investments in Mexico, Brazil, and elsewhere generally seemed to show reputable Canadian behaviour,[24] this is not the case with respect to Canadian-owned gold mines in Nicaragua. To backstep a bit, consider the following 1947 analysis offered by the Canadian ambassador to the U.S.

> Mr. Bernbaum [of the U.S. State Department] appears to think that the [Nicaraguan] rebels have a legitimate grievance against the Canadian and United States owned gold mines as they are, in a manner of speaking, the backbone of the Somoza regime. Mr. Bernbaum stated that Mr. Cameron, the Canadian manager of the La Luz mine, admitted

to him that he first began to pay General Somoza direct one per cent of the gross output of the mine and that he later added a further one and a half per cent which was paid into the National Bank.[25]

It would appear that a Canadian corporation helped to finance the notoriously dictatorial Somoza regime in order to operate a profitable venture in Nicaragua.

A few years later, Canadian labour caught wind of the appalling situation at the Nicaraguan mines, resulting in complications between government, labour, and business. This was revealed in a 1954 letter from the undersecretary of state for external affairs to the Canadian ambassador in Washington, DC:

> Mr. Pearson has received a letter from the Canadian Congress of Labour concerning the conditions of work in their [Noranda and Ventures] Nicaraguan subsidiaries ... [The secretary-treasurer of the congress] stated, however, that the Transport Workers Federation of Nicaragua [which issued the complaint regarding working conditions] was a very weak organization and he feared that, if Noranda and Ventures knew that the Federation had made representations to the Canadian Congress of Labour, they might take measures to crush the Federation.[26]

Three decades later, the Canadian government would decide that the working conditions in the mines had been deplorable. Daniel Ortega told a Canadian House of Commons standing committee in the early 1980s that the mines had 'destroyed hundreds of workers from tuberculosis and ... looted our national resources' – a view that paved the way for Nicaraguan nationalization of the Canadian mines.[27] So while Canada, in the 1950s, officially argued that poverty and inequity fed into the hands of the communists, there is at least one significant episode in which Canada's own corporations contributed to such conditions.

A fifth contradiction concerned Ottawa's general support for U.S. objectives in the Cold War, despite Canada's dislike of the intense ideological clamour which marked the McCarthy era. One such example involves the blacklisting by the U.S. of Lauchlin Currie, a Canadian-born economist who advised the Roosevelt administration. He later became a resident of Colombia and was quite influential as a commentator on the economic development of that country. Canadian government officials, then and now,[28] have a great deal of respect for Currie's social democratic views, and applaud his contributions to the development of the Colombian political economy. As a DEA document reveals, Currie's 'retirement here [Colombia] has probably been caused to some extent by the fact that his name has come up periodically in the United States as linked to subversive communist activities by various witch-hunting committees now in operation there.'[29] Thus, while Canadian officials shared many U.S. objectives, there was also a great deal of doubt about the disconcerting intensity of American ideological crusades – crusades which often conjured up images of the Inquisition.

A striking pattern to emerge regarding Canada's reaction to revolutionary developments in Guatemala, Cuba, and the Dominican Republic was its distaste for the leaders of these movements in tandem with both strategic and economic concerns. Accompanying this was a general alignment with U.S. objectives and, crucially important, a profound disagreement by Canadian officials regarding the means Washington used to achieve these objectives as well as the tone of U.S. ideological proclamations.

It was observed earlier that Canadian officials had been scathingly distrustful of Arbenz even before he assumed the presidency of Guatemala in 1951. In 1953, the Canadian ambassador to Mexico observed that 'there are indications that the Soviet Embassy here is the contact through which Communists in Guatemala are directed.'[30] Hence, certain Canadian officials seemed to concur with the U.S.-inspired argument that the Guatemalan government was involved in a Soviet conspiracy to spread communism throughout Latin America.

Although Canada clearly was not happy with Arbenz and his colleagues, there were some Canadian diplomats who did not fully embrace the U.S. argument that Guatemala represented a strategic threat to its neighbours. A case in point concerns a shipment of arms transported through Sweden to Guatemala, which, Washington argued, would serve the purpose of communist aggression throughout the Caribbean Basin. Canadian analyses suggested that this shipment may have represented part of an attempt to defend the Guatemalans from what they correctly perceived to be an impending U.S. invasion. A report on this matter from the Canadian high commissioner in London suggested

that Guatemala has, at present at least, no aggressive designs on neighbouring states, being too much plagued with domestic problems to embark on external adventures; [and] ... that the Guatemalan Government is itself nervous of attacks from Honduras, and to a lesser extent from Nicaragua and Salvador.[31]

In other words, some Canadian officials suspected that the U.S. was overreacting.

Placing this in historical perspective, the conservative American historian Thomas Leonard suggests that 'after World War Two, Central America became a microcosm of U.S. Cold War responses to communism.'[32] In an analysis which parallels the Reagan administration's perception of Nicaragua in the 1980s, former U.S. secretary of state John Foster Dulles observed in 1954 that

in Guatemala, international communism had an initial success. It began ten years ago, when revolution occurred in Guatemala. The revolution was not without justification, but the Communists seized on it, not as an opportunity for real reforms, but as a chance to gain political power ... If world communism captures any American State, however small, a new and perilous front is established which will increase the danger to the entire free world and require even greater sacrifices from the American people.[33]

That explanation, however, is less than convincing. It appears that the U.S. overthrew Arbenz largely due to his policy of land reform, which ran counter to the interests of American-owned banana plantations in Guatemala. Arbenz's policy included the redistribution of 234,000 acres of unused lands owned by the United Fruit Company to landless peasants.[34] The company was to be compensated at market rates for the confiscated parcel. As historian Walter LeFeber notes,

United Fruit launched a massive lobbying campaign for U.S. intervention [in Guatemala]. It began with enviable connections to the Eisenhower Administration. Secretary of State John Foster Dulles and his former New York law firm, Sullivan and Cromwell, had long represented the Company. Allen Dulles, head of the CIA, had served on UFCO's board of trustees. Ed Whitman, the company's top public relations officer, was the husband of Ann Whitman, President Eisenhower's private secretary. Ed Whitman produced a film, 'Why the Kremlin Hates Bananas,' that pictured UFCO fighting in the front trenches of the Cold War.[35]

Subsequently, through U.S. military intervention, the democratically elected government of Arbenz was replaced by a dictatorship loyal to U.S. interests. While the Canadian government was no friend of Arbenz, Ottawa did not believe that U.S. military intervention was necessary or wise.

By the late 1950s, Canadian diplomats maintained their resolve to forestall communist penetration of the Western Hemisphere, but once again they were at odds with the U.S. as to how best to achieve this goal. Canada's ambassador to Peru, echoing Washington's concerns, emphasized the 'clear and present danger presented by the communists in Peru,'[36] especially regarding communist infiltration of the labour movement, the danger of which '[could not] be overestimated.'[37] The ambassador hoped that Canadian labour leaders could teach their Latin American counterparts the 'virtues of non-political trade unions.'[38]

Canada's ambassador to Colombia, while still regarding communist influence as a threat, took exception to U.S. recipes for eliminating subversives in Latin America. Moreover, the ambassador perceived as dangerous the diminishing levels of U.S. developmental assistance to the region, a somewhat ironic point, given Canada's lack of direct aid to Latin America.[39] The decline of such assistance was viewed as likely to result in Latin American nations seeking assistance from the Soviet bloc, undoubtedly a negative development for the Western strategic alliance.

It is of interest to note that the ambassador to Colombia suggested that increased significance ought to be attributed to Latin America due to its strategic role in the Cold War. He also made the important observation that 'in the United Nations it is obvious that the Latin American bloc has lost a great deal of the influence that it originally exercised when it represented almost one third of the total votes.'[40] It will be recalled that, in the late 1940s, one of the central reasons Canada attributed any significance at all to Latin America was due to the votes it wielded at the U.N.

Not only was the Canadian government conscious of the strategic implications of communist influence in Latin America, so was Canadian business. In 1957, the Canadian ambassador to Brazil stated: 'During a recent conversation a senior executive of The Light [Brazilian Traction, Light and Power] told me that his office had been keeping track of the number of Brazilian politicians who had been officially invited to visit the USSR and that during the last eighteen months the list of visitors had grown to some 300.'[41] In the face of declining U.S. popularity,

Canadian business was concerned with subtle inroads being made by the Soviets, sometimes through their allies, the Poles. Obviously, 'The Light' was concerned about Brazilian hostility to foreign capital, which it felt might be precipitated by Soviet influence. It is of interest to note that 'The Light' was nationalized by the Brazilian government in 1964, apparently due to indigenous, leftist nationalism rather than to Soviet directives.[42]

The successful Sputnik operations, coupled with a precipitous decline in U.S. popularity, due to perceived American bullying, suggested the possibility that Moscow could gain popularity in the Western Hemisphere. The disastrous visit by Vice-President Nixon to Latin America in the spring of 1958 illustrated just how deeply U.S. popularity had plunged. The vice-president encountered wild protests and riots contesting U.S. policies in Latin America.[43]

Related to the issue of U.S. unpopularity in the region is a letter of instructions from the DEA to Canada's new ambassador in Peru, which indicated Ottawa's profound concern over the matter. 'A continuing deterioration of the relations between the United States and a number of Latin American countries would disturb us, not only because it would affect the value of the OAS as a regional alliance, but because it would weaken, politically and economically, our neighbour and most important ally.'[44] Ultimately, Canada linked its own security and interests to the success of the U.S. – a trend which has continued into the present.

Despite their respective positions on the philosophical spectrum, from Francis Fukuyama on the Right to Fred Halliday on the Left, many contemporary international relations experts would agree that the Cold War contained an important component of legitimate ideological contestation.[45] A similar position was expressed over three decades ago by Canada's ambassador to Venezuela.

> In the clash of economic ideologies which divide the world today, Latin American thinking is unquestionably closer to the collectivism of the communist camp, than it is to free enterprise capitalism as advocated by the United States. This gives the Communists a sharp advantage in the battle to win the allegiance of South America and is a factor which must be considered in any attempt to gauge the chances of ultimate communist victory in this area.[46]

This ideological chasm between Latin America and the West was responsible, according to the Canadian ambassador, for the volatile demonstrations against Vice-President Nixon during his ill-fated visit to South America in 1958.[47]

Even though the U.S. was the central target of Latin American hostility, Canadian diplomats worried about a possible threat to Western capital in general, which would threaten Canada's business interests (these being centred on banking, insurance, resource extraction, and infrastructure development).[48]

> So far, we have managed to escape the hostility which has been the lot of the United States, but this will not go on forever. The good name of the companies involved and of Canada itself depend upon the proper course being taken before it is too late. The Gordon Report underlines the shortcomings of certain foreign investors in Canada. It is important that where Canada is the source of the foreign capital, we should not practice what we condemn in others.[49]

Hence, the crucial analytical and practical point emerged that Canada's sensitivity to U.S. investment within its own borders should lead it to be more sympathetic to Latin Americans, who were in a similar predicament.

Written in 1957, the Royal Commission on Canada's Economic Prospects, chaired by Walter Gordon and dubbed the Gordon Report, provided a critical assessment of U.S. investment in Canada. It would herald a ground swell of similar views that would continue into the Trudeau era.

> At the root of Canadian concern about foreign investment is undoubtedly a basic, traditional sense of insecurity vis-à-vis our friendly, albeit our much larger and more powerful neighbour, the United States. There is concern that as the position of American capital in the dynamic resource and manufacturing sectors becomes ever more dominant, our economy will inevitably become more and more integrated with that of the United States. Behind this is the fear that continuing integration might lead to economic domination by the United States and eventually to the loss of our political independence.[50]

The view that Canada, due to similarities between Canadian and Latin American relations to U.S. capital, could understand Latin America better than could the U.S. would find expression not only in the Trudeau government but also in Latin America itself.[51]

Canada and International Hemispheric Institutions: 1949-58
The central focus in the discussion above has been upon the influx of
the Left into the Western Hemisphere in the form of the so-called
communist threat. We shall now turn to the issue of how Canada's
relationship with the OAS and other regional institutions was affected
by the Cold War. I begin in 1954, which marked Canada's first major
rethinking of its interests vis-à-vis the OAS since the institution's creation
in the late 1940s. In a DEA memorandum to Cabinet, it was argued that

> developments of very considerable significance have taken place since
> the last submission to Cabinet in 1947, not only in Canada's relations
> with Latin America, but also in the importance of the countries of Latin
> America in world affairs, particularly at the United Nations. United
> States policy towards Latin America is more cooperative and flexible,
> thus reducing the possibility of friction; Canadian trade has increased
> more than fifteen-fold, but competition, particularly from continental
> European countries, is becoming keener; the importance of retaining
> the good will of Latin American countries in the cold war is not
> negligible.[52]

Thus, Ottawa seemed to be displaying a warmer attitude towards the
OAS than had been the case seven years earlier, since U.S. friction with
the rest of Latin America had subsided. By the early 1950s, Canada had
eleven diplomatic missions in Latin America, whereas before the Second
World War there had been none. No doubt this development correlated
with Canada's discovery of Latin America's economic significance.

Along with Canada's continued general support for the U.S. against
the USSR, it appears that Ottawa's fears regarding a potential disagreement with U.S. policy in Latin America had faded considerably. With
respect to debates which arose at the annual OAS conference in 1954,
the Canadian representative observed: 'In most cases we would have
agreed with the United States.'[53] The days of Canada having to side
either with the U.S. or with the British were long gone, and now Ottawa
found itself more or less ideologically aligned with the U.S. While it is
true that Canada concurred with Washington on many of the major
issues in inter-American affairs (with the notable exceptions discussed
earlier), it is also the case that Ottawa began to wonder what purpose
would be served by joining the OAS and, therefore, having to side with
either the U.S. or with Latin America when disputes inevitably arose.

In 1957, Canada's ambassador to Colombia observed that, with respect to diplomatic relations, Ottawa had more to gain by working with Latin America through the U.N. than through the OAS.

> The only two international organs in which the Latin Americas can effectively exercise their influence are the United Nations and the Organization of American States. Since the latter is limited geographically and politically in its usefulness to the Latin Americans by the over-whelming strength of the United States, it is probable that the United Nations will continue to be the field in which Latin American diplomatic activity will be most actively conducted. And it is in the United Nations, therefore, that in my opinion, we ought to concentrate our diplomatic effort to prevent a shift towards neutrality, on the part of the Latin Americans, and to try to control and influence their twenty votes, now far more important in crucial issues than they were when the West could almost automatically count on a majority in the United Nations.[54]

Prudently, then, Canada decided that diplomatic relations with the Americas should be conducted outside the OAS. Overall, there was little Canadian interest in joining the OAS in the 1950s. There was not one question regarding the institution in the House of Commons during 1949-54 and only a flurry of interest in the late 1950s. The enthusiasm that did emerge came from Prime Minister Diefenbaker's new secretary of state for external affairs, Sidney Smith, who travelled to Latin America in 1957 and was keen on the idea of Canada joining the OAS, but the notion perished with his death in 1959.[55]

In sum, the tables had turned and now Canada was welcome to join the OAS, that is, the U.S. was comfortable with Canadian membership given the new postwar global arrangement. Policymakers within Canada, however, were torn – certain quarters encouraged Canadian membership, while weightier elements opposed it on the grounds that it would mean being caught in battles between the U.S. and Latin America – a no-win situation. Moreover, Canada preferred to use the U.N. as the chief venue for its multilateral policy.

Conclusion

The period following the Second World War witnessed the dawning of the Cold War. It was characterized by a world order dominated by two superpowers, with the USSR somewhat successfully playing catch-up to an always more powerful U.S. The world was caught in a bipolar contest between capitalism and Soviet-style communism, and Canadian policy in Latin America should be viewed in this context.

Canada's alliance with the West and, particularly, with the U.S. was solid and unquestionable. While Canada shared the U.S. goal of trouncing Soviet interests and promoting capitalism in Latin America, Ottawa often disagreed with the means Washington chose to achieve those objectives. Canadians, as the period wore on, increasingly viewed U.S. policy as too heavy handed, too Manichean.

With Canada's former ties to British hegemony long gone, Canadians began to glimpse the dark underbelly of a world order dominated by the U.S. This was apparent both abroad and at home. Domestically, the 1957 Gordon Report ushered in profound fears that U.S. control of the Canadian economy could result in U.S. control of Canada. Gordon would later become finance minister under Prime Minister Lester Pearson, an experience that, in 1966, led him to write: 'During the two and one-half years I held that office [Finance], the influence that financial and business interests in the U.S. had on Canadian policy and opinion was continually brought home to me.'[56] As shall be seen in subsequent chapters, a parade of Canadian doubt regarding ties with the U.S. would become more prominent as the 1960s wore on and would dominate the early Trudeau era. Slowly, Canada's state structure began to alter in order to protect itself from U.S. economic and political encroachment.

The issue of American economic domination of Canada also had an effect upon Canadian relations with Latin America. The Gordon Report led Canadian diplomats in Latin America not only to question Canada's economic dealings with the poorer states of the Americas, but also placed Canada in a better position to understand the region's attitude to the U.S. in particular and to the North in general. It would suggest the potential for Canada's role as a mediator or balancer between the U.S. and Latin America – a salient topic during the Trudeau period. Thus, while Canada remained committed to capitalism and generally shared U.S. objectives, there were some important ideological differences between Canadian and American foreign policies (which is not at all surprising, given their distinct positions in the world order). In addition to its greater tolerance for socialist experiments in the Western Hemisphere, Ottawa also distinguished itself from the U.S. by displaying sympathy towards economic nationalism.

This was also a period during which Canada's ability to be a significant actor in Latin America grew considerably. Canada by now had established diplomatic relations with all countries of the region, a Latin

American division of DEA was opened, and Ottawa became active in the Interamerican Development Bank (IADB) and ECLA. The notion of joining the OAS became a more serious topic of discussion, but, ultimately, fears of U.S. domination prohibited a definitive move. With respect to this issue and others, the Canadian diplomatic community was not always in agreement.

Although Canada's economic and diplomatic interests in Latin America expanded rapidly during this era, the focus of Canadian foreign policy remained upon the North Atlantic and its major hemispheric international organization, NATO. As well, Canada favoured working through the U.N., as its broad membership reduced the possibility of Ottawa offending either Washington or particular Latin American states.

3
Ideological Pluralism: Cuba and the Dominican Republic

With the Cold War solidly in place, some decisive events occurred during the period under study here. With respect to inter-American affairs, foremost among these were the developments surrounding the Cuban Revolution. These shall be explored in some depth, as shall the episode involving U.S. intervention in the Dominican Republic.

To begin, Canadian diplomats during this era made some interesting analytical observations. In 1959, Canada's ambassador to Peru offered the insightful view that 'somehow the United States must devise means of identifying itself with the social and economic change which a knowledge of the American way of life [has] stimulated.'[1] In other words, having become more familiar with the materially richer way of life enjoyed by North Americans, and having been provoked by U.S. propaganda which flaunted the wonders of capitalism, Latin Americans were becoming increasingly impatient with their sluggish pace of economic development. It was believed that this impatience could prove to be a recipe for socialist or communist revolution, and it is significant that the ambassador's 1959 analysis presaged the Relative Deprivation Theory developed by Ted Robert Gurr in 1970.[2]

Another striking observation emanating from Canadian diplomatic personnel in Peru was: 'To most of the sierra Indians life is now little or no better, and sometimes worse, than it was under the Inca empire.'[3] Interestingly, the same point is currently being advanced by Peru's leading revolutionary guerrillas, Sendero Luminoso.[4] In any case, it is clear that Canadians had considerable sympathy for the plight of Latin Americans, who were disenfranchised from the benefits of growth in the global political economy.

Canada and the Cuban Revolution

Innocently foreshadowing developments that would soon greatly affect his country, in the late 1950s the Cuban permanent representative to the U.N. recognized the ascendency of Soviet global power. The Canadian ambassador to Cuba stated: 'It is of interest to note here that when I called on Dr. Guell and "Sputnik" was discussed, he referred to it as a fantastic development and an obvious defeat, both technically and propaganda-wise, for the U.S.'[5] Despite Soviet success in space, however, officials at the time did not appreciate the possibility of Moscow's imminent inroads into the Caribbean. In 1957, Canada's chargé d'affaires in Havana was certain that the sheer 'physical strength' of the Cuban government could subdue revolutionaries. The state's array of force included a 'goon brigade [as well as] the ranks of the police, secret police, army, navy and air force.'[6]

In 1958, Castro presented himself as a force to be reckoned with. With remarkable skill, this dedicated revolutionary called for a general strike to be supported by labour and students, a moratorium on paying taxes to the Cuban state, and, perhaps most alarming of all, a mutiny by the armed forces.[7] The Canadian ambassador was now entertaining the 'frightful' notion of the 26th of July Movement, a guerrilla force bent on overthrowing the Cuban government, controlling a portion of the island, especially in the province of Oriente.[8] Moreover, the ambassador's description of Castro was not at all flattering: 'From his background he appears to be nothing but a plain rebel and a revolutionary.'[9]

Although Canada has maintained diplomatic relations with Cuba throughout Castro's reign, and has enjoyed lucrative commercial relations with the island, it should not be thought that the Canadian government was fond either of Castro or of his ideological leanings during the beginning of the revolutionary period. In 1959, only a few months after the Cuban Revolution, Canada's ambassador to Cuba expressed his desire 'to halt this cancerous growth.'[10] Interestingly, in the first few months after Batista was overthrown, the Canadian ambassador to the island, while appreciating Castro's nationalistic leanings, did not think he was a communist. Rather, the new Cuban leader was portrayed as a weak figure who was being manipulated by the Communist party.

The communist party, since the fall of the Batista government, has attempted to use its united front technique; has, in fact, become more revolutionary than the revolutionaries and more nationalistic than the

26th of July Movement. In this way, they have made of several Castro appointed governmental leaders unwitting tools for communist activities and have kept the inexperienced government largely off balance, so that no effective means of controlling the communist party has been instituted.[11]

Clearly, the ultimate question was whether or not communist tendencies would eventually dominate the Cuban government.

In April 1959, Canada's ambassador to the island offered a portrait of Castro to interested members of the Department of External Affairs (DEA). It was a worrisome picture indeed. He was presented as an enemy of democracy and as a fanatic recklessly plunging Cuba into the depths of chaos, where communists would opportunistically seize power.[12] Furthermore, he was described as rather frail, as incapable of leadership, and vulnerable to the influence of the more formidable personalities of the communistic duo composed of his brother Raul and Che Guevara.[13] More indicting still:

Finally, according to the doctors who have been looking after him, they are more and more convinced that he is not normal. He has been during the last three months living by absorbing stimulants during his 18-to-20-hour days and then massive doses of barbiturates to get an hour or so's sleep every day. They fear that sooner or later he cannot carry on under this sort of treatment and that he will collapse. This will be the time for his brother and his chief adviser Guevara, both known for their Communist affiliations, no doubt to attempt the seizure of power.[14]

Castro would later prove himself to be considerably sturdier, on both a personal and a political level, than these early reports would suggest.

In April 1959 Castro visited Canada, in part to allay concerns that his government was communist or, worse, that he might be bent on exporting revolution – as though revolution were a commodity, like bananas, which could be exported. This visit, however, did not bolster his approval rating among Canadian government officials and/or diplomats. They still worried that he was capable of executing his enemies but incapable of creating a democratic state complete with freedom of the press. Canada's ambassador to Cuba expressed his fear that Havana had designs on the fragile governments of Haiti and Panama. Canadians, however, remained confused as to whether or not Castro was, indeed, a communist, and even worried that during his trip to Canada the true reds in Cuba might take advantage of his absence and seize greater power.[15]

By the autumn of 1959, voices within Canada seemed to exhibit a somewhat more balanced and relaxed assessment of Castro and his ambitions, at least compared to those originating from Canadian diplomats. In a letter of instruction from the DEA to Canada's new ambassador to Cuba, policymakers were optimistic that the global political reality dictated that Havana attempt to cultivate cordial relations with the U.S. But still there were problems. Ottawa worried that Castro was slowly abandoning any rightist elements which supported him and continued to fear that he was fully capable of exporting revolution. Significantly, Canada's fresh objective would be to attempt to influence Cuban foreign policy, especially at the U.N. and the OAS.[16]

Despite its differences with Havana, Ottawa may have felt that the workable economic relationship between the two countries might allow Canada to influence Cuba. With the overthrow of the Batista dictatorship, the new government in Havana nationalized all banks except for the Royal Bank and the Bank of Nova Scotia – seemingly a friendly gesture. While it is unclear why the Canadian banks were the exception to the rule, they nevertheless chose to vacate Cuba as a result of what they considered to be a difficult financial and commercial atmosphere.[17] The banks negotiated with the revolutionary Cuban officials and accepted compensation for the nationalization process. Apparently, Canadians felt they could deal with the Cubans, even when the situation was not exactly perfect.

Despite their ability to work effectively with the Cubans, in 1960 Canadian diplomats maintained their distrust of the Caribbean's most notorious leader. Canada's ambassador to Argentina, following the visit of a Cuban delegation to Buenos Aires in commemoration of the 150th anniversary of Argentina's independence, arrived at the conclusion that 'Cuba is not content with a revolution confined to its own borders but is anxious to export it to other Latin American countries as well.'[18] That analysis followed pro-Cuban demonstrations in the streets of the Argentine capital, though 'no proof' existed that the Cubans were involved.[19] The same Canadian diplomat would later call Castro an 'infection,' which, even when confined to Cuba, would tarnish the appeal of Latin America in general to foreign capital.[20]

The strategic implications of Soviet influence through Cuba were enough to set the alarm bells ringing for diplomats and political analysts in the hemisphere. But, in the eyes of Canadian officials, the introduction to the region of the world's second-ranked communist power, China, was gasoline on the fire. The Canadian trade commissioner in Hong Kong observed that the Chinese were 'desperately striving' for official recognition from Havana, which was to culminate in an exchange of embassies. While such a move would bolster Peking's (now known as Beijing) international prestige, Canada held that it would also promote Cuba's interest by echoing and, therefore, legitimizing its international ideological proclamations.

> In general terms the Chinese line has been that the United States is intervening in Cuban internal affairs, practicing economic aggression against Cuba and plotting military invasion to stamp out Cuban independence and democracy in order to check the growing tide of national independence movements in Latin America and prolong and extend U.S. plunder and control of Latin America.[21]

The same analysis went on to note that Latin Americans 'harbour secret admiration' for Castro's Cuba simply for its remarkable capacity to defy the U.S.[22]

When diplomatic relations were established by the autumn of 1960, Canada's trade commissioner observed: 'It represents a breakthrough in Latin America for China after protracted and strenuous efforts in recent years. It also means support in the United Nations for Communist China and adds one more to the inexorably growing list of Chinese U.N. supporters.'[23] Once again, it was clear that Canada often assessed Latin American affairs in the context of its consequences at the U.N. Beyond that, Canadian officials began to wonder whether Chinese involvement in Latin America meant the progression of communism or the beginning of a competition between Moscow and Peking that would result in a withering of both their interests.[24]

Canada sustained normal economic and diplomatic relations with the Castro government. This, with the exception of Mexico, stood in contrast to its sister states in the Americas. This peculiar scenario prompted Canadian officials to breathe a sigh of relief when Ottawa opted not to join the OAS[25] – a point developed more fully below. Still, Canadian diplomats persisted in their exhortations of dissatisfaction with the Castro government. Canada's ambassador to Peru, for instance, applauded the severance of relations between Peru and Cuba when documents were discovered which allegedly linked Havana to subversive plots in Lima.[26] Ottawa's partial alignment with Washington on the Cuban issue crystallized in a joint communique:

> The President and the Prime Minister ... were in accord that the alignment of a regime in the Western Hemisphere with communist leadership abroad was a matter for concern, threatening as it did the peaceful and democratic evolution of the Latin American peoples. The Prime Minister assured the President of Canada's continued and increasing interest in Inter-American affairs.[27]

Not only was the concern strategic, but, as was mentioned earlier, Cuba's entry into hemispheric politics initiated a contest of ideas. As the Canadian ambassador to Venezuela noted, the Americas were now caught 'between two different methods of forcing upwards the standards of living and, in the end, of gaining the minds of men.'[28] Hence, there emerged a 'Great Contest' in the Americas between two competing developmental models.

In conjunction with pronounced ideological struggles, the early 1960s witnessed some important military-strategic episodes involving Cuba and the U.S. Amidst an assortment of desperate and unsuccessful U.S. schemes to oust the Castro regime, the ill-fated Bay of Pigs invasion was perhaps the most dramatic as well as the most embarrassing. Some notable distinctions and similarities emerged between U.S. and Canadian policy with respect to this episode. At the U.N., on 18 April 1961, Canada's secretary of state for external affairs, Howard Green, warned that the U.S. invasion would spark a dangerous and protracted civil war directed by the two superpowers.[29] Although Prime Minister Diefenbaker would continue to insist on Canada's right to conduct trade with Cuba despite the U.S. embargo, he more or less echoed Washington's view. In the House of Commons he raised concern with respect to a 'dispatch by Chairman Khrushchev of a message which revealed beyond doubt the extent to which international communism is prepared to go in consolidating its foothold in Cuba, a bridgehead from which the penetration of the whole of Latin America could be launched.'[30] Diefenbaker proceeded to suggest that Cuba, 'like so many small and defenceless countries,' had become part of a global 'ideological contest,' in which the 'interests of the Cuban people have been subordinated to the interplay of outside forces beyond their control.'[31] Despite Ottawa's regret that Cuba was caught in a hegemonic power play, and the fact that Canada found Castro's regime ideologically objectionable, Diefenbaker insisted that 'no matter what our disagreements may be with other nations as far as their philosophy is concerned, we have endeavoured to conduct normal relations.'[32]

The distinction between the Diefenbaker and Kennedy governments regarding the trouble-prone island became vividly clear during the Cuban Missile Crisis of 1962, when Washington requested that NORAD (North American Air Defense Command) forces join the U.S. military in a state of alert. This was three days prior to the official alert announcement. Strikingly, at the request of Washington, the Canadian minister of defence overtly disobeyed Diefenbaker's explicit directions not to place Canadian forces on wartime alert.[33] The prime minister wished to wait until more information on the matter could be provided by an international organization such as the U.N. Diefenbaker simply did not trust the U.S. on this matter. Overall, the extent to which the prime minister lost control of the Canadian armed forces to the directives of the U.S. was shocking.[34]

Certain Latin American officials were audibly discontent with Diefenbaker's actions (or inactions) and with official Canadian policy in general, as is exemplified by Peruvian criticisms of Canadian trade with Cuba.[35] Similar protests were raised by other Latin American governments. Costa Rica, which 'had previously criticized Canada for its trade relations with Cuba ... [is] now commenting that, in this crisis, Canada did not play the part which had been expected of it.'[36] Prime Minister Diefenbaker must have had the same attitude towards the Canadian armed forces.

More broadly, Ottawa's reaction to the twin crises involving Cuba in 1961-2 symbolized the independence of Canadian foreign policy during this period. True, there were other significant examples of Ottawa's go-it-alone attitude. These included Diefenbaker's misplaced attempt in the late 1950s to diversify Canadian trade by channelling 15 per cent of it away from the U.S. and towards Great Britain, and the crucial point that 'Canada ... differed more in its voting pattern [at the United Nations] from that of the United States than most other members of NATO.'[37] Canada's push for disarmament at the U.N., along with its dispute with the U.S. over the DEW (distant early warning) line and the stationing of nuclear weapons on Canadian territory, also signified Ottawa's autonomous foreign policy during this period. It is in this context that Canada's independent stance with regard to Cuba assumes 'critical importance.'[38] With the Cuban example in mind, a prominent analyst at the time suggested: 'It is not too soon for Canada to conclude that her influence upon the United States is in direct proportion to the reality of her independence.'[39]

By 1964, Canadian policymakers maintained their balanced view of the Cuban situation. Ottawa recognized that, like it or not, Castro was firmly in power, and that, therefore, any attempts by Canada to isolate Cuba diplomatically or economically would not bear positive results.[40] While arguing that 'Cuba could scarcely be regarded as a very attractive Communist show-case in Latin America,'[41] a DEA review again asserted that Canada was willing to conduct normal economic and political relations with countries regardless of their ideology[42] – an assertion that has since become a hallmark of Canadian foreign policy.

Ottawa figured that the most fruitful position would be to occupy a sometimes ambiguous middle ground. On the one hand, Canadian officials would refuse to utter hostile statements regarding Cuba, since this policy had 'been helpful in protecting individuals and firms and at least ... [enabled] them to secure compensation for their Cuban interests with a minimum of loss, as the banks [had] already been able to do and as the life insurance companies [would] endeavour to do shortly.'[43] On the other hand, Ottawa would avoid committing the obvious mistake of alienating the U.S. In this regard, Prime Minister Diefenbaker pledged 'to President Kennedy at the Hyannis Port meeting last year that the Canadian Government would do or say nothing to show support for the Castro government.'[44] Canada would also sweeten its deal with the U.S. by utilizing the Canadian embassy in Havana for the provision 'of information of interest to the United States.'[45] Thus, in some important ways, Canada was willing during this period to act in concert with the U.S.

Canada held more or less the same position in 1966. By this time, however, Ottawa was slightly more critical of both the U.S. and of Havana. The Canadian government feared that U.S. attempts to isolate Cuba would produce the unwelcome result of pushing that country closer to the Soviet orbit, thereby rendering the problem increasingly intractable.[46] Ottawa was also more critical of the revolutionary Caribbean government, especially for what it viewed as Castro's agenda to export revolution. Worse, Canada was quite perturbed by Cuba's suspected attempt in 1964 to utilize Gander Airport to transport Cuban military personnel to revolutionary adventures in Algeria.[47] Ottawa was also concerned that Havana was abusing diplomatic immunity by employing 'diplomatic cover' to import from Canada an assortment of badly needed U.S. civilian goods to the island.[48] At any rate, the Cuban situation provided the Canadian government with ammunition to argue that Ottawa, indeed, was pursuing an independent foreign policy at a time when Canadian nationalists turned up the volume of anti-U.S. protests.[49]

More Intrigue in the Caribbean: The Dominican Republic

Having barely digested the troubling implications of Castro's Cuba in the Caribbean Basin, Ottawa was particularly disturbed by events in the Dominican Republic in 1965. That imbroglio pointed to the rising tide of leftist nationalism in the region, raising possible threats to foreign capital and perhaps introducing security concerns. Equally significant, Ottawa did not see eye-to-eye with the U.S. on how best to deal with the situation. As well, the inadequacy of Canadian intelligence in predicting the crisis was exposed. A DEA analysis, released in early 1966 (and which was confidential at the time), is worth quoting at length.

> The prospect that political stability can be established in the Dominican Republic is not bright and there are not yet grounds for optimism that the issues and grievances which erupted in the civil war can be resolved by the June elections, if, indeed, these elections take place. At the time the civil war broke out, the breadth and resilience of Dominican support for the rebels had not been foreseen; insufficient weight had been given to the social, political and economic origins of the civil war; and the extent of extreme left-wing participation in the rebel movement had been exaggerated. Results of these miscalculations have been the protraction of violence and destruction, the dislocation of the Dominican Economy, the entrenchment of anti-American feeling, some polarization of political views at the expense of the moderates, and the preservation thus far of a corrupt military establishment.[50]

Clearly, Ottawa was not pleased with the results of U.S. intervention.

As the DEA analysis cogently argued, Washington's actions achieved the superficial goal of removing a government by which it felt threatened, but the underlying structures of economic, political, and military perils either remained intact or were exacerbated. While the U.S. insisted that the Dominican military would represent an obstacle to socialist foes, Canada worried that the power vested in the armed forces would only perpetuate the inequitable social and economic relations which had provoked the rebellion in the first place.[51] As well, Ottawa strongly resented the unilateral nature of the U.S. action, which, it felt, diminished the power of the rest of the Americas and went against the grain of multilateralism, which was the centrepiece of Canadian foreign policy.[52] Even more worrisome, Canada feared that, ultimately, the U.S. intervention would backfire.

> Cuban officials, initially alarmed by the swift U.S. intervention, consider that the Dominican crisis left them with a net gain as the prestige of the OAS and the U.S. fell within the hemisphere. There is reason to believe that the Dominican Episode undermined much of the goodwill which the Kennedy Administration had generated in Latin America.[53]

Beyond the concerns mentioned above, later Canadian analyses would reveal that Ottawa worried that U.S. intervention in the Dominican Republic would provide Washington with the impetus to intervene militarily in Cuba – with potentially explosive results.[54]

Canada and Hemispheric International Organizations: 1959-67
Canada's relations with revolutionary Cuba have been explored at length in this chapter. The Cuban case has been employed by numerous Canadian analysts as ammunition in arguments against joining the OAS. Although Secretary of State for External Affairs Howard Green supported Canadian membership in the institution, members of Canada's diplomatic corps disagreed and utilized the Cuban case in their arguments. In 1961, for example, Canada's ambassador to Colombia suggested a hypothetical scenario whereby Canada, being a member of the OAS,

> would have the doubtful honour of casting a deciding vote on the hemisphere's relations with Cuba, and thus be placed in a most difficult situation. The pressure on us from the United States and to a lesser extent from countries like Colombia would be enormous. Nevertheless, to follow their lead would surely force a reversal of our present Cuban policy, and perhaps a cooling of existing close relations with such probably dissident voters as Mexico, Brazil and Argentina. The prospect of such a future policy squeeze should surely be taken into account in any evaluation of the actual advantages to be gained from joining the OAS.[55]

Thus, the Cuban example illustrated once again how joining the OAS could alienate Canada either from the U.S. or from certain Latin American powers. Certainly, the 1962 expulsion of Cuba from the OAS, along with the organization's American-directed economic boycott of Cuba, would have presented Ottawa with a dilemma if Canada had, indeed, been a full member.[56] That is, it seemed to demonstrate that Canada's autonomous foreign policy might be rendered vulnerable by membership in the OAS. Not only would pressure be exerted upon Ottawa by the U.S. and Latin America, the Canadian government would also come under domestic fire from those who supported Cuba versus those who argued that Canada should be a member of the OAS in order to 'avert a fatal eruption of the spread of Communism in the Western Hemisphere.'[57] These points would be resurrected on numerous occasions over the next three decades by Canadian opponents to full membership in the OAS.

Despite arguments opposing Canadian membership in the organization, many vigorously supported it. A prominent business magazine in Canada published an editorial urging Canadian membership. The OAS was viewed as a vehicle for augmenting Canadian commercial opportunities in the region, and it was argued that 'we must increase our relations with Latin America if we don't want to be frozen out of their markets by their plans for economic integration.'[58] Proponents of Canadian membership fortified their position by suggesting that, with Secretary of State for External Affairs Howard Green pushing for Canadian membership and with a new section at the DEA having been created especially for Latin America, Canada was more prepared than ever to join the OAS. Moreover, Canada had entrenched its interest in Latin America by finally becoming a member of the Economic Commission for Latin America (ECLA) in 1961, largely as a result of Green's efforts to bolster the Canadian presence in inter-American affairs and to tap into economic trends in the region.[59] Also, by 1961, Canada had completed the process of establishing diplomatic relations with all Latin American countries. In the context of Canada's immersion in Latin American affairs, Canadian reluctance to join the OAS was becoming increasingly conspicuous.

With the strategic implications of Cuba in mind, in 1964 certain Canadian officials argued that if Canada joined the OAS, it would be harassed into becoming a signatory to the Rio Treaty. Furthermore, 'Canadian membership in the OAS would inevitably lead to increasing pressure for Canadian aid to Latin America in the wake of the Alliance for Progress.'[60] While the prospect of defence obligations, along with

burgeoning pleas for increased developmental assistance, seemed to have compounded the reasons for Canada's decision not to join the OAS, Ottawa began thinking about joining the Inter-American Development Bank (IADB). Membership in the bank, according to Canadian analyses, might increase economic gains to Canada from Latin America.[61] In 1964, Ottawa therefore decided to contribute $10 million annually to that institution.

Political uprisings and the subsequent U.S. intervention in the Dominican Republic in 1965 raised additional doubts for Ottawa regarding the efficacy of the OAS. A Canadian embassy official in the Dominican Republic suggested that events there had led him 'to wonder whether the OAS as an organization [could] keep in touch with the belated "nationalism" and desire for democratic government that [seemed] to have finally affected the Southern portions of the hemisphere.'[62] (Future events, especially the Falklands/Malvinas crisis and the Central American imbroglio, would prompt similar concerns.)

The issue of the Dominican Republic raised a number of questions for Canada. First, the unhappy possibility of Ottawa being caught between U.S. imperial ambitions and Latin American nationalism resurfaced. A Chilean official asked: 'Would the dictatorships of the Hemisphere, together with Washington, have been able to carry the day against the democratic nations in debate on the Dominican crisis last May, if Canada had been in the OAS?'[63] Similarly, a Peruvian diplomat argued that the communist scare was being overplayed by the U.S., and that, 'more than anything else, this is why I would like to see Canada as an OAS member: to help provide the voice of reason that is so much needed.'[64] On the other hand, a Bogota newspaper suggested that Canadian membership in the organization would only contribute to 'Anglo-Saxon domination of Hemispheric matters.'[65] Obviously, Latin Americans disagreed as to the implications of Canadian membership in the OAS.[66]

The debate continued, although the substance of the arguments remained largely the same. Noted foreign affairs analyst John Holmes, in a piece written in 1967, echoed the views of Vincent Massey in the late 1940s by arguing that Canada had little in common with Latin America, and therefore should not pursue interests there.[67] In contrast, others argued that by remaining aloof from the OAS, Canada was allowing itself to be uninformed or, worse, disinformed on issues of direct interest to Canadians.[68]

Conclusion

The Cuban issue demonstrated an important degree of independence with respect to Canadian foreign policy and, at the same time, exposed the limits of that autonomy. An ideological chasm emerged between Canada and the U.S. during the Cold War era. Clearly, Ottawa, unlike the U.S., viewed revolutionary turmoil in the region to be a result of indigenous socio-economic inequities, rather than accepting the view prevalent in the U.S. that international communist subversion represented the culprit behind such developments. Events such as the Bay of Pigs invasion suggest that the U.S. failed to comprehend that the Cuban Revolution was, in part, an anti-American revolution, not a communist coup. Without the consent of the majority of the local population for U.S.-supported dictatorships in Cuba, the Dominican Republic, and elsewhere in Latin America, Washington chose to rely on military force to suppress the population into accepting U.S. dominance. It is here that Ottawa and Washington parted ways. While Canada shared the U.S. goals of capitalism and democracy for Latin America, Ottawa differed with its superpower neighbour as to how to attain them.

Amidst this rather confrontational Cold War atmosphere, Canada continued to regard the U.N. as the most appropriate multilateral forum for addressing global and hemispheric crises. The OAS continued to be viewed as too dominated by the U.S. to be useful to Canada. Hence, while some had argued for Canadian membership in the organization, the balance of power rested with those who opposed it. It is also important to emphasize that a Latin American division had been created within the DEA, and that, by the mid-1960s, a Canadian diplomatic corps had been established to deal with all Latin American countries. Overall, however, Ottawa viewed Latin America as trouble-prone and continued to view the North Atlantic region as the centrepiece of Canadian foreign policy.

The choices that Canada made with respect to Cuba have, in some important ways, represented a guiding light for Canadian policy in Latin America ever since. Ottawa learned that it was worth the trouble to assume an independent line vis-à-vis the U.S. regarding Latin American affairs in cases where Canada fundamentally objected to U.S. policy. Overall, this approach has served to win the respect of Latin American states, who could not view Ottawa as simply a puppet of Washington's policy. Similarly, the people of Canada were assured that their country's foreign affairs did not merely echo those of their southern neighbour.

Last but not least, Canada benefited economically from its maverick stance towards Cuba. The following chapters will examine how Canadian-Cuban ties were strengthened during the Trudeau era.

Part Two:
The Trudeau Years

4

New Approaches

The early Trudeau years were a watershed for Canada's role in the world. It was an exciting period – a period that led some observers to characterize Canada as a 'principal power' rather than as a 'middle power.' This was ironic, given that Trudeau himself suggested a demotion of Canada's international position. At any rate, it was in the Trudeau era that Latin America was first viewed as truly significant to Canada. While progress was made in fostering a greater Canadian presence in Latin America, much early promise was simply not realized, as will be seen in subsequent chapters.

Foreign Policy for Canadians

A radical rethinking of foreign policy was reflected in *Foreign Policy for Canadians (FPC)*, a series of six intellectually rigorous pamphlets released in 1970, which established new international vistas for Canada. Many of the most important views reflected in that work, however, were presaged by decisions enacted by Pierre Elliott Trudeau during the preceding two years. In 1968, for example, Canada afforded diplomatic recognition to Communist China, beating the U.S. to the punch and, hence, waving a banner of independence. And, in a move which startled its Western allies, in May of the same year Ottawa announced its decision to cut Canadian troop commitments to Western Europe by one-half. Both these decisions reflected the Trudeau government's acceptance of a new distribution of global power and, coupled with this, a significantly reduced threat from international communism. Trudeau posed a number of pointed questions in this regard.

Will the U.S. sacrifice Europe and NATO before blowing up the world? ... What is the point of having large conventional forces if they are going to lose the conventional battle anyway? ... Is NATO the best way to secure peace at the moment? ... When are we going to arrive at a plan to achieve peace by not getting stronger militarily? ... Can we assume that Russia wants war because it invaded Czechoslovakia? We do not want war but we (ie, the United States) landed troops in Lebanon, we sent troops to the Dominican Republic. Are these not similar? ... In what way is NATO of value to Canada?[1]

This profound questioning of the world order coincided with an atmosphere in which Canadians were critical of U.S. foreign policy, especially with regard to Vietnam, and in which they were also concerned about increasing American penetration into Canada's political economy.[2]

Also in 1968, Trudeau announced that

we have to take greater account of the ties which bind us to other nations of this hemisphere – in the Caribbean, Latin America – and of their economic needs. We have to explore new avenues of increasing our political and economic relations with Latin America where more than four hundred million people will live by the turn of the century and where we have substantial interests.[3]

Hence, the Trudeau government signalled early in its tenure that Latin America was a rising international power and required greater Canadian attention. In 1968, Canada's most extensive government mission ever sent to Latin America – a mission lasting one month and including five cabinet ministers – represented the initial phase of Ottawa's new Latin American policy.[4] A Latin America Task Force was assembled in 1969, consisting largely of academics and businesspeople, who, upon deliberation, recommended that Canada take out full membership in the OAS,[5] a point elaborated upon below.

Turning to *FPC*, I begin with the introductory document, which established general themes for Canadian foreign policy, and then shift to an analysis of the pamphlet devoted to Canada's Latin American policy. *FPC* asserts that Canada's global power had declined precipitously since the Second World War, a natural occurrence given the reconstruction of Europe and Japan.[6] This analysis stood in vivid contrast to the assessment of previous Canadian governments, which deemed Canada's rank to be certainly among the upper tier of states. According to *FPC*, Germany and Japan were the world's 'new great powers.'[7]

Among other striking challenges to conventional Canadian analyses, the Trudeau government contended that once-sacred international organizations had withered and grown irrelevant, and that the global ideological contest had become blurred. 'Western Europe had not only fully recovered from the war but was taking steps toward integration that put strain on transatlantic ties and, combined with changes in the Communist world, called into question the continuing Canadian participation in NATO.'[8] The problems of the Third World ranked increasingly high in global significance and demanded Canadian attention.[9] Once again, key components of the foreign policy doctrines of previous administrations underwent radical restructuring.

Although the absence of a pamphlet devoted specifically to U.S.-Canadian relations was particularly conspicuous (other pamphlets were devoted to Europe, international development, Latin America, the Pacific, and the U.N.), what appeared salient were analytical tidbits indicative of a distinctly new tenor regarding Ottawa's attitude towards its southern neighbour.

> Criticism tended to gather in a hard lump of frustration – accentuated by the war in Vietnam – about having to live in the shadow of the United States and its foreign policy, about the heavy dependence of Canada's economy on continuing American prosperity, and about the marked influence of that large and dynamic society on Canadian life in general.[10]

The preservation of Canada as an independent state was among the highest priorities for Ottawa in the face of enormous, though apparently unpopular, U.S. power.[11] Nationalism was an important bond between Canada and Latin America in the 1970s and early 1980s.

It was also deemed to be in Canada's interest to court new international partners as political and economic 'counterweights' to the U.S.[12] Latin America would become a case in point. Not only would this diversification protect Canadian independence and sovereignty, according to *FPC* the position of the U.S. would soon decline relative to that of other powers.[13] Therefore, it would be prudent to foster relations with the world's up and coming powers, rather than to cling to one that was waning. The Trudeau government was surely ahead of its time in conceptualizing the contentious issue of U.S. hegemonic decline, since the serious debate regarding the slippage of American power did not occur in mainstream academia until the late 1970s and 1980s.[14]

Related to the centrality of Canada maintaining its sovereignty and independence was the conviction that Canadian foreign policy should serve domestic needs. 'External activities should be directly related to national policies pursued within Canada, and serve the same objectives.'[15] In this light Ottawa questioned previous defence spending and commitments. Did they really serve Canadian interests, especially in a changing international environment? Trudeau observed that 'Canada's present military establishment was determined not to impress our enemies but rather to impress our friends,'[16] and that 'it should be your foreign policy which determines your military policy,'[17] not the other way around.

Six foreign policy goals that would advance Canadian domestic interests were identified by *FPC*: (1) economic growth; (2) sovereignty and independence; (3) peace and security; (4) social justice; (5) the enhancement of quality of life; and (6) a harmonious natural environment.[18] The first goal, economic growth, would be accomplished through trade diversification, conducted with not only the rising industrial powers in mind, but also with Latin America. The diversification of Canadian political and economic policy would also lead to the achievement of the second goal, sovereignty and independence.

Unlike previous administrations, the Trudeau government did not consider European peace and security to be a problem. In the era of détente, with a huge arsenal of nuclear weapons pointing east and west, and with the developed Northern powers having too much to lose to embark upon a devastating war, stability in Europe was seen as more or less assured. The real threats to world peace would, increasingly, emerge from the Third World.

> The frustration of developing countries during the next decade will increase as they feel more acutely the limitations on their own technological and material progress, compared with that of industrialized countries. Their sense of impotence to gain quickly and effectively a more equitable distribution of needed resources will become more bitter if the signs of flagging interest and disillusionment on the part of more-developed countries are not reversed.[19]

Thus the third goal, peace and security, would be achieved through the creation of developmental assistance programs, along with a call for the erosion of First World protectionism towards Third World products. The attainment of the fourth goal, social justice, would be secured through focusing upon human rights and, therefore, development issues in the Third World. Thus, the focus on North-South relations provided an important context for Canada's new policy towards Latin America.

The fifth goal, enhancement of quality of life, would 'involve such activities as cultural, technological and scientific changes which, while supporting other foreign objectives, [would be] designed to yield a rewarding life for Canadians and to reflect clearly Canada's bilingual and multicultural character.'[20] Finally, the sixth goal, ensuring a harmonious natural environment, would entail a recognition of the threat to human life posed by the deterioration of the global environment.

Foreshadowing trends that would not fully take shape until the late 1980s and 1990s, FPC predicted the increasing importance in world affairs of transnational production[21] – a point that is key in the current global political economy and which is central to the North American Free Trade Agreement. The review contained other prophetic aspects as well, not the least of which was the prediction of a 'worldwide trend toward regionalism in one form or another.'[22] The current shift towards world trading areas – the European Community (EC), the Asia Pacific region, and the Americas – is the manifestation of a phenomenon which Ottawa predicted two decades ago. The crucial point, then, is that FPC represents a watershed in governmental conceptualizations of Canadian foreign policy – and, in some important ways, correctly predicts trends in international history two or three decades into the future.

But this radical rethinking alarmed and angered mainstream commentators of the time. Peyton Lyon, a professor at Carleton University, for example, could not accept the Trudeau government's approach, arguing, falsely as it turned out, that a retreat from Europe could be equated with a Canadian retraction from the rest of the world.[23] Elsewhere, he claimed that FPC was 'nationalist, self-centred,' and represented a reversal of Canada's internationalist bias.[24] Similarly, there could be no question that Trudeau's predecessor, Prime Minister Pearson, was not enamoured of the new thinking in Ottawa. Pearson argued that the Trudeau government had defined its national interest too narrowly by not taking into account the significance of global security concerns.[25] Pearson was certainly correct in arguing that some of Canada's traditional allies were less than pleased with FPC, with the most notable example being the Europeans, who would refuse Ottawa's overtures for trade diversification in the face of Canadian troop cuts in Europe. Nevertheless, other parts of the globe, such as the Third World, applauded Trudeau's fresh approach, as did many Canadians.

As noted earlier, one pamphlet of *FPC* was devoted entirely to Latin America. It began with the observation that, although geographically screened from Canada by the U.S., Latin America was a rising power and that Canadian influence there was on an upswing.[26] *Latin America: Foreign Policy for Canadians (LA:FPC)* argued that the U.S. would 'pose a challenge to Canadians to maintain their own cultural and entrepreneurial identity when dealing with Latin Americans.'[27] One is reminded here of Trudeau's classic analogy with regard to having the U.S. as one's neighbour: 'Living next to you is in some ways like sleeping with an elephant: no matter how friendly and even-tempered the beast, one is affected by every twitch and grunt.'[28]

It is significant that, in *LA:FPC*, Ottawa drew a parallel between Canadian and Latin American economic dependence upon the U.S.

> Since Canadian producers export to the United States market and the United States investment in Canada is substantial, there is a certain correspondence between the Canadian and Latin American situations vis-à-vis the United States, and the Latin Americans tend to look to Canada for understanding of their attitude toward the United States on economic questions.[29]

Hence, the contention arose that perhaps both Latin America and Canada could to some degree escape their dependence upon the U.S. by fortifying commercial relations with each other. 'Increased trade with Latin America and judicious Canadian investment there would augment Canada's capacity to pay its way in the world.'[30]

It was believed that, with the proper focus, Canada and its Latin American counterparts could reach mutually beneficial arrangements. As Latin America developed economically, a process that could be assisted through the initiation of bilateral developmental assistance,[31] there would be more demand for Canadian products. Furthermore, Canada's expertise in a number of fields could help to develop the region through direct foreign investment – especially in the areas of telecommunications, grain storage facilities, hydroelectric equipment, port-handling equipment, forest fire-fighting equipment, pulp-and-paper machinery, specialized aircraft, subway, road, and rail equipment, nuclear reactors, airport construction, aerial survey, and so on.[32] Canada would also make a commitment to reduce protectionist measures against Latin American goods, and the Canadian government would intervene to promote Canadian trade with, and investment in, Latin

America.[33] This was an era in Canadian history during which it was acceptable for the state to involve itself in the economy in a manner that would be considered taboo after 1984.

There was also a debate within the review regarding the undying matter of Canada's option of joining the Organization of American States. While a government-formulated task force recommended joining the OAS in 1969, as was noted earlier, *LA:FPC* argued that such a move would disproportionately channel Canadian resources to the organization's membership dues. Hence, the Trudeau government suggested that the most propitious move for the moment would be to bolster bilateral relations with Latin America. Short of full membership, *LA:FPC* promised that a 'formal link between Canada and the OAS countries [would] be established at a suitable level.'[34] This would result in permanent observer status.

In sum, the review was analytically path-breaking for Canadian policy towards Latin America. The region was identified as a focus for Canadian foreign policy for the first time in history. Other firsts included the initiation of bilateral aid, a commitment to engage more fully with the OAS, and a dedication to increase trade and investment to the region in order to diversify Canadian relations away from the U.S.

As noted earlier, in a glaring omission, *FPC* contained no substantial discussion of U.S.-Canadian relations. It was not until after four years in office that the Trudeau government managed to produce a document on this obviously crucial topic, which led some analysts to say that Canadian foreign policy was being held in a state of suspended animation.[35] The long-awaited commentary came in the form of an article by Secretary of State for External Affairs Mitchell Sharp in *International Perspectives*, entitled 'Canada-U.S. Relations: Options for the Future.'

Although consistent with the general tone of *FPC*, which argued that Canada needed to actively protect its sovereignty and independence as well as to diversify its political and economic partners, Sharp's article was also a reaction to three events in U.S.-Canadian relations which had occurred over the previous four years. First, as von Riekhoff observes, was the so-called 'Nixon doctrine,' which promoted independent economic relations between developed states.[36] Second was the U.S. administration's reduction in purchases of Canadian petroleum in retaliation for Ottawa's Arctic Waters Act, which created a 100-mile pollution control zone in the Arctic, thereby extending Canadian sovereignty in the region and so curtailing U.S. encroachment in the Northwest Passage.[37] Third, and most important, was the announcement in August 1971 of a 10 per cent U.S. surcharge to be levied against all foreign imports, including those from Canada. That, together with the collapse of Bretton Woods, signalled the retreat of U.S. leadership in the global economy.

Sharp's article began with the premise that the traditional global distribution of power was changing in some important ways. No longer would the U.S. and the USSR dominate international relations. There were important new powers to be reckoned with – a reconstructed Europe and Japan, an emerging China,[38] as well as regions such as Latin America. It was particularly important for Canada to incorporate economic diversification into its foreign policy, because the U.S.-Canadian relationship was one of 'unequal dependence; the impact of the United States on Canada [being] far greater than Canada's impact on the United States.'[39]

Sharp then proceeded to cite public opinion polls which demonstrated that 88.5 per cent of Canadians wanted Canada to have more control over its economy. Further, these polls showed that a majority of Canadians would even prefer a lower standard of living in efforts to diminish what was viewed as unacceptably high levels of U.S. investment.[40] Canadian public opinion seemed to support a policy leading away from the 'dependence' observed by Sharp.

Sharp saw three options, the first being to maintain more or less Canada's present relationship with the United States.[41] Although that avenue might have been the easiest to pursue, it was not in keeping with the view of global politics defined by *FPC* and by Sharp himself in the introduction to his essay. It was also inconsistent with public opinion polls.

Option two, pursuing integration with the U.S., was even more unthinkable at that historical juncture.[42] This possibility, if carried through, was viewed as irreversible for Canada, while the U.S. would have the power to retract. Sharp also argued that further integration with the U.S. would limit Canada's capacity to develop links with other rising powers, and, worse, it would pave the way for political union between the two countries. As the process towards political union occurred, Canada would witness a diminishing capacity to control policies which affected it.[43] Brian Mulroney would pursue an integrationist policy a decade-and-a-half later.

The Trudeau government selected the 'Third Option.' The objective would be to curb Canadian vulnerability to the U.S. by directing economic activity to other global powers.[44] It would require substantial state intervention.[45] Ultimately, the Third Option would fail in its goal of diversifying Canadian trade. Western Europe, angered by the Canadian troop reduction there, was not interested in bolstering commercial relations with Canada. With respect to the rising star of the East, the Japanese showed little interest in Canada, and when they did, they complained about Canada's low productivity, high wage levels, and propensity for strikes.[46] Trudeau's principal secretary lamented that the policy, while appropriate, generally failed due to an increasing lack of will by the government to carry it out.[47] Despite those shortcomings, the Third Option did succeed in Latin America. As shall be seen, it was instrumental in reinforcing Canadian trade and investment in the region, and in carving out a new role for Canada in the OAS.

Overall, the Trudeau government's revision of Canadian policy suggested that Canada's orientation towards the global arena should be more nationalistic and, particularly, should be independent of U.S. policy. In a more multipolar world, Canada would endeavour to form close bonds with states of roughly similar international power and disposition. These potential allies would be found not only in the First World but also in the Third World. It was in this context that Latin America found a new place in Canadian foreign policy.

Conclusion

The early Trudeau years were a watershed in Canadian foreign policy. Sweeping new analyses of international relations led Ottawa to formulate a new set of global objectives. The shifting global context was an instrumental factor in the revision of Canadian foreign policy. Arguably, the late 1960s and early 1970s saw the end of Pax Americana. U.S. destructive capability was confronted by Soviet military parity as well as by new and formidable security concerns in the Third World. U.S. productive capability was challenged by a reconstructed Europe and Japan, while the collapse of Bretton Woods signalled a retreat by Washington from leadership in the global economy.

Paralleling challenges to U.S. productive and destructive capabilities was the new ideological complexion of the international arena. Instead of the intense ideological hostility that existed in the bipolar Cold War era, the emergence of a more multipolar global environment placed relations in a less Manichean ideological context. In the West, this sometimes took the form of social democracy. In Latin America, it was often manifested in nationalism and anti-American sloganeering. Accompanying these changes was a rethinking of both the models of state structure and of international organizations. Thus, the early Trudeau government's refashioning of foreign policy was commensurate with shifts in the world order.

As Canada attempted to diversify its economic and political relations in order to ensure independence from the U.S., Canadian foreign policy began to focus on Latin America. The Latin American Task Force was created and embarked on what was then the largest official Canadian contingent ever to visit the region. Bilateral aid was promised, as was the lifting of protectionist measures against Latin American products. There was a reconsideration of Canada's relationship with the OAS, with eventual progress in this realm as well. Ottawa seemed intent upon penetrating the so-called U.S. screen to enrich its relations with its Latin neighbours to the South.

But while there was progress in furthering Canadian ties to Latin America, actual policy did not live up to the promise of the late 1960s and early 1970s. There were a number of reasons for this, which will be elaborated upon in subsequent chapters. Among these, government policy sometimes proved to be incoherent, recommending on the one hand an entrenchment of Canadian interests in Latin America, while on the other hand implementing the closure of embassies in key Latin American locations. Also, at this stage, Canadian academics, nongovernmental institutions, and the business community were quite immature regarding inter-American affairs, and had much to learn about the region before ties would be enhanced.

5
1968-73: Early Promise

Almost five centuries after Christopher Columbus made his ethnocentric claim, Canada, during the Trudeau years, 'discovered' Latin America. The Trudeau era will be divided into three distinct periods, 1968-73, 1974-9, and 1980-4, and Canada's ministerial mission to Latin America will be given considerable emphasis here. Among the other issues discussed are Canada's interests in hemispheric institutions, regional security, trade/aid/investment, key aspects of bilateral relations, and the birth of important domestic groups interested in Canadian policy.

Ministerial Mission
In May 1968, as a component of a general review of Canadian foreign policy, Ottawa decided to send a ministerial mission to Latin America from 27 October to 27 November 1968. The mission, which included visits to nine countries,[1] had a number of objectives. The first of these was an effort to explore possible benefits from closer political, economic, and cultural relations with Latin America. Ottawa hoped that Canadian ministers would be able to establish direct contact with their Latin American counterparts and thus improve bilateral relations. As well, Ottawa wanted to explore similarities and distinctions between Canada and various Latin American countries regarding an array of global issues. Finally, Canada wanted to be better known in Latin America.[2] Five ministers took part in the mission, in addition to representatives from the Exports Credits Insurance Corporation (ECIC), the Canadian International Development Agency (CIDA), the National Film Board (NFB), the Canadian Broadcasting Corporation (CBC), and the press.

Among the issues of concern to the mission was the significance of the Latin American trend towards integration, particularly regarding the Latin American Free Trade Agreement (LAFTA), the Central American

Common Market, the River Plate Basin Group, and the Andean Group. The mission was especially concerned with the erection of protectionist barriers that might result from such integration, and so it endeavoured to establish 'reasonable terms' of trade between Canada and Latin America.[3] However, reports from Canadian posts throughout Latin America indicated that progress towards integration was occurring at a laggard pace, and that the prognosis for success was not especially bright.[4] Thus, while Canada was concerned with the possible consequences of Latin American integration, it was aware that this was not likely to reach fruition in the short term.

Economic issues were the mission's primary concern. Canada was keenly interested in expanding trade on a number of fronts. These included telecommunications, resource extraction equipment, transportation equipment, and nuclear reactors. Along with promoting specific products, the mission was also concerned with the transportation of Latin American goods to Canada. Many Latin American products were shipped first to the U.S. and then to Canada, inflating prices through the addition of service charges and also distorting trade figures.

Not only was the mission responsible for bolstering trade, it was also supposed to promote Canadian investment in Latin America. In the era of import substitution, the mission was quite aware that many parts of Latin America were sensitive to foreign ownership and investment. But it was also convinced that Latin America craved additional Canadian investment as long as it could control it through such arrangements as joint ventures.[5] Perhaps the bottom line for many Latin American countries was that Canadian investment would provide the area with technology and know-how and, crucially, would serve as a substitute for U.S. investment.

One of the most important issues on the mission's agenda was the announcement of the establishment of a Joint Mexico-Canada Committee. The committee would deal predominantly with matters of economic concern but would also address political and even cultural issues.[6] The idea behind it had been planted in 1965 by the Mexican foreign minister, Antonio Carillo Flores, during a meeting in Mexico with Canada's minister of finance, Mitchell Sharp.[7] Mexico had already established similar committees with other countries. The committee would begin meeting in 1969 at an interval of not less than every two years. In addition to providing important, if belated, recognition of the significance of Mexico to Canada, the move also signalled Ottawa's increasing economic interest in Latin America. In many ways, the formation of this committee foreshadowed the integration process of the 1990s.

In addition to the issues of regional integration, trade, and the formation of the Canada-Mexico Joint Committee, the subject of Canadian developmental assistance to Latin America was prominent during the government's 1968 tour of that region. Latin America received a mere 3 per cent of Canada's developmental assistance in that year,[8] and Canadian exports insured by the Export Development Corporation (EDC) represented only 13.7 per cent of the total insured by the EDC.[9] At that point aid was channelled through the Inter-American Development Bank (IADB), the World Bank, and the Canadian International Development Agency (CIDA). Canadian diplomatic personnel in Latin America strongly favoured the establishment of Canadian bilateral developmental assistance, since it was hoped that this would fortify Canada's Latin American presence as well as promote Canadian products through a tied aid provision.[10] Although bilateral aid would not be implemented for another three years, in 1968 CIDA created the Non-Governmental Organizations (NGO) Division, which would subsidize approved projects by up to half of their total cost.[11] This was a controversial move, since it was opposed by key personnel at Canadian embassies in Mexico and Argentina, apparently because they preferred the funds to be directly controlled by the government.[12] It is significant that provision of such funds to NGOs would strengthen their domestic influence upon Canadian policy in Latin America, a point to which I shall return.

Security issues also arose during Canada's reconsideration of its relations with Latin America. The government could not help but notice that in some of the countries visited the armed forces played a significant political role.[13] It will be remembered that, since 1945, the predominance of military dictatorships had been a major factor in Canada's reluctance to establish closer relations with Latin America. By 1968, Ottawa was still unclear as to the repercussions of dealing with the region's military regimes, but it now accepted them as a reality that must be coped with in order to realize clearly formulated economic and political objectives.[14]

Nuclear issues also appeared on the mission's agenda. Canada strongly supported the creation of a nuclear-free zone in Latin America.[15] With the exception of Cuba, Guyana, and Barbados, all countries in Latin America and the Caribbean had signed the Latin American Nuclear-Free Zone Treaty by 1968. The treaty banned testing, use, fabrication, production, or acquisition of nuclear arms in the region as well as the receipt, storage, and installation of such arms.[16] There was a rift among the signatories, however, regarding peaceful explosions of nuclear devices. As the Disarmament Division of the DEA noted,

> Mexico and other like-minded parties interpret the article defining a nuclear weapon as 'any device which has the characteristics of a nuclear weapon' to mean that peaceful explosions carried out by Parties to the Treaty are prohibited. Brazil, Argentina and some others, however, give precedence to an article which they contend specifically permits peaceful explosions.[17]

The Disarmament Division of the DEA warned the ministerial mission visiting Latin America that Brazil, especially, was sensitive to the issue of peaceful explosions of nuclear devices, and it was this that kept it from signing the Nuclear Non-Proliferation Treaty (NPT).[18] Although Canada signed the NPT on 23 July 1968 and strongly promoted it at the U.N., Argentina, Bolivia, Chile, Uruguay, and Cuba failed to become signatories. The Disarmament Division urged the Ministerial Mission to convince non-signatories to become Parties of the NPT, although Canada's efforts had little apparent effect.

The mission was also equipped with DEA briefings regarding the question of 'stability' in various Latin American countries. The region was divided into three categories. The first comprised countries witnessing 'Castroite-type subversion' complete with guerrilla warfare, as exemplified by Central America, Venezuela, and Peru. The second category consisted of nations plagued by dysfunctional political systems, such as in Ecuador, the Dominican Republic, Mexico, and Brazil. Chile was deemed to be the only stable country, although the Latin American Division of the DEA had the uncomfortable premonition that Chile had 'a large, legal Communist Party which might perhaps be in a position to assume power through future elections'.[19]

Other security issues that would confront the ministerial mission included the situation in Cuba as well as a simmering dispute in the Falkland (Malvinas) Islands. Regarding the former, Canadian trade with Cuba continued to be a sore spot for some Latin American governments, especially those dealing with leftist subversion. However, Canadians argued that the economic boycott of Cuba had not yielded positive results and was simply producing the undesirable effect of pushing Havana closer to Moscow.

Regarding the Falklands-Malvinas question, prior to the mission's visit to Latin America the Argentine ambassador had attempted to lobby the Canadian government to support Argentina's historic claim to the islands. The DEA noted that 'the Ambassador concluded that although he recognized that Canada would find it difficult to support Argentina against the United Kingdom on this issue, he hoped that Canada would keep Argentina's interest in mind.'[20] As an aside, he pointed out that Antoine Louis Bougainville, along with other French Canadians who had served in Quebec under Montcalm, founded the first settlement on the Falkland (Malvinas) Islands upon fleeing Canada after the British conquest.[21]

Not surprisingly, the issue of Canada's role in the OAS was highlighted during the mission's tour. Ottawa indicated that 'it appeared that the governments of all the countries visited would welcome Canada as a member of the OAS. However, while some urged Canadian membership, others did not.'[22] Presumably, one of the countries which did not encourage Canadian membership in the OAS was Mexico. The Mexican foreign minister, Carillo Flores, advised Ottawa a few months prior to the mission's tour that Canada would do well to stay out of the OAS and, instead, to focus upon bilateral relations with Latin America.[23] Although the Mexican official gave no reasons for his position, it is likely that he viewed the OAS as dysfunctional because of U.S. domination.

On the heels of the ministerial mission's tour of the region, a Latin American task force was created in 1969. Consisting largely of academics and members of the business community, the task force considered three options for Canada vis-à-vis the OAS: (1) it could maintain the status quo; (2) it could decide to join the OAS immediately; and (3) it could take steps short of joining the OAS to strengthen relations, and to defer the question of full OAS membership until the subject received further consideration.[24]

The task force recommended option two, joining the OAS immediately. As was indicated in Chapter 4, the Canadian government eventually chose option three. Part of the decision to avoid full membership had to do with financial costs – with dues estimated at $5.5 million annually.[25] Also, as was previously mentioned, full membership would mean that Canada would be pressured to support political and economic sanctions against states such as Cuba,[26] and would also leave itself open to becoming caught up in U.S.-Latin American disputes. Option three, viewed as the safest course of action, entailed appointing an observer mission to the OAS and, therefore, satisfying Latin American demands that Canada become involved in the organization while, at the same time, avoiding the necessity of voting on sensitive issues. This option would necessitate constructing bilateral relations with key Latin American countries. As was noted in Chapter 4, *LA:FPC* argued that option three afforded the most appropriate course of action.

Turning to other issues, it was during this period that a web of domestic interests would appear and eventually have a substantial influence upon Canadian policy towards Latin America. Brascan, a Canadian company with a massive investment in Brazil, was instrumental in the formation of the Canadian Association for Latin America (CALA) in 1969. This business lobby group attempted to strengthen Canadian-Latin American economic relations. Its links with Ottawa were tight, and, after 1973, it managed to achieve an arrangement whereby it received half of its funding from the Canadian government. Ottawa was crucial to expanding Canadian economic relations with Latin America, as, generally, business tended to follow the government's lead.[27]

Another important interest group, the Canadian Association of Latin American Studies (CALAS), was also formed in 1969 and published the journal *North/South: Canadian Journal of Latin American and Caribbean Studies*. CALAS worked to encourage increased academic relations between Canada and Latin America. Although the group received government funding, its editorials often criticized Ottawa's policies. The crucial point here is that, by 1969, an array of domestic forces sprouted within Canada which would concern themselves with inter-American affairs. Some of these would serve as an important domestic influence upon Canadian foreign policy. Such groups included Canadian NGOs, CALA, and an assortment of church groups, as well as roughly 2,000 missionaries working in the region.

While on some fronts Canadian relations with Latin America seemed to be advancing at an unprecedented rate, in other respects they seemed to be retreating. For example, Canada closed its embassies in the Dominican Republic, Ecuador, and Uruguay in late 1969 in order to reinforce the Canadian presence in francophone Africa and the Vatican.[28] Although the embassy closures occurred in rather small countries, the closure in the Dominican Republic, in particular, sparked criticism due to Canada's economic interests there.

The year 1970 was key, witnessing the publication of *LA:FPC*. As was mentioned in Chapter 4, this document pledged to reduce Canadian protectionism with respect to Latin American goods. This was especially important, as it shielded Canada from potential protectionist measures emanating from Latin American regional integration (e.g., LAFTA, the Andean Group, and the Central American Common Market). Canada viewed such integration as an attempt to pressure developed countries into adopting policies that accommodated the needs of the Third World.[29] Hence, there was the possibility that if Canada did not reduce its tariffs on Latin American goods, its products could be shut out by regional trading blocs.

Also in 1970, the DEA released an important set of Canadian objectives in Latin America. Ottawa stressed the need for Canadian-Latin American cooperation concerning human rights promotion and environmental protection. It was noted that

> closer relations with Latin American countries [would] serve to strengthen Canada's independence and national identity; at the same time, such associations [would] offer an opportunity to diversify Canada's external relations and make more significant Canadian influence on the policies of these countries and indirectly, on the policies of the United States in this area.[30]

Thus, even prior to the announcement of its Third Option in 1972, the Trudeau government was committed to bolstering Canadian sovereignty by placing less emphasis on the U.S. and more emphasis on regions such as Latin America, which was identified as a 'growing force in the world.'[31]

Once Latin America was established as a priority, Ottawa constructed a hierarchy indicating which countries were most important to Canada. Because of their economic potential, the first level of importance included Mexico, Brazil, Argentina, and Venezuela. For political, geographical, as well as economic reasons, Mexico was especially important to Canada. Colombia, Peru, and Central America occupied the second level of importance, as they were the focus of Canadian bilateral aid. The DEA added that 'Chile should also be included as significant for political reasons and potential economic interest.'[32]

The importance assigned to Latin America occurred amidst a myriad of significant global changes. The world seemed to be moving away from bipolarity, which had characterized international relations since 1945, towards multipolarity. Canada diplomatically recognized Communist China in 1970, years before the U.S., and, in so doing, formally acknowledged its power. Europe and Japan emerged as major economic contenders in the global arena and, therefore, as major political powers. Parts of Latin America were booming, and Canada saw it as an emerging world power. Other Third World states would soon be inspired by the power of the Organization of Petroleum-Exporting Countries (OPEC), prompting developed nations to appreciate not only their dependence upon oil but also the possibility of Third World countries asserting their collective power in the international arena.

In contrast to the rising star of various countries and regions of the world during this time, the U.S. was beset with enormous problems. This was discussed at the first Canada-Mexico ministerial meeting in 1971. Canada's secretary of state for external affairs, Mitchell Sharp, confided to his Mexican counterparts that the U.S. was less than pleased with Ottawa's policy on a number of fronts, such as its recognition of Communist China, its policy of sovereignty in Arctic waters, and its maintenance of friendly relations with Cuba. Both Mexico and Canada believed that the U.S. had been weakened by its protracted involvement in the Vietnam War. Domestic economic problems, particularly 'stagflation' (flat economic growth combined with relatively high inflation rates), also served to weaken U.S. power. Both Canada and Mexico lamented the 1971 American surcharge on exports, but viewed this as evidence of declining U.S. power. Much of Latin America seemed less willing to follow the U.S. This was apparent by an intellectual flirtation with dependency theory in certain parts of Latin America – a theory that argued, in part, that Third World countries must retract from the world capitalist system (dominated by the U.S.) in order for true development to take place. As a result of U.S. debilitation and the diffusion of global power, the Mexican minister, Emilio Rabasa, suggested that the time was ripe for Canada to join the OAS, implying that the institution would no longer be dominated by the U.S.[33]

With the emergence of détente, Canada under Trudeau avoided the anti-communism and anti-Sovietism that were apparent in earlier periods. Prior to Trudeau's visit to the USSR in 1971, the DEA prepared a background paper on Soviet policy towards Latin America. The paper suggested that the Soviets were attempting to gain influence in the region through diplomacy rather than through insurrection and revolution. For example, Moscow saw Chile as capable of illustrating the peaceful election of a socialist government. The paper went on to note that the Soviets wished to avoid another Cuba, due both to its expense and to its general isolation within Latin America.[34] The relaxation of superpower tensions may have been another reason why Canadian participation in the OAS now appeared more favourable than it had in the past.

In 1971, Salvador Allende, the Marxist president of Chile who had come to power a year earlier, extended an invitation to Pierre Trudeau to visit the country. The DEA weighed the pros and cons of such a visit, arguing that acceptance of this invitation might offer an opportunity for the Chilean government 'to diversify its foreign relations and to obtain some leverage in resisting communist pressures.'[35] The socialist government in Chile also raised some concerns for Canadian businesses – concerns which could be discussed during Trudeau's visit. A declaration that all mineral deposits in Chile were the exclusive property of the state led a small Canadian venture to wonder whether its operation would be nationalized. Ottawa was optimistic that this would not occur, since Canada possessed valuable mining expertise and because 'we [were] not labelled with the unfortunate association of attributed imperialist tendencies.'[36] Ottawa ultimately decided to reject any visit for fear of alienating rightist elements in Chile and elsewhere.

There were other developments in 1971 that were particularly important to Canada's relationship with Latin America. A $10 million bilateral aid program was established for the region, and negotiations began in April for Canada's permanent observer status in the OAS. In pursuing expanded trade with its hemispheric partners, it was acknowledged that Latin America ranked second – after the U.S. and ahead of Europe – in terms of importing fully manufactured products from Canada.[37] The Trudeau government opened a new department, the Bureau of Western Hemisphere Affairs, to deal with increasingly important inter-American issues, and Ottawa continued to work with CALA and NGOs in order to further Canadian involvement in the region.

The year 1972 was pivotal for Canadian foreign policy towards Latin America. Not only was it a time to trace the progress that had been made during the first Trudeau government, it was also a time that witnessed important milestones in Canada's relationship with the Americas. Perhaps foremost among these was Canada's official status as permanent observer in the OAS, which was approved on 2 February 1972.[38] As the DEA observed, since the status of permanent observer was not envisaged in the organization's statutes, 'Canada was asking the OAS not only to accept a special Canadian relation but also to amend its procedures to make this feasible.'[39]

The formulation of Canada's Third Option, discussed in Chapter 4, paralleled Canada's formal entrance into the OAS in 1972.[40] Trade prospects looked good at this point, with Canadian exports rising from $395 million in 1968 to $613 million in 1972.[41] One potential problem for increased Canadian trade, however, was that Latin American products were, increasingly, manufactured goods rather than staples and, thus, were beginning to compete with Canadian goods. This was exacerbated by the popularity of import substitution models, which were adopted in some of Latin America's most developed countries. Furthermore, in order for Canada to increase trade with Latin America, it would have to understand certain Latin American realities. According to Galo Plaza, secretary general of the OAS:

> The new Latin American nationalism is characterized by a desire to assert the national identity more boldly, and to chart the course for development without foreign interference or well-meaning paternalism ... If Canada understands the new Latin American nationalism, and acts accordingly, the door in Latin America will be open for Canadian cooperation and investment ... Canada, for reasons of her own enlightened self-interest, cannot afford to remain aloof from developments in Latin America.[42]

Being nationalist itself, Canada had no problems appreciating Latin American sentiments.

Canada also joined the Inter-American Development Bank in May 1972, having provided $74 million in developmental loan funds to that institution since 1964.[43] Canada would commit $100 million to the bank between 1972 and 1975.[44] Ottawa hoped that joining the IADB would both stimulate Canadian trade and provide Canada with more control over its contributions.[45]

There were other developments regarding Canada and international organizations. Sympathetic to Ottawa's policy of attempting to diversify trade away from the U.S., the Andean Community (Ancom), a subregional group within LAFTA, granted Canada permanent observer status in 1972. CIDA, the first outside contributor to the group, dispersed almost $6 million to finance studies on economic integration in Latin America.[46] Canada, however, viewed Ancom as a regional exception, as Latin America was considered to be increasingly nationalist as opposed to interdependent or integrationist.[47]

As can be seen, 1972 witnessed an unprecedented level of Canadian participation in inter-American organizations. This was accompanied by a $50,000 DEA stipend to devise methods to increase Canadian participation in hemispheric organizations.[48] In addition to the developments mentioned above, Canada also increased its inter-American role by joining or strengthening its position in a number of smaller agencies within the OAS.[49]

There were also some important advances in the bilateral realm during 1972, as by this time Canada had established fourteen diplomatic posts in Latin America. There was strong recognition on the part of Ottawa as to Brazil's special place in Canadian relations. Canada's $1 billion investment in Brazil was its largest outside the U.S., and most of it involved Brascan. In the face of fantastic Brazilian growth rates, which reached 11 per cent in 1971, Ottawa wished to increase its exports to the country. While appreciating the potential demonstrated by Brazilian growth, Canada was also concerned about its political economy. For example, Ottawa noted that only 5 per cent of the Brazilian population benefited from five years of unprecedented growth, and that 45 per cent of the population saw their standard of living decrease during the same period.[50] There were additional Canadian concerns regarding human rights violations in Brazil as well as the fear of protectionism fostered by Brazil's role in LAFTA. Hence, although Brazil represented an economic powerhouse, there were some important obstacles to expanding relations with it.

Mexico, too, remained high on Canada's list of favoured countries. The DEA noted that 'Mexico is the only Latin American country which has a land-border with the U.S.A. and has bilateral problems (energy policy, foreign ownership, resource management and utilization, etc.) with the U.S.A. which are similar in kind, although not always in degree, to Canada's interests.'[51] Mexico was also a target for expanding Canadian exports through the Third Option. The country's stability, along with its average growth rate of 6 per cent between 1960 and 1972, were attractive. Canada was also important for Mexico in that 100,000 Canadian tourists visited the country in 1972, and that number was growing each year. Not only was this important economically, but it increased Canada's profile in Mexico. Finally, Canada, Mexico, and the U.S. began negotiations to reach a narcotics control agreement, thus paving the way for future trilateral negotiations.

Venezuela was also among the four Latin American countries at the top of Ottawa's list, largely due to its per capita wealth, economic growth, and political stability. The role of Venezuela as a major oil producer was crucial for Canada. Since the first OPEC oil crisis, Eastern Canada had become increasingly dependent on Venezuelan oil. (Venezuela's relationship with OPEC made it the first Latin American country to form an extra-hemispheric alliance.)[52] Not only was Venezuela important to Canada in terms of imported oil, but, as oil producers, the two countries shared similar interests.

Argentina, at this point, was perhaps the least important country targeted by Ottawa. Although it had great economic potential, its economy was deteriorating as its political instability was burgeoning.[53] Still, Argentina represented a major Latin American market for Canadian goods, and it aroused Canadian interest because of its geographical similarity to Canada. Argentina's antarctic region was particularly intriguing to Ottawa, which was keen on exploring its own polar region. Perhaps most important was the prospect, eventually realized, of the sale of Canadian nuclear power generating equipment (i.e., the CANDU reactor).[54] I shall return to this topic (as well as to the special case of Chile) in Chapter 6.

Nineteen seventy-two was a year of enormous and fateful turmoil in Chile – turmoil which would create implications for Canada for the remainder of the decade. (This turmoil is discussed more fully in the next chapter.) Some Canadian economic interests there – which included CP Air, Bata, Noranda, Atlas Explorations, and Hindrichs Mining – were threatened. Bata, for example, was included on a list of ninety-one companies whose fate was undecided: Would it remain private, shift to a joint venture with the state, or be nationalized? One of its plants was occupied by what the DEA thought were 'left wing extremists.'[55] Ottawa believed Chile to be sliding into economic and political chaos, and, predictably, the Export Development Corporation refused to finance Canadian exports to the country.[56] The Canadian government noted that 'the nation's economy virtually ground to a halt and talk of civil war or army intervention were rife.'[57] Despite this move by the EDC, President Allende, during a speech in October 1972, spoke warmly of Canada and indicated that Ottawa had been quite supportive of Chile in the face of widespread hostility by many other states, especially the U.S.[58]

Trouble also confronted Canadian interests in the Dominican Republic. In late 1971 and early 1972, a Dominican Republican newspaper began a strenuous campaign criticizing Canada's Falconbridge nickel mining operations. *El Nacional* charged that nickel mined by Falconbridge in the Dominican Republic was being used to assist the U.S. in the Vietnam War and raised the possibility that it might be utilized for other 'imperialistic' purposes in the future. The same paper was also critical of the pollution produced by the mine, and by the fact that most of the mine's profits went to foreigners.[59]

In 1973, the Trudeau government attempted to gauge the success of its foreign policy initiatives over the previous five years and tried to cope with a changing international political economy. In a document which traced these changes on the eve of Mexican president Luis Echeverría's visit to Canada, the government made the following observations:

> The international system has evolved in recent years from its Cold War bipolarity to a mixed pattern of major power relationships. The two superpowers, the United States and the Soviet Union, have lost their position of near dominance of the world. China is emerging as a great power in Asia, potentially a superpower. Western Europe and Japan are economic powers in their own right and are now rivals to the United States. Other factors have modified the structure of the international system: the growing economic problems in the formulation of foreign policy, which are supplanting security problems.[60]

Thus, bipolarity was giving way to a multipolarity dominated by five powers – the U.S., Western Europe, Communist China, the USSR, and Japan. From the Trudeau government's point of view, this meant potentially greater international influence for middle powers such as Canada and Mexico, 'largely because the five poles [would] not be able to really "control" the system.'[61] Ottawa and Mexico saw eye-to-eye on a number of specific issues, particularly nuclear disarmament and the Law of the Sea.[62] The relationship between Mexico and Canada grew closer both because of their common neighbour, the U.S., and because they were middle powers with increasing international influence.

Reviewing Canada's relations with Latin America in light of the objectives established in *LA:FPC*, the Trudeau government was justifiably pleased with its progress. The amount of Canadian developmental assistance to the region quadrupled with Canada's full membership in the IADB, Canadian trade with Latin America increased roughly 10 per cent between 1971 and 1972, and the EDC's global exposure in Latin America doubled in 1972 to reach $1 billion. In addition to joining the OAS as a permanent observer, Canada also entered into hemispheric talks concerning narcotics control and disarmament.[63] Ottawa had also established solid bilateral relations with key countries throughout Latin America.

It was now incumbent upon Canada to decide how the objectives formulated in *LA:FPC* could be implemented in 1973-80 (obviously, Trudeau was convinced he could win the 1974 election). There was a renewed commitment to Latin America. With government stimulation, the domestication of Canadian trade towards Latin America, now the fastest-growing region of the Third World, would be further emphasized. Particular emphasis would be placed upon exports with high technological content, and special attention would be devoted to Mexico and Brazil. Latin American nationalism and integration would be scrutinized for potentially negative implications for Canada, and Ottawa would implement programs to increase immigration from Latin America.[64]

With regard to international organizations, Canada's mission at the OAS observed that there was 'much cause for satisfaction that Canada is not a member.'[65] Among other factors, this was due to a substantial degree of anti-Americanism and a widespread sentiment that the OAS required considerable restructuring to overcome its inefficiency. Thus, Canada's observer status demonstrated this country's symbolic commitment to the Americas, without having to pay the price of being fully immersed in the organization's distressing problems.

With respect to the IADB, Canada took its position seriously. For example, it criticized the U.S. for using the bank 'as a lever and a whip to punish recipient countries involved in "bilateral" disputes over expropriation and compensation.'[66] That is, Canada charged that the U.S. was using the IADB in retaliation for what it found to be the disagreeable policies of the Allende government in Chile. Thus, Canada stood up to the U.S. at the Bank regarding issues it deemed to be important.

Turning to bilateral issues, Chile would emerge as a major object of Canadian foreign policy during the remainder of the decade. The Trudeau government was aware of the increasing chaos in the country in 1973, prior to the U.S.-backed coup. The suspension of EDC credits prompted Chile's minister of finance to criticize Canada's 'banker's attitude,'[67] although, as was noted earlier, Allende himself spoke warmly of Canada.

While the issue of Chilean refugees will be discussed at length in Chapter 6, it is worth noting that the coup which ousted President Allende on 11 September 1973 was met with uncertainty in Ottawa. Canada's ambassador to Chile recommended that Canada grant immediate recognition to the new regime. In a communiqué to Ottawa, he stated: 'I can see no useful purpose to withholding recognition unduly. Indeed such action might even tend to delay Chile's eventual return to the democratic process.'[68]

Ottawa's recognition of the new regime on 29 September met with considerable domestic resistance. Approximately 80 per cent of the cables Canadians sent to Ottawa were critical of the decision. The press was mixed, with, for example, the *Winnipeg Free Press* and *La Presse* favouring the decision and the *Montreal Gazette* and the *Toronto Star* opposing it. A plethora of interest groups, especially church organizations, staunchly criticized Ottawa's recognition of the regime which had militarily ousted South America's first democratically elected socialist government.[69]

Conclusion

These were truly remarkable years for the advancement of Canadian relations with Latin America. Notable achievements were accomplished on both bilateral and multilateral fronts. In addition to constructing durable relations with specific key countries, a policy of bilateral aid was established. Canada's new-found role in the OAS and the IADB represent milestones. This era also witnessed the birth of an important domestic constituency within Canada that was interested in Latin American affairs.

Ideologically, both Canada and many of the Latin American countries found themselves with strikingly similar views on many matters. This shared ideological outlook included a critical rethinking of the role of the U.S. in the hemisphere. Canada and many Latin American countries attempted to strengthen relations with each other, while diversifying relations away from the U.S. In certain quarters of Latin America, this took the form of an intellectual flirtation with dependency theory, which condemned U.S. interference in Latin American economies, and which, among other things, advocated alternative socialist models of development. Also heralded were the benefits of import-substitution models, as well as the importance of state-led development. The state, in this new conceptualization, would assume greater responsibility for incorporating a greater sense of equity within society. Here, then, was a new theoretical framework of the state-society relationship, with a considerably stronger role for the state.

The Canadian state, too, broadened its horizons. This country's economic advancement in Latin America would be led by Ottawa, and, in the main, private business would tag along. Remarkably, the state was even instrumental in developing a domestic constituency which would evolve into a critical force with respect to the formulation of Canadian policy towards Latin America. This was accomplished through Ottawa's support for NGOs, academic groups such as CALAS, business lobby groups such as CALA, and others. Hence, there existed a correspondence of sorts between Canada and Latin America regarding strong state models.

There was also a convergence of ideological sentiment between Canada and Latin America in other realms. One of these was nationalism. While the presence of nationalism in Latin America has been explored here, it should also be noted that the early Trudeau government played upon nationalist sentiment in Canada. This was expressed on a number of dimensions, and was most strikingly embodied by pronounced criticism of the role of the U.S. in the Canadian economy. To some extent, then, nationalism overlapped with anti-Americanism. For Canada this was exemplified by chilly assessments of U.S. influence in the Canadian political economy and with open hostility directed towards U.S. international adventures in Vietnam, Chile, and elsewhere.

While the presence of left-leaning dependency theory in Latin America has been noted, international socialism and communism were also given a warmer reception in Canada during this era. Certainly Trudeau was ideologically less hostile to global leftism than were the Americans. Significant here is Canada's recognition of Communist China, which preceded U.S. recognition by years, as well as the cordial diplomatic relations that existed between Ottawa and the Soviet Union during this period.

Regarding international institutions, Canada's plan to increase its role in Latin America produced concrete results with Canada's new-found position in the Organization of American States, the Inter-American Development Bank, the Andean Group and in smaller, specialized agencies. These multilateral progressions were matched by progress bilaterally with a number of countries, particularly Mexico, and also through a newly established policy of bilateral aid to the region as a whole.

Finally, a changing world order had ramifications for Canadian capabilities in the global arena, and this was apparent with respect to Canadian relations with Latin America. With the international distribution of power moving from a bipolar to a multipolar arrangement, the Trudeau government viewed this as an opportunity for the so-called middle powers to have greater international influence. While endeavouring not to overestimate Canadian power, the Trudeau government took advantage of Canada's potential capabilities by strengthening ties with other middle powers such as Mexico.

6

1974-9: Gathering Strength

Pierre Trudeau and his Liberal government, having secured a parliamentary majority, returned to office in July 1974 and remained there until 1979. The Canadian government found itself in a world order characterized by détente and multipolarity, and it was during this era that the basis was established for Canada to be reconceptualized by academic observers as a 'foremost' or 'principal' power in the global arena. Against this backdrop, an array of significant episodes occurred in the realm of Canada's inter-American relations. These included Trudeau's celebrated and controversial tour of Latin America in 1976, Canada's sale of the CANDU nuclear reactor to Argentina (at a time when the latter was one of the world's worst human rights abusers), and Canada's acceptance of 7,000 refugees (mostly leftists) from Chile. This chapter examines some of the most prominent aspects of Canada's relations with Latin America during this significant period and provides a portrait of the global context in which they occurred.

The momentum generated with respect to Canadian-Latin American relations during the 1968-73 period spilled over into 1974. Ottawa was encouraged by trade figures which indicated that Canadian exports to Latin America were up 83 per cent from the previous year, with imports rising 105 per cent. In contrast to serious recessionary pressures in the North, Latin America in general was booming, with an average annual 7 per cent growth in gross domestic product (GDP) between 1970 and 1974.[1] Brazil, Venezuela, Mexico, and Cuba now appeared on the list of Canada's top twenty global trading partners.[2] Adding to the network of Canada's growing connections to the region were a quarter million Canadian tourists, who, each year, flooded into the tropical environs of Mexico, Central America, and Cuba.

While it is true that Canada was successful in its endeavour to broaden its access to Latin American markets, there remained much to be accomplished. Canada only supplied 3 per cent of Latin America's imports, while the U.S. supplied 37 per cent, Germany provided 9.7 per cent, and Japan accounted for 7.2 per cent.[3] Furthermore, amidst Latin America's appealing prosperity, Ottawa discovered a worrisome current of nationalism and anti-imperialism in certain quarters of Latin America, as well as a trend towards acceleration of the regional integration process. In 1974, 16 of 20 Latin American countries, representing over 93 per cent of the population, were engaged in one of three regional free-trade schemes – LAFTA, the Andean Group, and the Central American Common Market. This led to concerns that Latin America might eventually shut Canada out from the region's booming success.

On the heels of the Trudeau victory in 1974, Canada's ambassador to Cuba argued, in part, that *FPC* was now 'obsolete.'

> During the last five years many of the aims of our 1969 policy prognosis have been achieved and there is little left in it that will enable Canada to keep pace with the accelerating technological revolution and the increasingly critical problems of inflation, escalating costs of energy and primary materials, hunger, widening development disparities, and rising political tensions. Our international objectives and priorities are in urgent need of review for reorientation toward much longer-term global and integrated projections of Canadian interests that will contribute to world stability.[4]

The ambassador also argued that Canadian credibility in Latin America, during a period of ardent nationalism there, ultimately depended upon Ottawa assuming a staunchly distinct regional policy from that of the U.S. On the whole, the most significant point of the analysis was that Canada risked getting lost if it failed to create new policies in order to meet the current reality. But as shall be seen, the Trudeau government clung, with considerable success, to its original policies and objectives throughout the 1970s. While the world had no doubt changed between 1968 and 1979, the initial policies established by Ottawa were sufficiently broad and pertinent to guide the government's relations with Latin America throughout the 1970s.

Also in 1974, Chile and Cuba emerged as special objects of Canada's bilateral attention. Regarding Chile, the DEA argued that the military junta's austerity plan offered 'reasonable prospects for economic recovery and growth,' but that it would be impossible, in 1974 alone, for Pinochet to 'regain all the ground lost during the previous regime.'[5] Remarkably, while providing refuge for Chile's displaced leftists, the foreign policy establishment accepted the policies of the newly installed right-wing government.

Also in 1974, a significant dispute arose between the U.S. and Canada when a Montreal company, MLW-Worthington, Ltd., attempted to sell thirty locomotives to Cuba. The problem was that the company was a U.S. subsidiary, and a U.S. blockade was still in effect against Cuba. Therefore, according to the U.S. State Department, a 'trading with the enemy' law was in effect. Exacerbating the predicament, the U.S. State Department refused to acknowledge Ottawa's notes urging a reconsideration of the issue. It was later discovered, however, that the 'trading with the enemy' law only pertained to U.S. citizens. Thus, Canadians eventually found their way around the problem when the U.S. officer of the company voted 'no' to the sale, therefore exonerating himself, but was outvoted by Canadian officers. This issue brought to light this important distinction between U.S. and Canadian policy, and highlighted potential problems surrounding extraterritoriality vis-à-vis U.S. corporations in Canada.[6]

The following year, 1975, witnessed the emergence of issues regarding the OAS, the role of Canadian domestic interest groups, and the reconceptualization of Canada's position in the global arena. With respect to the OAS, Canada radically, if temporarily, altered its views of the organization. Ottawa's mission to the OAS continued to observe the U.S.'s 'declining dominance of OAS affairs in the face of the more vociferous left-wingers and the more economically powerful Brazil, Venezuela and Mexico,'[7] and this phenomenon (along with others) seemed conducive to Canada's becoming a full member. Canada's observer suddenly witnessed an atmosphere of 'compromise' in the OAS.[8]

> Canada's traditional fear that membership in the OAS would only lead us into situations where we would be obliged to side either with the U.S. or with the Latin Americans to the detriment of our bilateral relations, is no longer valid ... Many of the interests of the U.S. are no longer entirely incompatible with these nouveau rich members (e.g., Venezuela, Brazil and Mexico). Mexico's strongly nationalistic or third world position at the OAS has not interfered to any extent with its relationship to the U.S. – Canada's specific concern.[9]

Canada's permanent observer noted other hopeful signs in the OAS that rendered full membership a wise move. The Latin America Economic System (SELA), for example, was viewed as 'the weapon of the future for confronting U.S. (and Japanese and European) imperialism and could take considerable pressure off OAS debates.'[10] Full membership would also promote, according to this review, accelerated commercial and bilateral relations with important OAS members. Furthermore, this was seen as a time of restructuring for the OAS, with the result that a position as full member would allow Canada to 'help shape the OAS to better suit [its] own interests.'[11] The same review concluded that the Rio Treaty did not represent the obstacle that it once did, since Barbados and Jamaica were now full members of the OAS without having signed it.[12]

Interestingly, it was thought that Canada, due to its distinct economic and political relationship with Latin America, was in a position to make an important contribution to the OAS.

> Canada should evaluate its future relationship with Latin America from the standpoint of a challenge to be met rather than an opportunity to be exploited. OAS participation could give Canada tremendous influence by bringing a large group of nations together to act in a responsible (ie, Canadian) manner in world affairs and at the U.N. American treatment of Latin America as a business opportunity, as a source of raw materials and as a potential market, has cost them dearly in credibility and it will be many years before they are trusted again. Canada could perhaps fill the gap.[13]

This review is enormously significant, as it foreshadows a Canadian relationship to the OAS that was still fourteen years in the future.[14]

Canadian trade with Latin America continued to grow, largely due to government efforts. Five ministerial trade missions visited the region between 1968 and 1976, and commerce grew at an annual rate exceeding 20 per cent – a higher rate than that with the U.S., the EC, or the U.K.[15] The EDC increased its share of credits to regional trade from 13.7 per cent in 1968 to 38.1 per cent in 1975,[16] totalling $300 million.[17]

But as Canadian trade and investment expanded in Latin America, some observers criticized its effects. Two Canadian critics cited CALA as a 'powerful corporate lobby for trade and investment in Latin America,'[18] which promoted economic relations that were not always in its best interests. These authors noted that Canada had the largest foreign investments in three Latin American countries: Falconbridge in the

Dominican Republic, INCO in Guatemala, and Brascan in Brazil. While indigenous criticisms of Falconbridge were mentioned in the last chapter, the Canadian critics suggested that the aforementioned investments perpetuated inequity and social injustice. They noted, for example, that a Brazilian officer of Brascan was a self-proclaimed fascist.[19] Thus, as Canadian economic interests in Latin America grew, they also came under increasing scrutiny.

The role of Canadian NGOs in Latin America continued to expand, with fifty-four such organizations operating in the region by 1975 and with CIDA picking up 28 per cent of their tab. Not only did the NGOs deliver grass-roots developmental assistance, they also became an increasingly significant interest group with respect to Latin American affairs, especially in the 1980s. Regarding the larger picture of Canadian aid, however, Latin America received only 4 per cent of Canada's total developmental assistance projects, a rather low figure given the importance attached to the area.[20]

Finally, 1975 also witnessed an important attempt to redefine Canada's place in the global arena. In a thought-provoking analysis, James Eayrs argued that Canada had been transformed from a middle power (a term which, he points out, was first coined in 1945), and also transformed from 'the largest of the small powers' (Trudeau's 1968 description), to the status of a 'Foremost Power.'[21] Eayrs maintained that there were two central reasons underpinning what he saw as Canada's remarkable ascent in the world order. First, resources were now viewed as more important than technology. Thus, since Canada was rich in resources, especially oil in the context of the crisis inspired by the OPEC cartel, it catapulted into the top ranks of global power. Second, as U.S. hegemony was in decline, there was more room for Canada to manoeuvre internationally.[22] Eayrs's 'Foremost Power' status was similar to the 'Principal Power' status later bestowed upon Canada by Dewitt and Kirton, although they viewed Canada's strength to lie not only in resources but also in population, technology, and so on.[23] Obviously, the line of argument entailed in that sort of rethinking of Canada's international position is quite debatable. The central point is that while academics had reconceptualized Canadian policy, the Trudeau government had not altered its policy with respect to inter-American affairs since the early 1970s.

Nineteen seventy-six was important both with respect to specific aspects of Canadian-Latin American relations and the context in which they occurred. Bilateral aid to Latin America had almost quadrupled in the period 1970-6 to $31.95 million but still represented only 6 per cent of the total aid disbursement,[24] while EDC credits to the region trebled.[25] On a somewhat disappointing note, Canadian exports to Latin America as a whole increased only 6.2 per cent in 1976. If Ottawa wanted Latin America to be a viable target for its Third Option, it would have to work harder.

And Canada did work harder in 1976. That year marked the first time a Canadian prime minister officially visited a South American country and, controversially, the first time a head of state from a NATO country ever visited Castro's Cuba. Trudeau toured Mexico, Venezuela, and Cuba in January and February. Why those three countries? Together, they absorbed roughly 50 per cent of Canadian exports to Latin America and represented about 80 per cent of Canada's Latin American imports. As well, each of these countries was politically important.[26]

Cuba was perhaps the high point of the visit. Trudeau's visit to Cuba was controversial not only because of its outcast status in the Western Hemisphere, but also because, in 1976, Castro began sending Cuban troops (ultimately numbering 50,000) to the conflict in Angola. Castro rolled out the red carpet for Trudeau, who spoke before a mass rally of about 25,000 Cubans at Cienfuegos. Fanning the flames of exuberance at the rally, the prime minister, to the delight of Castro, shouted: 'Viva el Prime Ministro Comandante Fidel Castro! Viva Cuba y el pueblo cubano! Viva la amistad cubano-canadiense!'

Regarding Cuban participation in the Angolan imbroglio, and the controversy surrounding it, Trudeau indicated that he initiated three hours of 'frank and brutal' discussion with Castro on the matter.

> One of the points of view that I took was, that apart from the destabilizing effect of any foreign intervention, particularly by nations from outside the African continent, I felt that Cuba, and I said so, was making a very serious mistake from the point of view of its own involvement in that Angolan situation. Regardless of the harm that they might be doing in Africa, I thought they were doing a fair amount of harm to themselves and I made that quite clear.[27]

On the whole, however, the visit was a success. Castro, in his reception of Trudeau, noted: 'Today the difficult years are behind us, we are less and less isolated, but we shall never forget those who behaved correctly towards us in those difficult years.'[28] Trudeau would later tell the press that he found Castro to be 'a man of great integrity ... within his own ideological framework, a man of world stature ... [who] has a great feeling for international affairs, a man who has assessed very well the qualities and weaknesses of various leaders.'[29] However, officials from Latin American countries dealing with leftist insurrections felt uncomfortable with the warmth of the Cuban-Canadian visit, as did conservative elements both internationally and within Canada. Nevertheless, Trudeau believed that, due to social inequities, the Cuban model would be replicated elsewhere in Latin America,[30] and, therefore, that it was important that Canada demonstrate its tolerance of ideological diversity. It also underscored the ideological distinction of Canada's policy in Latin America from that of the U.S., which government analysts had long argued was instrumental for solidifying Canada's relations with the region.

Less conclusive and colourful was Trudeau's visit to Venezuela, with which, due to its mounting reliance on Venezuelan oil, Canada had a trade deficit amounting to nearly $1 billion. In vain, Trudeau and President Pérez discussed ways in which that imbalance might be corrected. Because it was one of Latin America's richest countries as well as an OPEC member, the visit to Venezuela was diplomatically important, even if it did not produce immediate results.

Many observers considered Mexico to be the least successful leg of the tour. Although Canada's purpose was to increase trade, including a failed but vigorous attempt to sell Mexico a CANDU nuclear reactor,[31] the Mexicans were noncommittal to Canadian commercial proposals.[32] President Echeverría's term in office was due to expire at the end of the year, and this reduced the possibility of long-term agreements. A journalist who accompanied Trudeau on the tour noted that, 'Mr. Echeverría seemed more interested in talking than listening, and he and his officials took up much of the limited discussion time with the long-winded lectures on Mexican positions ... Mr. Trudeau frequently had difficulty getting a word in edgewise.'[33]

Trudeau failed to visit Brazil, probably due to the ideological gulf between Cuba and the right-wing Brazilian government. However, Canada's minister of agriculture, Eugene Whalen, visited Brazil in 1976, and the Canada-Brazil Joint Committee was formed in June of that year. As it was considered to be a key player in Canada's Latin American Third Option policy, by 1976 there were Canadian bank loans of more than $1 billion to, as well as substantial Canadian investments in, Brazil.[34] Ottawa, however, was concerned about the military government's domestic policy, especially in view of the increase in income disparities since it attained power, as well as the regime's authoritarian nature. These unpalatable aspects of the Brazilian government made it difficult for Ottawa to establish high-profile policies in Brazil.[35]

Canada was especially concerned about changes in Brazil's global position and was attentive to important alterations in Canadian/Brazilian trading patterns. The Trudeau government noted that Canada's position as an important Brazilian trading partner was slipping as Brazil's global rank was climbing.[36] Furthermore, there was a disturbance in the traditional pattern whereby the First World sells manufactured products to the Third World, and the Third World sells staple products to the First World. In 1976, this relationship between Canada and Brazil was reversed, with Brazil's exports being 42 per cent manufactured and Canada's exports being 11 per cent manufactured.[37]

Interestingly, during Trudeau's trip to Latin America both President Pérez and President Echeverría broached the topic of Canada's relationship to the OAS. Trudeau promised them that Canada would re-examine its status in the organization. But, in 1976, official Canadian assessments did not favour the OAS. A report from the Canadian delegation to the meeting of the OAS's General Assembly, for example, argued that

> if we were to become members of the OAS at present, we might end up with somewhat less influence than we now enjoy in Latin America, for we would then be forced to take a position on many of the subjects discussed at the OAS. In so doing, we would, because of the great disparity of interests between us and many of the members, probably quite often risk offending a large proportion of them without being able to further to a significant extent the interests and subjects we might hold to be important.[38]

The same review recounted other perceived problems associated with full Canadian membership in the OAS, including Canada's distaste for the authoritarian governments which dominated Latin America at the time and the view that the organization was irrelevant to Canadian national interests.[39] Other analyses during the same period suggested that the OAS was in disarray, lacking a clear view of either interests or duties.[40]

The year 1976 witnessed events which would seriously affect Canadian relations with Latin America. Within the Canadian political landscape, the resource-rich provinces of the West provided the Trudeau government with time-consuming problems, while the rest of the country witnessed economic stagnation. Even more important was the rise to power of the Parti Québecois, with its strikingly separatist rhetoric. Hence, domestic issues, especially the Quebec situation, began to consume more of Trudeau's time than did international ones. While Trudeau relegated more power over foreign policy to the Cabinet, one exception to this was North-South issues,[41] especially those concerning Latin America.

Internationally, the election of Jimmy Carter in the United States ensured a thawing in U.S.-Canadian relations, especially with respect to Latin America. Carter's emphasis on human rights, particularly in Third World countries, ushered in a less militaristic U.S. attitude towards Latin America than had previously been the case. This prompted a convergence of U.S. and Canadian attitudes.

Nineteen seventy-seven witnessed the dawning of an important review of Canadian policy in Latin America. Analysts at the DEA celebrated the election of President Carter, noting that 'Canada and the United States probably share more common interests and have a greater similarity of policy in Latin America than we ever had before.'[42] The analysis also emphasized Latin America's continued economic significance, as it was Canada's most important trading partner after the U.S., the EC, and Japan. During 1970-7, Canadian trade with Latin America trebled. By 1977 Canada had about $3 billion worth of investment there, and, commencing an ominous trend, there were outstanding Canadian bank loans to the area of around $2 billion.[43]

There was also concern regarding the relative paucity of Canadian aid to the region. Latin America, on the grounds that it was richer than were other Third World areas, was still receiving much less developmental assistance than were Asia or Africa. But Ottawa feared that Latin America would consider this arrangement to be unfair. A partial attempt to redress the imbalance would be the establishment of non-traditional aid projects, which would fall under the heading of 'new forms of cooperation.'[44]

In 1978, Ottawa focused on bilateral relations with Mexico, a country with which Canada had meant to augment its commercial relations since 1867.[45] The joint ministerial commission met three times between 1972 and 1978, exploring ways to advance Canadian trade to Mexico. A slight rift occurred in 1978, however, when Mexico suggested that Canada, Mexico, and the U.S. enter into a trilateral summit to discuss a variety of issues. An official at the DEA noted: 'I very much doubt that Canada would ever seriously consider diluting its relationship with the United States through participation in tripartite activities on anything except specific and technical matters, e.g. narcotics and the like.'[46] It was felt that Mexico wished to enter into negotiations with the U.S., but, in order to avoid the domestically unpopular move of appearing to negotiate directly with the Americans, it wanted Canada to be involved as well.[47] A decade or so later, in the light of globalization, Ottawa would amend its reluctance towards trilateral negotiations.

With respect to multilateral affairs, in 1978 Canada continued to take its position in the IADB quite seriously. Finance Minister Jean Chretien publicly criticized the U.S. for being $265 million in arrears at the bank,[48] thus impressing Latin America with Canada's independence from Washington.

Canada and the Southern Cone

Issues in the Southern Cone would dominate Canadian policy in Latin America during the closing years of the 1970s. Although Ottawa found Latin America's horrendous and widespread human rights violations very troubling, the Trudeau government was reluctant to initiate policies which could have a detrimental impact upon Canadian economic interests. For example, at the U.N. Canada had spoken and voted against human rights violations in Chile, but Ottawa maintained that economic sanctions against that country would only hurt Canadian economic interests and would have little effect in altering Chilean policies.[49] Another example concerned Brazil. While the U.S. under President Carter was quite critical of human rights violations in Brazil, Canada remained silent, in stark contrast to Ottawa's expressed distaste for abuses in Chile and Argentina. One can only surmise that this was due to a careful effort to avoid jeopardizing sizeable Canadian investments in Brazil.[50]

There were also some blemishes in Canada's relations with Argentina, which was Canada's fifth largest trading partner and home to many Canadian investments (e.g., Massey-Ferguson, Hiram Walker, Alcan, Seagrams, the Royal Bank, and CP Air).[51] Given Argentina's enormous human rights abuses, Canada's sale of a CANDU nuclear reactor to that country became quite controversial. Exacerbating the situation, Canadians absorbed a loss of $140 million due to cost overruns entailed in the reactor's construction.[52] Argentina had also been slow to comply with safety provisions, thus dragging the progress of bilateral nuclear cooperation.[53]

Additional complications arose in 1978 and 1979. While the prospect of a second CANDU sale represented the most important aspect of

Canadian economic relations with Argentina during this period, the human rights situation became even more intolerable.[54] Combatting what many observers regarded as the most potent leftist insurrection in South America, the military government, which assumed power in a 1976 coup that toppled the elected government of Isabel Perón, initiated brutal repression, resulting in the 'disappearance' (i.e., politically sanctioned murder) of between 10,000 and 20,000 people. The official Canadian position was 'to recognize the difficulties in which the Argentine authorities found themselves, and to urge a relaxation in the policies of the Argentine government as the internal situation improved.'[55]

Throughout the late 1970s, Canadian interest groups vigorously protested the sale of the CANDU to Argentina, as they did the fact that Canadian materials had gone into India's 'successful' explosion of a nuclear device in 1974. One such group argued that Canada should suspend the sale of nuclear equipment to Argentina because of the 12,000 political prisoners held without charges, the estimated 17,000 disappeared,[56] and the additional 10,000 allegedly murdered by authorities. Furthermore, the group deplored the purchase of $1.6 million in military equipment by a country which denied basic rights to its citizens.[57]

Ultimately, the Trudeau government faced a contradiction: it wished to promote trade with Argentina and was especially interested in the sale of a second CANDU nuclear reactor, but it could not defend Argentine human rights abuses and was being pressured by well-organized interest groups that provided strong arguments against the sale of nuclear equipment. Ottawa's reaction was to work within the U.N.'s Commission on Human Rights in an effort to implement a special investigation of countries where disappearances were occurring, without mentioning Argentina specifically. Although that attempt was unsuccessful, Buenos Aires took offence at the Canadian manoeuvres.[58] To assuage Argentina, Canada's ambassador noted that it would be wrong to criticize human rights abuses in South American countries without appreciating the context in which they were occurring and without recognizing the problems facing South American governments.[59] This did not placate Buenos Aires.

Canada's bid for a second CANDU, made in February 1979, paralleled Ottawa's intense and thinly veiled criticism of Argentina at the U.N. Secretary of State for External Affairs Flora MacDonald, appointed by the Clark government (which came to power in May 1979), pointedly attacked Argentina's human rights policy at the U.N. on 15 September 1979. It was this event, some observers say, that was the basis for the eventual failure of Canada's bid for the second CANDU.[60] In this case, well-deserved criticism of basic human rights violations took precedence over commercial opportunities.

Canada and the Chilean Refugees

With the overthrow of the first democratically elected Marxist government in Latin America and the subsequent assassination of Salvador Allende, virtually an entire class of Chileans, often well-placed supporters of the overthrown government, now became disenfranchised and in danger of suffering from the enormous abuses that the Pinochet regime would enact. In a truly path-breaking move, the Canadian government during the 1970s accepted over 7,000 political refugees from Chile, mostly leftists, who might otherwise have become the target of Pinochet's torturers and death squads. Although aspects of Canada's policy were the object of legitimate criticism, ultimately, the episode demonstrated Canada's genuine commitment to human rights in Latin America, and also indicated its clear ideological independence in accepting leftists displaced by a U.S.-supported coup that installed the Pinochet regime.

Following the overthrow of Allende in September 1973, a number of Canadian interest groups, including the Inter-Church Committee for Human Rights, the Canadian Labour Congress, the Chile-Canada Solidarity Committee, the Canadian Association of University Teachers, and the Association of Colleges and Universities of Canada, vocalized their support for displaced Chileans. United in their criticism of the coup, these groups demanded that the Canadian government allow those Chileans who wished to come to Canada safe passage into the country. While the Swiss, Swedish, and Mexican embassies provided a safe haven for a number of disenfranchised Chilean leftists immediately after the coup, the Canadian embassy in Santiago accepted only seventeen individuals. By the end of September, with over 10,000 Chileans living in church-run camps under the auspices of the United Nations High Commission for Refugees (UNHRC), Canadian minister of manpower and immigration Robert Andras indicated that Canada was prepared to cooperate fully with UNHRC but would only accept, as top priority, about seventy Chileans who wished to emigrate to Canada.[61] The primary reason behind this cautious Canadian approach and for subsequent delays was a process of 'security screening' – a process which was instituted because of the ideological persuasion of the Chileans seeking refuge.[62]

Stirring controversy during this early period, Canada's ambassador to Chile deemed some potential émigrés to be the riffraff of Latin America,[63] and, in an apparent expression of sympathy with the newly installed Pinochet regime, he propounded upon the thankless task faced by the Chilean military and police.[64] Allaying to some extent any ideological anxiety perceived by Ottawa regarding potential émigrés, UNHRC assured the government that refugees with the most extreme political views were being sent to Sweden and Cuba.[65] By late November, Ottawa indicated that it was prepared to accept between 300 and 1,000 Chilean refugees and to provide them with public assistance once they reached Canada. Near the time of the decision, Allende's widow toured Canada and had an audience with Prime Minister Trudeau, urging the country to accept the disenfranchised from Chile.[66]

By the end of January 1974, 706 Chileans were permitted entry into Canada, with 4,000 additional applications being processed. Many were assisted by free fare on Canadian chartered flights and by Canadian loans. Given that the minority Trudeau government was facing an election in 1974, and with the brewing of right-wing criticism regarding the admittance of leftist Chileans, Canada's immigration minister Robert Andras noted in January of that year that there would be 'hell to pay' for the government's policy.[67]

While the Trudeau government was criticized by the Canadian Right, the Canadian Left was also less than enthused with Ottawa's handling of the situation, especially considering the slow pace of the immigration process, the Canadian ambassador's aforementioned hostility to Chilean leftists, and the tedious security investigations of the would-be refugees. Many such observers argued that refugees from Eastern Europe and from Uganda (refugees whose ideological positions were generally right of centre) received quicker and better Canadian attention.[68] Racism may also have come into play. As two Chilean refugees to Canada noted: 'We believe that the reluctance of the Canadian government to accept Chileans was linked to both our political stories and to the fact that we are "Hispanic," not "white" Europeans.'[69]

The number of Chilean refugees accepted into Canada would grow in the late 1970s. By 1976, the Canadian Department of Manpower and Immigration established a policy of admitting up to 5,000 Chileans affected by the coup.[70] But many more wished to emigrate to Canada. In 1976, as Patricia Tomic and Ricardo Trumper observed,

Of 16,320 applicants, less than one third had obtained visas (5,300); 740 had been rejected for security measures; 60 for health reasons; 1,450 because immigration officers 'were not satisfied the refugees could successfully establish themselves in Canada'; 7,960 applications had been withdrawn or cancelled; the rest of the applications were being processed.[71]

By November 1977 the Trudeau government had agreed, in principle, to accept 7,000 Chileans,[72] with the actual number reaching 6,610 by March 1978.[73] This made Canada the largest single provider of asylum for Chileans displaced by the coup. The concentration of these Chilean refugees in Canada's largest cities also ensured that they contributed to the emergence of a growing constituency that would pay close attention to Latin American affairs and to Ottawa's position in inter-American relations.

Despite legitimate criticisms regarding aspects of Canada's immigration policy,[74] on the whole, the Trudeau government is to be commended for achieving the status of the world's single largest provider of asylum for Chilean refugees and for saving them from a country infamous for its horrendous human rights abuses during the Pinochet years. The fact that many of the refugees were socialists demonstrated the courage of the Trudeau government, which had to endure an election in 1974, and which, like all Canadian governments, was obliged to maintain cordial relations with the U.S.

The episode also bolstered a number of pillars of Canadian foreign policy. First, it underscored Canada's strong commitment to human rights in the global arena. Events in the southern cone raised, in a major way, the issue of human rights in Latin America, an issue that would become more visible in the 1980s. It also demonstrated this country's continued support for the United Nations (which served as the lead agency in the process of emigration). Further, the Chilean case brought to light the government's willingness to take heed of the position of Canadian interest groups which urged the provision of asylum. This was also an important instance of interest groups uniting effectively on a Latin American issue. Finally, Ottawa's policy regarding the Chilean refugee situation was indicative of the government's independent policy in Latin America.

Conclusion
On a number of fronts, this period witnessed the continued

advancement of Canadian interests in Latin America, as well as a blossoming harmony with the region. In the ideological realm, the Trudeau government maintained its support for ideological diversity in the hemisphere, as evidenced by the prime minister's celebrated visit to Cuba. The possibility that the model of state adopted by the island might be replicated in other parts of the region did not seem to particularly worry Canada at the time. And Ottawa's ideological tolerance was especially demonstrated by this country's acceptance of nearly 7,000 Chilean refugees, many of them leftists. More broadly, Canada and Latin America, both in a nationalist and somewhat anti-U.S. mode (especially prior to the Carter presidency), found themselves sharing mutual ideological concerns.

Canadian capabilities appeared to expand during this period as well, within a world order characterized by the perceived decline of U.S. power – a decline precipitated by the Vietnam debacle, the disgrace of the Nixon administration, and the rising politico-economic challenge of the Europe-Japan-OPEC triad, and compounded by the military challenge of the Soviet Union. While Trudeau initially deemed Canada to be the largest of the small powers, Ottawa appreciated that the multipolar global climate of the decade would ultimately afford Canada more power and room to manoeuvre, especially if the country acted in tandem with other 'middle powers' such as Mexico.[75] The government wisely clung to its initial assessment of Latin America, concocted in the late 1960s and early 1970s, disregarding internal critics who argued that Ottawa should take a second look. Academics began to reconceptualize Canadian capabilities, with Eayrs elevating Canada's role to a 'Foremost Power,' and with other observers later writing that this period exemplified the country's 'Principal Power' status.

Regarding institutions, Canada maintained its unconditional support for the United Nations, and chose that organization to voice many of its concerns with respect to Latin America. Canadian reservations regarding human rights violations and nuclear proliferation, for example, found their expression at the U.N. Although Canada had entered the OAS as a permanent observer in the early 1970s, this appeared to be largely a symbolic move. Towards the end of the decade Canada began to criticize the effectiveness of the organization, and wisely chose to raise its concerns regarding inter-American affairs elsewhere. Ottawa continued to take the IADB seriously, as was noted, and also appreciated the significance of attempts by Latin American countries to integrate through trade packs such as LAFTA.

In terms of state-society relations, it is important to observe that Trudeau himself continued to afford significant attention to inter-American affairs during this period despite increased economic difficulties in certain parts of the country, which were accompanied by the rise of deep social tensions within Canada. The separatist movement in Quebec and the election of the Parti-Québecois in 1976, absorbed much of the prime minister's attention, as did disputes between central Canada and the resource-rich Western provinces. But still, Trudeau made Latin America a priority, as evidenced by his high-profile tour of the region.

With respect to the formulation of Latin American policy in particular, the 1970s were enormously important due to the rise of domestic interest groups in this realm. During this period, the formidable role of such groups can be observed as they affected Canadian policies towards the Southern Cone. Particularly significant was the role of these groups in prompting the government to criticize Argentine human rights abuses at the U.N., which ultimately cost Canada the sale of its second CANDU, as well as the insistence of these groups that the Canadian government accept leftist refugees from Chile. While one could conceivably argue that the government would have adopted those positions anyway, it is more probable that the well-organized and vocal Canadian interest groups wielded a substantive impact upon policy formulation.

Overall, the late 1970s saw Canada move towards stronger relations with Latin America, building upon the momentum begun earlier in the decade. The foundation established during this period was crucial for the expansion of Canadian interests in the region in the 1980s – interests which would expand even more, especially as a result of this country's role in the Central American imbroglio and the Latin American debt crisis.

7

1980-4: Crisis and the End of an Era

A new era began in 1979. Vast changes occurred on the global landscape, as they did on the Canadian domestic scene. Against what the U.S. perceived to be a threatening international environment, the Reagan administration was elected in the hope of reasserting U.S. hegemony. In Canada, after the country's remarkably brief flirtation with the Progressive Conservative government from May 1979 to February 1980, the Trudeau government returned to power for its four-year finale. Ottawa's bilateralism and a renewed sense of nationalism were the orders of the day. And in Latin America, a volatile mixture of debt accumulation, revolutionary tension, nationalism, and a craving for democratic structures produced profound changes in the region.

This is the context of Canada's relationship with Latin America during the period 1979-84. This era was enormously important to the evolution of Canada's Latin American policy. The Central American imbroglio and the Latin American debt crisis, among other issues, delivered to Canada's doorstep tangible interests which could not be ignored and which solidified Canadian relations with Latin America. Although Canada's role in Central America is the focus of this chapter, Canada's Parliamentary Report on Latin America, the debt crisis, Canada's interests in the OAS and the Falklands/Malvinas conflict, and Canadian bilateral relations with Mexico will also be examined.

The Context

For many Americans, especially those on the Right, the 1970s represented a lost decade. Perhaps it commenced with the resounding U.S. defeat in Vietnam, which resulted in a 'syndrome' that weakened U.S. resolve to engage militarily in developing countries, particularly those of dubious strategic interest. Also crucial was the establishment of the

OPEC oil cartel in 1973, which again revealed Washington's inability to control events in the Third World as fully as it wished. Stiffer economic competition from Japan and Europe challenged U.S. economic hegemony. 'Stagflation' worsened the U.S.'s economic predicament and further depreciated its self-image.

The horizon appeared even gloomier during the latter part of the decade. In the midst of the heated presidential campaign of 1979, Ronald Reagan incredulously claimed that the Soviet Union had deliberately taken advantage of détente by redoubling its efforts to achieve Moscow's long-time strategic ambitions with respect to both the arms race and the superpower contest in the Third World. Stung by the Carter administration's ineffectual manoeuvres in Iran in the wake of Islamic revolution, and alarmed by the bold but ultimately disastrous Soviet invasion of Afghanistan, by 1979 the New Right exaggerated U.S. inferiority and pledged to restore it to its premier position in the global hierarchy.[1]

Not only would the United States, under the newly elected Reagan administration, implement a generally interventionist and unilateral foreign policy explicitly fashioned to reassert American hegemony, but pivotal changes were also occurring with respect to U.S. state-society relations – changes which would belatedly affect the Canadian political economy with Canada's 1984 election of the Mulroney government. Emphasizing the significance of traditional ideological values, the Reagan era introduced what Robert Cox terms the 'hyperliberal state,' characterized by attempts to dismantle the welfare state, weaken the position of labour, and enhance the influence of market forces. All of this occurs against the backdrop of militarism and military Keynesianism.[2] Being the most powerful state in the global arena, the U.S.'s profound restructuring of its state-society relations had an international impact, particularly in the Americas.

Turning to the mosaic of Latin American affairs, 1980-4 witnessed drastic structural transformations. During the 1970s and early 1980s, the region embarked upon a borrowing spree that would detonate on Friday the 13th, August 1982, when Mexico announced it could no longer borrow enough money to pay the interest and principal on its accumulated debt, thus ushering in the so-called 'Debt Crisis.' Furthermore, revolutionary tension emanating from Central America, compounded by the devastating fallout from the Falklands-Malvinas conflict of 1982, served to introduce enormous strategic worries to the Western Hemisphere. These occurred upon a foundation of anti-

Americanism and widespread economic disaster. Also significant during this period was the obvious local discontent with authoritarian political structures – discontent which translated into a yearning for democracy.

This period also saw shifts in Canadian politics which would affect policy in Latin America. For example, the lengthy Liberal reign of Pierre Trudeau was interrupted by the Progressive Conservative government of Joe Clark, whose remarkably quick visitation to the office of prime minister lasted from May 1979 to February 1980. I shall indicate important distinctions, with respect to Ottawa's hemispheric relations, between the policies of the Clark government and those of the Liberals – policies which foreshadow the entirely new foreign policy agenda of Brian Mulroney.

The Liberals reclaimed their place with a revived sense of nationalism and with a clear emphasis upon bilateralism in foreign policy. With respect to nationalism, the Trudeau government bolstered the role of the Foreign Investment Review Agency (FIRA) and concocted the National Energy Policy (NEP), both of which were aimed at limiting U.S. encroachment of the Canadian economy. This corresponded with a resolve to fortify the Third Option, that is, to diversify Canadian economic and political relations so that Canada would no longer be so dependent upon the U.S., which, Ottawa believed, was in hegemonic decline.[3]

Thus, the Trudeau government attempted, once again, to enhance relations with rising global powers in order to balance Canada's gradual detachment from the U.S. A second OPEC oil crisis in the late 1970s would render Latin American oil important for Canada, which contributed to Ottawa's focus upon both Mexico and Venezuela as trading partners. A deep recession in the North in 1981 and the emergence of the debt crisis in the South, however, would limit the realization of Ottawa's ambitions of expanding economic ties in the region.

Canada's Parliamentary Report on Latin America

Canada's most significant overview of its relations with Latin America since *FPC* appeared in 1982. It was a report to the House of Commons by the Standing Committee on External Affairs and National Defence, and it began with a grim portrait of crisis in Latin America.

> Central America, in particular, is today a region of mounting violence.
> The war between Great Britain and Argentina in the South Atlantic has

cast inter-American security into disarray. Mexico has just suffered a major trauma of national insolvency. Countries like Brazil and Argentina, which emerged as important international actors in the past decade, are now burdened by heavy foreign debts.[4]

Despite being burdened with gargantuan challenges and problems, Latin America, for economic and security reasons, was considered to be the most important area of the Third World for Canada.[5] The achievement of stability was identified as the chief objective of Canadian foreign policy in the region. As well, the report emphasized Canada's special capacity to affect change in Latin America due to its unique position in the global political economy.

Our country is recognized as an industrialized nation which has to confront many economic problems similar to those that developing countries face; ... and while Canada is regarded as having some influence in the international community, it is not viewed as having the economic or military power to threaten or overwhelm other countries.[6]

In light of Canada's heavy reliance upon trade, Latin America was especially important. The report noted that during 1965-80, Canadian imports and exports to the region increased tenfold, with about 150,000 Canadian jobs dependent upon sales to Latin America. Intensifying the significance of this was the fact that 40 per cent of Canadian exports to the area consisted of fully manufactured products, compared to only about 10 per cent of exports to the European Community or Japan. Still, Canada's trade with Latin America represented only about 5 per cent of its global total, and so more work was required in order to seize apparent opportunities. Regarding investment, the report indicated that, between 1949 and 1979, Canadian direct investment in Latin America (as a proportion of its international total) rose from 8 per cent to 20 per cent, comprising 75 per cent of all Canadian investment in developing countries.[7]

Throughout 1980-4, and increasingly as the 1980s wore on, many interest groups argued that Canada should not trade with Latin American countries that were internationally recognized as human rights abusers. In contrast, having emphasized Latin America's economic significance to Canada, especially with respect to trade, the standing committee report maintained that 'trade sanctions should not be used to achieve human rights objectives abroad.'[8] Under the Trudeau government's Third Option, Canada would trade with any Latin American country if it was profitable to do so, regardless of human rights issues or ideological considerations. The only caveat involved instances in which the U.N. imposed sanctions or in which the sale of Canadian military equipment was contributing to political repression and unrest. The report suggested that, rather than inflicting punishment upon abusers, Canada should encourage improvements in human rights through the provision of EDC credits to countries that were attempting to improve their records in this regard.

Canada and Central America[9]

Instrumental in solidifying Canadian relations with Latin America were the twin crises of the situation in Central America and the Latin American debt. With respect to the former, why were the tiny isthmus nations so important to Canada? Canadian interest in Central America, according to officials at the DEA, was 'directly linked to its capacity for destabilization.'[10] Two obvious questions emerge with respect to Ottawa's concern for stability in the area. First, why was stability in Central America so important for Canada? Second, what factors bred instability in the region?

Regional stability was significant for Canada because of its commercial and economic interests, although these paled in comparison to U.S. hegemonic concerns in the area. While this country's direct economic interests in Central America were rather meagre, Canada enjoyed more significant business relations in areas surrounding the isthmus. Trade with Mexico alone surpassed the level of Canadian trade with all of Central America. Canada also had more sizeable trade relations with Venezuela and the Caribbean region than it did with Central America.[11] Against the backdrop of the second OPEC-inspired energy crisis, in the late 1970s and early 1980s Mexico and Venezuela became crucial sources of imported oil, thus acquiring greater economic and strategic significance for Canada.[12]

Hence, while Canada's direct economic interests in the isthmus were not considerable, it possessed a greater stake in neighbouring countries which may have been vulnerable if a regional war erupted. Of particular concern were Colombia, torn apart by civil war and violent conflicts associated with narcotrafficking, and Mexico and Venezuela, where the debt crisis had seriously exacerbated existing social tensions.

Perhaps the main reason that stability in Central America was important for Ottawa stemmed from Washington's perception that Central America posed a threat to U.S. and/or Western security.[13] Particularly alarming to Canada was the Reagan administration's 'whatever is necessary' approach to ridding the region of 'communism,' which Ottawa feared could be a recipe for inadvertent but massive destabilization.[14] According to Robert Miller, who served as director of research for the Canadian House of Commons Standing Committee on Central America, U.S. entanglement in this sort of crisis 'would distort the United States' political and economic relations with other parts of the world.'[15] That is, a full-blown war in Central America or a national conflict that spread to its neighbours might distract the U.S. from performing its global hegemonic role – both economically and militarily. The result could be a global crisis.

Particularly interesting with respect to Canada's involvement in the Central American crisis are ideological considerations, diplomatic and economic relations, and the crucial role performed by interest groups. To begin with, Canada's policy in Central America was fraught with contradictions, as Ottawa had to contend with a number of often conflicting considerations. Remarkably, when officials met to concoct policy on Central America, they consulted two groups of experts – one group which specialized in Canada's bilateral relations with Central American states, and another group whose expertise was U.S. strategic interests in the Western Hemisphere.[16] Not only were interests within the DEA and other elements of the bureaucracy rather frayed, but an assortment of interest groups, including business lobbies, regularly presented agendas which were clearly at odds with each other and with the government. Competing perspectives are a typical feature of the environment in which policymakers work. But in the case of Central America, the diversity of potential determinants affecting Ottawa's policy, combined with Canada's inexperience in affairs of the isthmus, was a recipe for contradiction.

Before going further, it is helpful to assess the ideological complexion of official Canadian analyses regarding the roots of turmoil in Central America. It is remarkable that these analyses have remained fairly consistent over the last three decades. When Canada opened an embassy in Central America in the early 1960s, Minister of External Affairs Howard Green sent a letter of instruction to the new Canadian ambassador in order to introduce him to the complex political landscape of the region. With great lucidity, the letter challenged the notion of a military solution to the area's political strife.

The reaction in [Central American] Government circles to these challenges tends to be unrealistic. They often fail to understand the causes of popular discontent. In a recent conversation with his Canadian colleague, the Nicaraguan ambassador in Washington outlined the challenges faced by his Government and concluded that 'the only solution consisted in the strengthening of military forces in order to provide a deeper sense of discipline for unruly elements.' Such a policy however could lead to recurrent disorders of greater magnitude as time passes.[17]

This analysis portended the revolution in Nicaragua, which would occur two decades later. It also pointed to indigenous factors in the Central American political economy, in conjunction with the region's history of subjugation first by the Spanish and later by the U.S., as the root of its turmoil.[18]

The DEA's analysis in 1961 of the political situation in Central America is quite similar in tone and content to a 1983 Standing Committee Report to the House of Commons regarding the Central American crisis. It differed substantially with respect to both its analysis and conclusions from its American counterpart. The U.S. analysis, *The Report of the President's National Bipartisan Commission on Central America* (also known as the Kissinger Report), was also published in 1983.[19] The major distinctions between the two reports centre around five basic issues: (1) the roots of the crisis in Central America; (2) the question of whether Nicaragua's Sandinista government represented a strategic threat to Western interests; (3) the debate over a military versus a diplomatic solution to the region's escalating problems; (4) the nature of the Sandinista regime; and (5) the role of the state with respect to plans for economic recovery in Central America.

The Kissinger Commission, a twelve-member body that was the brainchild of Jeane Kirkpatrick and which contained only two liberal members, suggested that the roots of the Central American crisis were 'both indigenous and foreign.' The U.S. report recognized that pressing socio-economic problems in conjunction with authoritarian political repression rendered Central American states ripe for revolt. However, it maintained that the potency of the guerrilla movements in El Salvador and Guatemala, and in Nicaragua prior to the 1979 revolution, was a direct result of foreign support, principally from the Soviet Union and Cuba.[20] Therefore, it argued, the Soviet Union and Cuba functioned as catalysts fomenting revolutionary sentiment in Central America of a sort that would not otherwise have flourished to such an uncontrollable degree.

In contrast, the Canadian report suggested that regional turmoil was fundamentally linked to North-South disparities, rather than to Moscow's international ambitions. It focused upon indigenous determinants of discontent in Central America. 'Many of the problems are a result of economic structures, rooted deeply in the past, which cannot respond adequately to powerful and frequently adverse international economic forces.'[21]

Another point of contention between the Canadian and American analyses concerns the question of whether or not the Sandinistas represented a strategic threat to Western interests in the hemisphere. The authors of the Canadian report were willing to provide the Sandinistas 'with the benefit of the doubt' that the expansion of Nicaragua's armed forces was for defensive rather than offensive purposes. While the report dismissed the contention that Nicaragua represented a base for Soviet expansionism, it nevertheless stated unequivocally that Canada was solidly committed to the protection of Western strategic interests in the hemisphere:

It should be clearly understood by all countries in the Caribbean and Central America that these regions are of strategic importance to the U.S. and to the Western Alliance of which Canada is a member. Any direct threat to vital U.S. and Western strategic interests will be resisted. The U.S., for its part, must be prepared to accept differing political regimes as a fact of life.[22]

This view is quite similar in tone to that of many American liberal commentators, who argued that the U.S. should accept ideological diversity in the hemisphere so long as those states pursuing socialism are not equipped with Soviet-Cuban military bases.

The Kissinger Report adopted quite a different perspective on this matter. It asserted that Nicaragua provided a 'crucial stepping stone for Cuban and Soviet efforts to promote armed insurgency in Central America,' and that the country was 'seen by its neighbors as constituting a permanent security threat.' Furthermore, the report claimed that the U.S. must prevent 'the erosion of [its] power to influence events worldwide that would flow from the perception that [it was] unable to influence vital events close to home.'[23] Again, the issue of the 'Sandinista threat' represented a major distinction between U.S. and Canadian analyses of Central American turmoil.

Another contrast between the two reports entailed the debate regarding a diplomatic versus a military solution to the crisis in the region. The Canadian report emphatically urged diplomatic negotiations 'between countries whose policies in these regions are in conflict, including the United States and Cuba.'[24] The American report, however, promoted elevated levels of American military support for its allies in Central America, and also espoused the threats of military force as an effective bargaining tool against the Sandinistas: 'We can expect negotiations to succeed only if those we seek to persuade have a clear understanding that there are circumstances in which the use of force, by the United States or by others, could become necessary as a last resort.'[25] Similarly, it suggested that the U.S.-directed Contra military incursions into Nicaragua constituted a favourable bargaining device for Washington.

The Kissinger Commission clearly indicated that the aim of the U.S. should be to eradicate the Sandinistas: 'We do not advocate a policy of static containment.'[26] Indeed, containment implied that the Sandinista regime should be permitted to exist so long as it did not sponsor revolutionary activity elsewhere. The policy employed by Ronald Reagan, who declared himself a Contra in the spring of 1986, was designed to topple the Sandinistas. Again, this stands in sharp contrast to the Canadian position that the U.S. should learn to tolerate ideological diversity in the hemisphere.

The Canadian Report also rebukes the polemic of 'authoritarianism versus totalitarianism' as resurrected by Jeane Kirkpatrick in the late 1970s. Simply put, Kirkpatrick argued that right-wing, authoritarian dictatorships are morally superior to left-wing, totalitarian dictatorships because the former possess the propensity to evolve into democracy, whereas the latter do not. While the Canadian report argued that Nicaragua is 'not a totalitarian state,' the Kissinger Commission suggested that 'regimes created by the victory of Marxist-Leninist guerrillas become totalitarian.'[27]

Canadians and Americans also clashed regarding acceptable avenues for economic revitalization in Central America. The Kissinger Commission maintained that the primary vehicle for economic acceleration in Central America ought to be the private sector, a view congruent with so-called 'Reaganomics.' The Canadian report, by contrast, urged 'new forms of economic development involving both government and the private sector. This economic pluralism preserves the greatest flexibility in dealing with an inherently unpredictable and increasingly severe environment.'[28] This recommendation was no doubt a product of Canada's unique history of relying upon the state for domestic economic development.

Predictably, the Kissinger Commission chastised its Western allies for providing its arch-enemies, the Sandinistas, with both foreign aid and moral support. Ottawa, which had provided bilateral developmental assistance to the Sandinistas since 1979, suggested that its ties with both Cuba and Nicaragua should be celebrated as representing important 'diplomatic assets' which could prove instrumental in any diplomatic settlement of the regional conflagration.[29]

Finally, the Canadian report urged the establishment of a Canadian embassy in Managua, which would significantly enhance Canada's rather limited intelligence-gathering capacity. Meyer Brownstone, who was then the director of OXFAM-Canada, astutely observed that the primary intelligence sources for Canada's Central American embassy in Costa Rica regarding Nicaragua were the U.S. embassy in Managua and the pro-American sector of the church there – sources that decidedly reflected a U.S. bias.[30] Although it exceeds the bounds of the period under study, it is worth noting that in December 1985, the DEA stated unequivocally that, due to 'budgetary restraints,' Canada had no intention of installing an embassy in Nicaragua.[31] The limits of Canada's intelligence-gathering capacity were a serious matter. When Canada's policymakers tended to 'rely on their Superpower ally for intelligence, they cut themselves off, in effect, from the informational basis for autonomous action.'[32]

Now that some important distinctions have been presented between U.S. and Canadian government analyses of the Central American imbroglio, let us turn to Canada's diplomatic relations with Central America. It seems proper to begin with Nicaragua, which, in many ways, was at the centre of the regional maelstrom. The Sandinista National Liberation Front (FSLN) became the official government of Nicaragua on 19 July 1979. In the weeks immediately prior to the Sandinista victory, however, the newly elected Progressive Conservative government of Joe Clark backed a U.S. proposal at the OAS for a 'peace keeping force, made up mostly of U.S. troops, to be despatched to Nicaragua to prevent the Sandinistas from taking power. The proposal died when no other country supported it.'[33] Clearly, the Clark government registered its concurrence with the Carter administration's ill-fated scheme to prevent the establishment of a socialist regime on the isthmus.

On 23 July 1979, just a few days after the Sandinistas came to power, the U.S. officially recognized the new government in Managua. A day after that, perhaps following the American lead, Canada also extended recognition. At this juncture, Canada's embassy in Costa Rica, which also served Nicaragua, had been without an ambassador for about a year. Appreciating the sensitivity of the situation, Ottawa assigned an ambassador to the region shortly after the Nicaraguan revolution. The Sandinista victory ushered in another test for Canada's tolerance of ideological diversity in the Western Hemisphere.

Canada's new ambassador to Nicaragua, R. Douglas Sirrs, appeared less than enthused with Nicaragua's socialist experiment. In an interview with a Costa Rican newspaper in 1980 (shortly after the Liberals returned to power in Ottawa), Sirrs complained that the Sandinistas seemed to be moving 'too far' to the left, and also indicated his dismay with the Marxist flavour of their literacy campaign, the exodus of the vice president of the State Council, and the 'overwhelming number' of Sandinistas on the State Council.[34] Sirrs himself, however, became the target of criticism by some Canadians concerned with Central American affairs. Progressive Conservative MP Flora MacDonald thought Sirrs to be 'uninformed as well as unsympathetic to aspects of development in Nicaragua which are positive,' while New Democratic Party MP Robert Ogle viewed the ambassador's analysis of Nicaragua to be 'very similar to the American line.'[35]

As American intervention in Nicaragua gradually intensified through 1983 with the presence of the U.S.-directed Contra forces, Nicaragua began to appeal to Canada to utilize its potential influence to mellow Washington's escalating belligerence. Nicaragua's minister for external relations, Miguel D'Escoto, arrived in Canada early in that year on a campaign to expose the nature of American adventurism in his country and, consequently, to evoke Canadian criticism of Washington's Central American policy.[36]

D'Escoto's mission was tarnished to some extent, however, when a couple of months after his visit to Canada a Nicaraguan diplomat was arrested and charged in Ottawa with cocaine trafficking and possession of an unregistered handgun. The Nicaraguan government persuaded Ottawa to grant diplomatic immunity to Rodolfo Palacios, first secretary of Nicaragua's embassy in Ottawa.[37] Despite this, the event represented a public relations setback for Nicaragua, since it fed into the hands of Washington's propaganda package, which alleged that, in a desperate effort to support the revolution, the Sandinista regime was heavily involved in drug trafficking.[38]

Also in 1983, Secretary of State for External Affairs Allan MacEachen voiced concern regarding the Canadian government's perception of the direction of the Nicaraguan Revolution. In a speech at the University of Ottawa, MacEachen stated:

> We are dismayed by the increasing tendency toward authoritarianism [in Nicaragua] ... Departures from professed non-alignment, and support for insurgencies in neighbouring countries only adds to the risks of violence and impedes progress toward peaceful change. For Canada, no ideology justifies the export of violence. It is clear that the interests of Canada are more closely linked with those of the hemisphere than ever before.[39]

MacEachen's position seemed to be moving closer to that of Washington's, and converged with arguments in the Kissinger Commission report.

In contrast to this and other criticism of Nicaragua, however, Canada opposed an attempt by the Reagan administration to halt all IADB aid to Nicaragua.[40] And, despite official Canadian statements that were clearly critical of Sandinista ideology, in 1983 Trudeau offered an analysis which may be regarded as the high-water mark of Canadian tolerance of ideological diversity.

> In our view states have the right to follow whatever ideological path their peoples decide. When a country chooses a socialist or even a Marxist path, it does not necessarily buy a package which automatically injects it into the Soviet orbit. The internal systems adopted by countries of Latin America and the Caribbean, whatever these systems may be, do not in themselves pose a security threat to this hemisphere. It is only when countries adopt systems which deliberately inject East-West rivalry or seek to destabilize their neighbors that a threat is posed.[41]

Thus, while Trudeau was clearly a supporter of ideological freedom, it seems that some members of his government had differing views regarding the Nicaraguan situation in particular.

In October 1983, the U.S. invaded Grenada. Canadians were particularly incensed, since, despite Canada's strong and historical ties with the Commonwealth Caribbean, Washington did not bother to inform Ottawa of the planned attack.[42] The episode demonstrated the Reagan administration's resolve to adopt unilateral policies in cases where multilateral consultation might impede U.S. national interests.[43]

Secretary of State for External Affairs MacEachen's position on Nicaragua seemed to soften a bit (compared to the critical views he expressed in 1983) following a fact-finding trip he made to Central America in 1984. In spring of that year, he became the first Canadian cabinet minister to visit Nicaragua. In April of 1984, MacEachen voiced tacit support for U.S. presidential candidate Gary Hart's proposal to withdraw U.S. troops from Central America.[44] A few days later, at a press conference in Honduras, the secretary of state for external affairs criticized the U.S. mining of Nicaraguan ports, an incident in which a Canadian ship narrowly escaped damage. MacEachen said, 'We oppose it, of course. We don't like what happened. We think it is a violation of international law.'[45]

MacEachen's visit to Central America seems to have made him more sympathetic to the trials and tribulations of the Nicaraguan Revolution. Upon his arrival in Canada, MacEachen indicated that the Canadian government had expressed to Washington its view of the situation in Nicaragua – a view which differed from official American analyses.[46] MacEachen also stated: 'I think that a state of emergency exists [in Nicaragua] and that is the justification for press censorship [there].'[47]

Near this time, Brian Mulroney, as leader of the Opposition, stated: 'I believe it is important that the political, economic, and social autonomy of all Central American countries be respected as their governments negotiate resolutions to civil and regional disputes.'[48] Thus, in the context of four years of escalating U.S. military intervention in Central America, there appeared to be growing Canadian opposition to Washington's interference in the region.

Francis Filleul followed Douglas Sirrs as Canada's ambassador to Costa Rica, Nicaragua, El Salvador, and Panama. During an interview in the summer of 1984, Filleul demonstrated that he agreed with his predecessor's analysis of the Nicaraguan situation – views which seemed to stand in contrast to the more liberal ones of Trudeau and of the secretary of state for external affairs. For example, Filleul was highly critical of the Cuban presence in Nicaragua.

Nicaragua has been penetrated so badly by Cuba and other [Eastern Bloc] countries that it is destabilizing. It was not that the people of Nicaragua ... chose to welcome the Russians and the Cubans. It was that the FSLN had gained control of the Revolutionary movement and that was their policy.[49]

Hence, Filleul suggested that the FSLN did not actually represent the will of the majority of Nicaraguans, and that it required the assistance of the Cubans and Soviets in order to maintain power.

Filleul also directed criticism towards the economic development policies of the Sandinistas. 'It is just pathetic to see what five years of this regime has done for the country. Instead of helping the people to develop, it has resulted in subdevelopment.'[50] Furthermore, the ambassador conveyed discontent with regard to what he saw as the Sandinistas' refusal to fulfil the original goals of the revolution. 'When the Sandinistas first took power, they established certain principles: non-alignment, a healthy private sector, and a pluralistic system. None of those conditions have been fulfilled.'[51]

In sum, Canadian diplomatic relations with Nicaragua seemed fragmented, with various quarters of the government expressing divergent views. This is one of many factors which contributed to a policy towards the region which did not always appear coherent.

While Nicaragua was the focus of the 'Great Contest' between capitalism and socialism in Central America, El Salvador was the scene of a ferocious civil war between the Left and the Right. Canada remained largely silent on the Salvadoran issue until the early 1980s. In January 1981, Secretary of State for External Affairs Mark MacGuigan met with members of El Salvador's leftist opposition groups, including Ana Guadelupe Martinez of the Farabundo Martí National Liberation Front (FMLN) and Hector Oqueli of the social democratic National Revolutionary Movement (MNR). During the meeting, MacGuigan voiced Canada's support for the principles of non-intervention and self-determination.

But the sincerity of MacGuigan's remarks and his gesture of goodwill towards opposition forces in El Salvador soon came into question. The Canadian government refrained from officially recognizing the Farabundo Martí National Liberation Front-Revolutionary Democratic Front (FMLN-FDR) as a legitimate and representative political force. Moreover, in February 1981, just one month after his meeting with

Salvadoran leftist forces, the Canadian secretary of state outraged some Canadian observers of Central American affairs by announcing that Canada would quietly submit to plans of heightened American military intervention in the tiny isthmus country. After returning from a trip to Washington for talks with U.S. secretary of state Alexander Haig, MacGuigan stated: 'I would certainly not condemn any decision the United States takes to send offensive arms [to El Salvador] ... The United States can at least count on our quiet acquiescence.'[52] Converging with Washington's policies, in 1981 Canada supported a U.S. initiative with the International Monetary Fund (IMF) concerning the approval of credit to El Salvador, despite the highly unusual circumstance of an adamant refusal by IMF staff to support the U.S. endeavour.[53] While it was unclear whether or not Washington could count on Canada's 'acquiescence,' perhaps what everyone could count on was Canada's unpredictability. Indicative of this was a series of Canadian abstentions between 1980 and 1982 at the Inter- American Development Bank (IDB) regarding U.S.-supported loan requests for El Salvador – abstentions which stood in direct contrast to Canada's support for Washington's initiatives with the IMF.[54]

While MacGuigan seemed, on occasion, to adopt a position that was close to the U.S. line with respect to El Salvador, the man who followed him as secretary of state expressed views which often seemed less compatible with those of Washington. In spring of 1984, Secretary of State for External Affairs Allan MacEachen planned an official trip to Central America, a visit which included travel to Costa Rica, Honduras, and Nicaragua. MacEachen had also arranged to meet with U.S. secretary of state George Shultz in Washington immediately prior to beginning his excursion to Central America. Shultz submitted a written appeal to MacEachen before the latter left Canada, requesting that he also include El Salvador on his agenda. MacEachen refused the request and was grilled by reporters at a Washington news conference as to why he chose to visit 'Marxist' Nicaragua to have an audience with President Daniel Ortega but refused to travel to U.S.-backed El Salvador. MacEachen responded by stating: 'My not going [to El Salvador] is not a political statement of any kind.' And he added that, despite the omission of El Salvador, he was convinced that his tour would provide him with 'a balanced perspective.'[55] While the secretary of state for external affairs claimed that he simply was unable to fit El Salvador into his itinerary, it also remains distinctly possible that he and the Canadian government were attempting to appeal to domestic interest groups that took out a full-page ad in the *Globe and Mail* prior to MacEachen's departure, urging him to criticize Washington's escalation of military tension in Central America. A last-minute inclusion of El Salvador in the tour might have provoked criticism reminiscent of that which erupted in the wake of MacGuigan's 'quiet acquiescence' remark.

Closely connected with Canada's diplomatic relations with El Salvador was the allegation of Sandinista support for Salvadoran leftist forces. It was commonplace for Canadian officials to balance criticism of the American-backed Contra forces, which violated international law by invading Nicaragua, with thinly veiled allegations of covert Sandinista assistance to the Left in El Salvador. For example, Claude T. Charland, former assistant deputy minister of the Latin American and Caribbean division of the DEA, made the following statement at a conference in the U.S.: 'Consistent with our opposition to third party intervention in Central America, we oppose continued military support for anti-Sandinista insurgents in the same way that we oppose the promotion of armed insurgency in El Salvador by outside powers.'[56] Opposition to any outside intervention in Central America was a hallmark of Canadian policy.

Canada's policy in Honduras, the Central American country that received the largest amount of Canadian developmental assistance, tended to centre around its role as landlord of the Contras. The geostrategic significance of Honduras to the U.S. derives from the fact that it borders with the strife-ridden Central American countries of Nicaragua, El Salvador, and Guatemala.

When Allan MacEachen first visited Honduras in 1984, he indicated at a news conference in Tegucigalpa that the only way to achieve peace in the region would be to demilitarize Central America and to eradicate foreign military bases.[57] He also warned Honduran officials that Canada would terminate its economic assistance if it ever became clear that the aid was being utilized directly for support of Contra forces or for related military purposes.[58] This warning was made in the context of Canadian funding in 1982 for what was initially thought to be a forestry road, but which turned out to be the infrastructure for a major Contra military base at Fort Mocoron.

Related to the points that Secretary of State for External Affairs MacEachen referred to above, Ambassador Filleul observed:

One big difference between the United States and Canada is that the United States has decided to strengthen Honduras militarily and make it a bastion against leftist regimes in the area. Our position is that the best thing to do is to stop all weapons deliveries, to demilitarize everywhere in Central America.[59]

Filleul also acknowledged that, 'if you are looking at it from a purely military point of view, you might say that the Nicaraguans could feel somewhat threatened by the Hondurans if the Americans were involved.'[60]

Turning to Guatemala, Canada's relations with that country have tended to centre around two issues: commercial opportunities and human rights. Historically, Canada has considered Guatemala to possess the most potential among Central American countries for lucrative economic relations. However, Guatemala's abysmal human rights record was a considerable worry to Canadian officials.

In 1982, Canada's trade office in Guatemala was upgraded to an embassy, with the resident ambassador's duties including Canada's relations with Honduras. The move was a result of the commercial significance Ottawa attributed to Guatemala as well as of the pressing need to install another embassy in the region in order to monitor more effectively the complex and rapid unfolding of political events. (In the name of fiscal restraint, the embassy in Guatemala was closed in 1986 but was reopened a few years later.) Also in 1982, Canada officially recognized the regime of Rios Montt, who was at the helm of one of the most monstrous dictatorships in Guatemala's troubled history.

Canada's relations with Costa Rica were dominated by economic concerns, and by the attempt to preserve peace and stability. Due to Costa Rica's distinct pattern of development,[61] it has not been plagued by the same degree of civil strife as have other states in Central America. Hence, matters such as violations of human rights, the legitimacy of national elections, and socialist insurgency have not been at the forefront of Canada's diplomatic relations with Costa Rica.

Canada and Central American Elections

Canada's position with respect to elections in Central America has been steeped in contradiction. Between 1984 and 1986, Canada sent official observers to elections in El Salvador, Guatemala, and Honduras. Ambassador Francis Filleul, an official Canadian observer during both the preliminary and final elections in El Salvador in March and May of 1984, indicated his satisfaction with regard to José Duarté's defeat of the ultra-right-wing candidate Roberto D'Aubuisson. Filleul also speculated that Duarté stood a 'good chance' of holding real political power in a country traditionally dominated by the military.[62]

But while components of the Canadian government seemed pleased with those elections, other observers were clearly critical of them. Maurice Dupras, former parliamentarian and chairperson of the 1982 House of Commons standing committee on Canada's relations with Latin America and the Caribbean, stated that the Salvadoran elections 'will only intensify civil strife.'[63] This was because, in his view, the elections offered only a facade of democracy. For example, the leftist opposition forces could not participate in the elections due to a bloody civil war that included death squad attacks against suspected socialists. Furthermore, Gordon Fairweather, chairman of the Canadian Human Rights Commission, criticized the administrative problems apparent in El Salvador's elections, which resulted in thousands of Salvadorans being turned away from polling stations. 'Democracy is affected if anybody who wants to vote can't vote.'[64]

While Canada sent official observers to 1984 elections in Washington's client state, El Salvador, the newly elected Mulroney government refused to send observers to elections in Nicaragua in the autumn of that year. Before he left office as external affairs minister, Allan MacEachen stated that Nicaraguan elections should be judged 'by the same criteria of objectivity and on-the-spot investigation' as were the Salvadoran elections.[65] Thus, while the Trudeau government seemed prepared to monitor the Nicaraguan elections, the Progressive Conservatives failed to do so. The Mulroney government offered no explanation for this course of action (or, more appropriately, non-action). Gordon Fairweather, considered by some to be Canada's premier election-watcher, commented: 'I don't see how we can accept an invitation from El Salvador in March and May and turn down Nicaragua in November.'[66] An unofficial group of Canadians, however, did attend the election.

The *Globe and Mail*, which sometimes adopted a critical stance towards the harsher aspects of Sandinista politics in Nicaragua, chastised the new Progressive Conservative government for its decision.

Canada has ... elected to wear the blindfold on Sunday as Nicaragua holds its election, evidently fearing that the presence of official Canadian observers will confer instant respectability on the proceedings.

Ignorance, while not exactly bliss, is considered to be at least safe in that it states dissatisfaction with the election arrangements and avoids irritating Washington.[67]

This decision by the Mulroney government signalled a major shift in Central American policy and appeared to indicate that the Tories would design policies that would be in closer alignment with the strategy of the Reagan administration – a topic which is discussed further in Chapter 8.

Canadian Trade, Aid, and Investment in Central America

The level of Canadian aid to Central America jumped dramatically in 1978, when 54 per cent of all Canadian bilateral assistance to Latin America was devoted to Central America, even though that region was home to only 6 per cent of Latin America's population.[68] The sudden escalation of Canadian aid coincided with increased revolutionary tension in El Salvador, and with the correctly perceived imminence of the 1979 Sandinista revolution in Nicaragua. Thus, the increase in Canadian assistance came at a time when stability in the region was obviously in jeopardy. Ottawa's aid to Central America grew enormously after 1979, when the isthmus became the centre of hemispheric crisis. While biltateral assistance totalled slightly over $5 million between 1971 and 1980, the figure catapulted to about $44 million from 1980-1 to 1983-4.[69] Since Canada believed the political upheaval in Central America to be a product of the latter's socio-economic problems, its aid package attempted, if only in a small way, to alleviate them.

The Canadian government provided considerable bilateral economic assistance to Nicaragua (see Tables A.3-A.4 in Appendix) despite the Kissinger Report's admonition that Western allies should refrain from supporting the Sandinistas. A DEA bulletin observed that 'Canadian aid to Nicaragua ... is more substantial than is generally appreciated, amounting to $33.5 million between 1980/1981 and 1984/85.'[70] The program included a wide assortment of projects, such as an $11 million geothermal plant, a $7.5 million potable water project, and a $2 million production involving the transport of 500 Holstein cows from New Brunswick to Nicaragua.

Honduras was the only country in Central America that CIDA had assigned 'core country' status, and it has been the target of most Canadian aid to Central America during the period under study here. In a sense, Ottawa's assistance to Honduras and Nicaragua represented something of a contradiction, since those two countries were essentially at war with one another. Indeed, it was charged that aid to Honduras was utilized, unbeknownst to Canadians, by the Contras in their regular but illegal incursions into Nicaragua.

> In 1980 Canada donated $200,000 to the United Nations High Commission to build a road to the Mocoron refugee camp in Honduras' unpopulated eastern border with Nicaragua. In 1982, the camp was cleared of refugees by U.S. helicopters during U.S.-Honduran military manoeuvres and the area turned into the home of a new battalion. The new Fort Mocoron is occupied by those troops remaining after the Big Pine II joint manoeuvres sponsored by the United States.[71]

Clearly, Canada could not have known that the road would be utilized by the Contras, since the donation preceded their inception by two years. However, aiding two countries that are engaged in hostilities always entails the possibility that well-intentioned aid might be employed as a buffer to divert some of the host country's domestic budget to military affairs.

In 1981, under the Liberals, Canada severed bilateral assistance to both Guatemala and El Salvador due to their horrendous human rights abuses. The cut in aid was a reaction to the imminent danger faced by Canadian developmental assistance personnel in the field. But, as shall be seen, the Mulroney government would soon reinstate aid to those countries.

Regarding Canadian trade with Central America, exports peaked in 1984 while imports peaked in 1982. Instability and civil war were the obvious reasons for curtailment of Canadian commercial relations with the isthmus countries during the 1980s. It is important to remember that Canada's trade with Central America was much less significant than was its commerce with the surrounding nations of Mexico, Venezuela, and Colombia. Maurice Dupras, former chairperson of the House of Commons Report on Central America, indicated that 'some 40 per cent of Canadian oil imports come from Mexico and Venezuela, countries immediately adjacent to the unstable and violence prone region of Central America.'[72] Hence there may have been a relation between Canada's interest in stability in Central America and its economic stake in surrounding areas.

Canadian corporations have had investments throughout Central America, although these have tended to be rather small. During the period under investigation, those interests included Bata Shoes in Nicaragua, Canadian Javelin (mining) and Moore Corporation (business forms) in El Salvador, in addition to a number of Canadian banks in Panama. Certainly, the instability of the 1980s did little to encourage any increase in investment. As a result of this tumultuous state of affairs, the EDC refused to insure private Canadian ventures in the isthmus, thus contributing to the halt of further investments in Central America. (It is of interest to note that the Royal Bank had outstanding loans to all seven Central American countries, and that it held 15 per cent of Nicaragua's debt to private foreign banks under the deposed Somoza regime.)[73]

While Bata Shoes was able to carry out operations in Nicaragua, two other Canadian-based ventures, Noranda and Windarra Minerals, had their mines expropriated by the Sandinistas. Addressing the question of whether or not the socialist Sandinistas represented a threat to Canadian business interests in the region, a senior political risk analyst at the EDC responded: 'The Sandinista socialist ideology is not a problem. It is the maniacal Reagan Administration's militarization [of the region] which has caused the biggest problem for the business climate.'[74] When asked the same question, a representative of CALA answered: 'It is the investment climate and particularly political stability that matters most. Socialist ideology probably does affect [adversely] Canadian business attitudes to some extent, but socialist Guyana has no trouble trading with Canada. Political stability is the key factor.'[75] Thus, it appears that Canadian companies might have been prepared to conduct business in Central America regardless of ideological considerations. However, warfare and political instability, coupled with the EDC's refusal to provide insurance to new Canadian investments, served to create an unfavourable business climate.

Canadian Counter-Consensus Groups and Central America

Counter-consensus interest groups (i.e., organizations whose interests and policy recommendations differed substantially from those of either official government policy or business groups)[76] constituted another reason for Central America's importance to Canada. With respect to Central America, these groups included, among others, OXFAM-Canada, the Latin American Working Group, the Inter-Church Committee for Human Rights, the Taskforce on the Churches and Corporate Responsibility, and the Canada-Caribbean-Central America Policy Alternatives (CAPA). They criticized what they regarded as exploitative

Canadian investment in the region, such as the defunct INCO mine in Guatemala and the two Canadian gold mines in Nicaragua.[77] They also complained that Ottawa provided excessive levels of developmental assistance to Honduras – Washington's chief ally in adventures launched against leftist forces in Nicaragua, El Salvador, and Guatemala – and not enough aid to Nicaragua, which was struggling with the effects of U.S.-supported Contra attacks, as well as with the impact of U.S.-imposed diplomatic and economic isolation.[78]

Counter-consensus groups also expressed their displeasure with aspects of Canada's diplomatic relations with Central America. CAPA, for example, criticized what it viewed to be Ottawa's double standard with respect to Central American elections, in that Canada sent official observers to elections in El Salvador and Guatemala but failed to do so in the case of Nicaragua.[79] Ottawa's refusal to open an embassy in Nicaragua and the dubious quality of Canada's intelligence-gathering capacity on the isthmus have also been the target of criticism.[80] In addition, counter-consensus groups voiced their discontent with regard to Canada's participation in unannounced naval exercises off the coast of Nicaragua.[81] It is particularly notable that the Taskforce on the Churches and Corporate Responsibility, through adroit publicity, was able to halt the sale of Canadian aircraft (with military capabilities) to Guatemala and Honduras.[82] This episode demonstrates how effective counter-consensus groups could sometimes be.

Generally, however, the expressed interests of the so-called counter-consensus groups were not reflected in government policy in Central America. Obviously, this is because the positions adopted by these groups tended to run counter to the interests of the dominant forces responsible for shaping Canadian foreign policy. While it is true that the preference for regional stability expressed by counter-consensus groups overlapped to some extent with state policy, it also appears that the positions of these organizations often clashed with U.S. policy in the region as well as with the interests of Canadian business, as manifested, for example, in the commercial orientation of Ottawa's aid programs. The government typically adopted a distant and unsympathetic approach to these groups. This was exemplified when External Affairs Minister Monique Vezina commented: 'According to our contacts, the views expressed by groups such as the Canadian InterChurch Committee lack objectivity and precision.'[83] Similarly, a DEA document reveals that in a meeting with the foreign minister of Mexico, Secretary of State for External Affairs MacEachen observed that, with respect to

Central America, 'There was considerable interest in Canada, largely stimulated by the churches – an interest which far exceeds Canada's real interest and involvement.'[84]

Despite their limited effect upon government policy in general, the expertise and organizational capacity of counter-consensus groups made them a force to be reckoned with. As a prominent theoretician of Canadian foreign policy has argued, there exists the 'possibility that political and educational activities [on the part of the counter-consensus groups] can initiate a shift in the operating assumptions on which the government bases its policies.'[85] Thus, counter-consensus groups wielded the potential to shift the parameters of Canadian foreign policy. In essence, these groups were instrumental in the government's defining Central America as a high priority.

At this point, a number of conclusions can be drawn with respect to Canadian involvement in Central America in the period 1979-84. The first conclusion concerns the significance of stability in key parts of the Third World, partly because this represents a crucial prerequisite for healthy commercial relations, but also because of reasons of global security. The Canadian government stressed the significance of stability in Central America in numerous commentaries regarding Canadian aid, trade, and investment. It was noted that Canada's economic interests in the areas surrounding Central America were much more important than were those in the isthmus itself. This was especially true with respect to oil purchased by Canada from Venezuela and Mexico in the wake of the oil crises of the 1970s.[86]

It is also the case that by trading with and/or providing developmental assistance to countries, such as Cuba and Nicaragua, which were enemies of Washington, Ottawa was able to satisfy the interests of both Canadian business, which profited from such moves, as well as counter-consensus groups, which often took an anti-American stance. Since dedication to profitable trade and investment appears to have been among the guiding principles of Canadian foreign policy, however, Ottawa alienated counter-consensus groups which criticized Canadian economic relations with countries that violated human rights.[87]

While there were economic motivations for Canadian policy in Central America, security considerations were perhaps more important. Canada possessed an interest in promoting stability in the face of a potential decline of U.S. hegemony in the Americas. Perceptions of declining U.S. influence in the region – which had some credibility in 1979-84 due to the wildly inequitable divisions of wealth in some U.S.

client states in Latin America, in addition to political repression, under-development, mounting external debt, anti-American sentiment pro-duced by decades of subjugation to U.S. strategic and economic interests, and so on – were linked to the prospect of explosive events occurring in the hemisphere. Hence, the Central American imbroglio was viewed as a fuse which could ignite a cataclysmic process through-out the region. Analysts at the time worried that, in a worst-case scenario, instability created by a regional war, beginning in Central America and spreading elsewhere in Latin America, might preoccupy Washington to the extent that the United States would be unable to perform adequately its important hegemonic role in the international arena – a concern expressed by the director of research for Canada's Standing Committee Report on Central America.[88] It was feared that such a predicament could generate increased global instability and perhaps even a hegemonic war. This is one of the motivations which led Canada to become involved in efforts at regional conflict resolution, such as Contadora, as will be seen in the next chapter.

Finally, counter-consensus interest groups were an important element in Canada's relations with Central America. While the government may not have translated many of the interests of these groups into actual policy, their expertise and organizational capacity made them a force to be reckoned with. As well, the counter-consensus groups made sure that debates regarding Canadian policy in Central America stayed in the press and, in so doing, served an important educational function.

Canada and the Latin American Debt Crisis

On 13 August 1982, Mexico announced that it was unable to borrow sufficient funds to pay the interest and principal on its loans. This event ushered in the Third World debt crisis, and, by the following year, forty-seven countries announced that they were in similar positions. While the evolution of the debt crisis is discussed at length elsewhere,[89] I will briefly discuss its genesis here. The OPEC oil cartel of the 1970s produced huge profits for Arab countries – profits which were placed in the stable confines of banks in developed countries. As an official Canadian review of the crisis noted: 'The net effect of the Arab OPEC deposits to the commercial banks in industrialized countries was to put the banks in the position of having to find outlets for these huge sums.'[90] Latin America, in particular, looked like a good bet for First World banks eager to lend money, since, in the 1970s, Latin American growth rates were generally high. Mexico's minister of finance told a Canadian committee investigating the matter that 'I had many bankers chasing me trying to lend me more money.'[91]

Latin Americans considered such loans to be quite attractive. There were no strings attached, as was the case with developmental assistance or foreign direct investment, and real interest rates at the time of initial borrowing were low or even negative. Ominously, however, these loans were made on 'floating' interest rates, and were largely pegged to U.S. dollars.

Disaster blew in during the early 1980s. A recession in the developed countries severely limited their capacity to purchase Third World products, plunging downwards the price of commodities from developing nations and, therefore, limiting their capacity to repay the debt. Compounding the problem, interest rates now soared to near 20 per cent, suddenly raising loan payments to exorbitant levels. Worse, the level of Third World currencies fell in relation to the U.S. dollar, the currency in which most of the debt was owed. Other factors were at play as well, including the use of loans for non-productive purposes such as military proliferation, and massive capital flight from developing countries as local economies collapsed. For instance, capital flight from Venezuela, Argentina, and Mexico amounted to $70 billion between 1979 and 1982, while capital inflows totalled $100 billion.[92]

How did Canadian banks become involved? The Canadian Senate Standing Committee on Foreign Affairs observed that 'several Canadian banking authorities told the Committee that they were personally aware that U.S. State Department and Treasury officials had urged the international banking community to "accept the responsibility of being the first channel for moving the new petrodollars" in the 1970s.'[93] Indeed, the U.S. secretary of the treasury urged developed Western nations to provide loans to Latin America, since private bank lending would channel financing from surplus to deficit countries.[94] In other words, U.S. officials seemed to believe that such loans to the Third World would have the doubly beneficial result of assisting growth and development in the South while simultaneously reaping profits for Western banks. Canadian officials familiar with the evolution of the crisis suggest that Canadian banks were generally willing to follow the U.S. lead and lend to Latin American countries.

By 1984, Canadian commercial banks had about $27 billion in outstanding loans to Latin American countries. Of that amount, 90 per cent was considered to be 'problem debt,' that is, debt which required rescheduling. Brazil owed Canadian banks about $5 billion and Mexico owed about $4 billion,[95] with Venezuela and Argentina together responsible for $6.4 billion.[96] Roughly 5 per cent of all Latin American debt was owed to Canadian banks. In 1982, Canadian banks had the following percentages of their international assets in Latin America: the Royal Bank had 22.4 per cent, the Canadian Bank of Commerce had 18.5 per cent, the Bank of Montreal had 21.2 per cent, the Bank of Nova Scotia had 20.5 per cent, and the Toronto Dominion Bank had 15.1 per cent.[97] Canadian financial institutions, then, were significantly exposed in Latin America.

The debt crisis had many implications for Canada and Latin America. From the Canadian side, between 1981 and 1983 Canada is estimated to have witnessed a reduction of $1 billion in exports to Argentina, Brazil, Mexico, and Venezuela, resulting in the loss of about 35,000 jobs.[98] During this period Canada's exports to Brazil fell 12 per cent, those to Mexico 50 per cent, and those to Argentina 55 per cent.[99] As shall be discussed in Chapter 8, the stocks of Canadian banks dropped precipitously in the late 1980s as a result of their exposure in Latin America. In addition to the loss of jobs and the perils of bank exposure, instability resulting from the debt crisis raised security concerns and threatened Canadian investment in the region.

Of course the majority of the population in Latin America bore the brunt of the suffering. Structural adjustment programs, which in some cases eventually resulted in greater economic efficiency, generally curtailed social welfare expenditures. These draconian measures had a devastating effect on the masses, who relied upon government assistance for housing, education, and health care. The termination of state-subsidized products, in conjunction with the drastic devaluation of local currencies, made even basic purchases of food excruciatingly difficult for many. This economic hardship forced a significant portion of the population to embark upon environmentally unsound subsistence practices.

In short, the debt crisis was a crisis for both Canada and Latin America. While the latter definitely would shoulder most of the suffering associated with the crisis, what became evident was that Canada and Latin America are interdependent with respect to security, economic growth, and environmental well-being.

Canada and the Organization of American States

The saga concerning the debate as to whether or not Canada should join the OAS flowed through the late 1970s and early 1980s. In 1979, CALA advocated full membership in the OAS, and urged Ottawa to 'take [its] full and rightful place in the Americas.'[100] In 1980 CALA surveyed over 250 businesses with links to Latin America and found that 69 per cent favoured full Canadian membership in the OAS.[101] By 1981, however, CALA had decidedly cooled to the idea. Perhaps its leading members were swayed by the position of highly placed officials at the DEA, who argued that it would be more propitious for Canada to focus upon its bilateral relations with Latin America than to deepen its ties with the OAS.[102] Despite Canada's reticence, the OAS continued to urge it to assume full membership.[103]

The 1982 House of Commons Committee Report on Latin America devoted a great deal of attention to the issue of OAS membership and considered the long and familiar list of pros and cons. CALA, in its submission to the committee, indicated that it had amended its previous view and now had 'no position' on the matter, since there was 'no perceived impact on Canadian business as a result of Canada not being a full member of the OAS.'[104] Committee members seemed acquainted with the formidable collection of positions that recommended not accepting full membership in the OAS. Not only had the OAS proven to be a failure with respect to conflict resolution in Central America, but the fallout from the U.K.-Argentina war over the Falklands/Malvinas was devastating to the credibility of the OAS. The report observed that

the very difficult division of loyalties and obligations which confronted the United States in the war exposed it to intense and bitter criticism in the OAS. It is argued plausibly that had Canada been a full member of the OAS during the conflict it might well have been more severely criticized than it was for its sanctions against Argentina.[105]

Critics pointed out that while Canada imposed sanctions upon Argentina and withdrew its ambassador in the wake of its invasion of the Falklands/Malvinas, Ottawa imposed no sanctions upon Buenos Aires when the local military slaughtered thousands of its own people during the dirty war of the late 1970s.[106]

The Canadian delegation to the OAS was also quite critical of full membership in the wake of the Falklands/Malvinas crisis. They thought that the results of the conflict were disastrous for both the U.S. and the OAS. The episode indicated to the Latin Americans that 'in a conflict of interest the U.S.A. would choose its partners in the industrialized western nations over its hemispheric allies.'[107] Equally important, certain quarters within Latin America were devastated to discover that the Rio Treaty would not be effectively invoked against British intervention. It was painfully clear that the treaty had been merely a U.S. device to protect itself against Soviet aggression during the Cold War, and would not be utilized to protect Latin Americans from intervention by industrialized allies of the U.S.[108] If Washington, the OAS, and Argentina were the losers in the complications surrounding the Falklands/Malvinas conflict, perhaps the clear hemispheric winner was Cuba, which gloated in its reiteration of the profound fallacies associated with the OAS.[109]

Canadian officials in Brazil interpreted all this to mean that, since the organization was no longer viewed as significant, the topic of Canadian membership in the OAS could once again be placed on the back burner.[110] It was also observed, however, that, although the OAS was ineffectual and the Latin Americans themselves seemed disinterested in it, many still hoped that Canada would take a more active role in the hemisphere. This was especially necessary due to the pernicious effects of transplanted 'Reaganomics' as well as to U.S. intervention in Central America. Latin Americans seriously hoped that Canada could influence the U.S. into devising more palatable approaches to the region.[111] Once again one can observe the region's desire that Canada act as both a bridge and a buffer between Latin America and the U.S.

The view of the majority of those who contributed to the House of Commons Committee Report on Latin America was that Canada should join the OAS as a full member but should refrain from signing the Rio Treaty. It argued that, despite the obvious shortcomings associated with the OAS, Canada's full membership would assist in the revival of what could become an important international institution.[112] Since the U.N. was overloaded, the report argued, a revived OAS could prove quite helpful with respect to handling the many hemispheric problems. Canada could make special contributions in the areas of human rights and developmental assistance[113] and, crucially, by encouraging Cuban membership in the organization – a move that was believed to be essential if the institution was to evolve as a meaningful forum for conflict resolution.[114] Minority committee members who argued against full membership did so for the familiar reasons: the OAS was weak and ineffectual, Canada would be better off focusing upon bilateral ties with Latin America, Latin Americans themselves seemed to have little interest in the OAS, and so on.[115]

Canada and Mexico – Key Bilateral Relations

Between 1980 and 1984 Mexico became Canada's central bilateral concern in Latin America. The reasons for this included Mexico's position as a leading target for Canadian exports and investment, its role as a supplier of oil for Canada, and its position as a global middle power with hemispheric interests quite similar to Canada's. With respect to commerce, in 1979 Canada hoped to sell Mexico four CANDU reactors worth $13 billion. This paralleled Canada's successful effort to triple the value of Canadian goods sold to Mexico between 1979 and 1981 to $715 million.[116] Since the Mexican government or state agencies controlled roughly 40 per cent of all Mexican imports, it was crucial that Ottawa foster healthy political relations with the country.[117]

Oil was also a factor in Mexico's importance to Canada, especially following the second OPEC price hike in 1979. Just prior to losing the 1979 federal election, the Liberals had arranged to purchase from Mexico 100,000 barrels of oil a day for ten years through Petro-Canada and the Mexican state-owned company Pemex. The Progressive Conservative government of Joe Clark hesitated signing the deal because it was ideologically opposed to the state-owned status of Petro-Canada. By the time the Liberals returned to office in February 1980, the Mexicans were no longer willing to promise 100,000 barrels per day, and Canada had to settle for half the original amount.[118]

When the Liberals returned to power in 1980, Mexico clearly became Canada's top priority in Latin America, and Mexico placed Canada on its list of top five countries (the others included Brazil, Sweden, Japan, and Spain).[119] In 1980, Canadian exports to Mexico increased 104 per cent and jumped a further 98 per cent in 1981. When the debt crisis erupted in 1982, however, the floor fell out of the Mexican economy. Canadian exports plunged 37.5 per cent, and, as was mentioned earlier, the CANDU deal evaporated.[120] Thus, the debt crisis unravelled much of the work Ottawa had put into increasing trade with Mexico. While there was discouragement on the economic front, Prime Minister Trudeau's 1982 visit to Mexico focused on such common political ground as the North-South Dialogue, the Law of the Sea, the Caribbean Basin Initiative, and the Central American crisis.[121]

In 1983, the Liberals attempted to bolster slumping trade with Mexico by raising EDC credits from $394 million to $700 million.[122] The following year, warm relations between the two countries continued with an official visit to Canada by President de la Madrid. The president and the prime minister celebrated the strong relations between Canada and Mexico, especially those fostered since 1980. As a DEA summary of private discussions between the two heads of state reveals, de la Madrid concurred with Trudeau's stinging assessment of the Reagan administration's foreign policy. The document summarizes Trudeau's position on the matter:

> Global economic problems could be traced to superpower rivalry and excessive military expenditures. These had created an economic environment dominated by the huge American deficit, high real interest rates, and overvalued U.S. dollar, trade deficits and protectionist sentiments. This chain of events was preventing other countries (such as Mexico) from benefitting from the economic recovery. All of this was due to the Americans' lack of vision and their inability to provide leadership for the Western world.[123]

Even if economic matters were not going well, the two leaders saw eye-to-eye on major global issues.

Conclusion

In the early 1980s, the Central American crisis and the Third World debt crisis erased any doubt as to whether Canada had prominent and tangible interests in the Western Hemisphere beyond those associated with the U.S. Not only did the significance of Latin America become even clearer to Canadians, but important global changes were brewing which, a few years later, would introduce an entirely new hegemonic structure.

With respect to ideology, there were some important developments within Canada, the U.S., and Latin America. With regard to Canada, Trudeau's address at St. Lucia underscored his government's position that ideological diversity was to be cherished and respected. Manichean attempts to classify countries as either communist or capitalist were no longer viewed as appropriate. Furthermore, Canada's 1983 Standing Committee Report to the House of Commons reached positions regarding the roots of turmoil in Central America that were strikingly distinct from the official U.S. view. Many of the policies pursued on the global stage naturally reflected ideas prominent within the domestic political economy. Economic nationalism on the home front, as manifested in the creation of NEP as well as in the fortification of FIRA, paralleled Ottawa's ideological support for the benefits of state intervention in the economies of many Latin American countries. As well, the revived Third

Option formula, a signal of the Canadian fear of U.S. economic and political encroachment, contributed to Ottawa's efforts to reinforce economic relations with key Latin American countries.

Finally, with respect to ideological considerations, Joe Clark's short-lived Progressive Conservative government in 1979-80 foreshadowed some of the changes that would occur with the Mulroney victory of 1984. The Clark government, for example, supported the U.S. with regard to Central American affairs, as was apparent in Canada's support at the OAS for President Carter's ill-fated scheme to prevent the Sandinistas from coming to power through the provision of a joint military force. As well, the Progressive Conservatives' ideological doubts regarding the notion of publicly owned corporations became apparent when the Clark government bungled an oil deal with Mexico by hesitating because it entailed the participation of Petro-Canada, a Crown corporation. Similar positions, although couched in a more coherent and wide-ranging package, would be apparent in the Mulroney era.

Crucially important was a major ideological shift in the world's most powerful state, the U.S. The Reagan administration's sharp turn to the Right, through both its foreign policy and its introduction of the 'hyperliberal state,' naturally generated a ripple effect throughout the globe. In the final Trudeau term of 1980-4, Canada was clearly out of step with Washington's ideological conversion – one that would produce an immense impact upon the hemisphere throughout the late 1980s and into the 1990s. In broad strokes, this new direction included a feverish resurrection of anti-communism, a predisposition to employ military force to accomplish political objectives, and a propensity to act unilaterally if multilateral fora seemed unsympathetic to U.S. objectives. 'Reaganomics,' with its emphasis upon the retraction of state intervention in the economy coupled with the retreat of welfare provisions, would be matched in Canada beginning in 1984. This economic formula was imposed upon Latin America through U.S. dominance in IMF restructuring programs in the late 1980s and 1990s.

After 1982, Latin American economic nationalism was torpedoed with the onset of the debt crisis. Restructuring under the IMF meant that Latin American countries had to surrender a significant portion of control over their political economies. If the region was pressured into complying with U.S. economic objectives through IMF directives, Washington was experiencing a more difficult task when it came to the

Central American crisis. Many Latin American states, Mexico and Brazil included, condemned U.S. intervention in the region during this period, and would later launch multilateral efforts that were at odds with U.S. policy (a point which will be discussed in later chapters).

Turning to the realm of capabilities for Canada, the U.S., and Latin America, some interesting developments can be observed here as well. Beginning with Canada, Ottawa revived its dedication to the Third Option formula, that is, to diversifying its political and economic relations. This paralleled an attempt to pursue closer relations with other so-called middle powers. Since the Trudeau government felt that Washington was failing in its capacity to lead the Western world, it was up to other states to fill the void and to promote stability. Canada's contribution towards this objective entailed fostering links with key powers across the globe and, whenever possible, aiding in conflict resolution. As a trading nation, Canada had a direct interest in preserving peace and stability.

Canadian exports to South America and Mexico peaked in 1981 (just over $3 billion), as did imports ($4.3 billion).[124] It was the debt crisis that would throw a monkey wrench into Canadian plans for increasing trade with Latin America during the 1980s. Particularly worrisome was a drop of almost 50 per cent in the amount of Canadian manufactured goods exported to South America and Mexico between 1980 and 1984.[125] Ottawa's scheme to increase trade with Latin America became a hostage of the Latin American debt crisis. Since diversification of trade was the centrepiece of Trudeau's foreign policy, the debt crisis and the related fall in trade posed a serious problem indeed. On the other hand, Canadian direct investment in South America and Central America (including Mexico) increased from about $1.3 billion in 1978 to $2.1 billion in 1984, with strife-ridden Central America representing the only area suffering a decline in Canadian investment.[126] Canadian capital had confidence in Latin America, even if the trade picture looked bleak. This process would accelerate in the 1980s and into the 1990s.

In terms of Canada's capacity to promote conflict resolution and stability within the Latin American context, it was observed that Prime Minister Trudeau attempted to stress the concept of ideological diversity in the Americas. In his view, the U.S. should come to accept that flirtations with socialism or communism did not necessarily mean an alignment with the USSR and strategic assaults against Western interests. Stability, then, was not necessarily threatened by socialist or communist political economies in Latin America. While that view may have been shared by key Latin American countries, such as Mexico, it was not adopted by the U.S. The increasingly compatible visions of Prime Minister Trudeau and President Carter evaporated during the Reagan years.

If there were failures to achieve what Canada was capable of, the noted economist G.K. Helleiner was quite adept at identifying some important components in this regard.[127] First, by 1981-2, after years in office, the Trudeau government had devoted only .42 per cent of its annual gross national product (GNP) to official developmental assistance, which was well below the .7 per cent targets set by global institutions. Furthermore, Canada had one of the highest levels of tied aid among major powers, a policy criticized not only for failing to provide the most appropriate assistance to the Third World but also for failing to assist in the process of increasing Canadian exports.[128] Finally, in general, Canada's tariffs on manufactured goods from developing countries were quite high, a policy which obviously ran contrary to the interests of developing countries.

In terms of U.S. capabilities, Washington decided that an aggressive foreign policy would catapult the U.S. back to its premier position in global politics. In Latin America, this was embodied by a strategy of 'low intensity conflict' in Central America. This strategy combined support for military counter-revolution in Nicaragua as well as military assistance for U.S. client states in the region in the face of serious insurgences, with a clever mixture of diplomatic, economic, and psychological warfare. All this was part of the Reagan doctrine, which attempted to reverse the revolutionary process in Soviet-supported socialist states and to make such experiments so costly that they would promote the eventual economic and political collapse of the USSR. Unilateralism was the order of the day, especially since some of the tactics entailed in the quest to make America number one might not please Washington's traditional allies. U.S. destructive capabilities were rising, although, as shall be seen later, U.S. productive capacity was falling.

Let us turn to Latin American capabilities. The Sandinista revolution in particular, as well as strong leftist insurrections in Central America, were largely interpreted as enormous challenges to U.S. influence in the region. The early 1980s demonstrated that Latin America had some capacity to contradict U.S. wishes, at least in the short run. But if Latin America was seen as defying Washington's interest, it could count on a tough fight during the Reagan years. More generally, the Third World debt crisis dissipated much of Latin America's ability to resist U.S. economic and political pressure. This became more obvious as the 1980s wore on.

From the Canadian perspective, institutions during this period were weak. It was felt by some that, since the U.N. was overloaded, it would be a good idea if the OAS could be strengthened in order to deal with the pressing issues in Latin America. In that spirit, the House of Commons Standing Committee on Latin America recommended full Canadian membership in the OAS. But the balance of power rested with those who thought that full membership in the OAS would be unwise, since the institution was unable to assist in the resolution of the hemisphere's most outstanding problems, such as the Falklands/Malvinas conflict, the Central American imbroglio, and the debt crisis. Perhaps the OAS reached its lowest ebb during this period.

Viewing the relationship among ideas, institutions, and capabilities, it can be seen that this era was one of great flux and incongruence. But the ball was rolling towards a firmer fit between these components that would take shape near the end of the decade, thus signalling an emerging hegemony.

State structures were undergoing careful examination and change in the early 1980s. The hyperliberal model employed by the Reagan administration, though out of step with Canada and most of the countries in Latin America, would represent the wave of the future. Nevertheless, one of the major components of Canada's politico-economic compatibility with key Latin American states was the celebration of state intervention in mixed economies – an idea in the twilight of its hemispheric popularity.

Important changes also occurred in state-society relations. For Canada, an important aspect of this was the emergence of counter-consensus interest groups as significant determinants of Canadian policy. Even if the interests of these groups were not often realized in actual policy, their impressive expertise and organizational ability allowed them to shape the context of debates by lobbying both the government and the public.

State-society relations underwent drastic shifts under the Reagan administration. A feverish sense of patriotism and militarism was evoked by Washington, as was a successful ideological campaign to dismantle the welfare state. The U.S. demographic shift towards the

South and West paralleled the new outlook that shaped American state-society relations – an outlook that would have international ramifications.[129]

The discussion above has alluded to a shifting world order. The U.S. embarked on a vigorous effort to bolster its global position. Washington's attempt to shape the world order was accompanied by efforts to alter state-society relations and state structures. The years between 1980 and 1984 witnessed events that created a process which would erode the bipolar world order – one which would render Soviet influence in the Western Hemisphere (or anywhere else) to be a non-issue. It was the beginning of the end for a long wave of pronounced anti-Americanism and nationalism in Latin America as well as Canada. By the end of the decade, the rest of the hemisphere would be more in step with the project launched by the Reagan administration. In that sense, out of the early 1980s came the building blocks for a hegemony that would develop over the next decade.

Part Three:
The Mulroney Years

8

1984-8: The Predominance of Central America

This period witnessed the beginnings of an unprecedented process of integration in the Americas. The debt crisis and, especially, the Central American imbroglio dominated Ottawa's attention with respect to Latin America. This chapter explores the global and domestic determinants of Canada's growing role in inter-American affairs during 1984-8. Since Central America largely eclipsed other issues in hemispheric relations during this period, this topic will receive considerable attention here.

The Domestic Context

With the landslide victory of Brian Mulroney in 1984 came profound changes in both Canadian foreign and domestic policy. Embracing the neoconservative agenda which was already in place in the U.S., ideological elements within the Progressive Conservative party supported a process of harmonization between Canadian and American policies, although some distinctions were visible. Not only was there a general convergence between Washington and Ottawa on many levels, there also appeared to be an increasingly shared world-view among hemispheric states in general.

It was noted in Chapter 7 that the philosophical underpinnings of the Trudeau government seemed out of step with the New Right agenda which emerged in the U.S. around 1980. Upon closer inspection, it is clear that the Liberal government during 1980-4 was ideologically fragmented, with key members refusing to support the reassertion of the Third Option, the fortification of FIRA, and the creation of NEP. Members of the business community, which, at one time, embraced Trudeau's style of economic nationalism, no longer did so. This component of the Liberals and their supporters now desired more amicable relations with Washington and even contemplated versions of free trade with the U.S.

Angered by NEP and FIRA, in 1981 Washington retaliated by threatening Canada's access to the U.S. market, the destination of roughly three-quarters of Canadian exports. Reflecting a global trend to transnational production and freer international capital flows, Canadian capital seemed to have an increasing stake in foreign countries and, especially, in the U.S. Between 1978 and 1983, Canadians invested $22 billion in the U.S.[1] Thus, the government not only had to ensure that Canadian capital was welcome abroad, it also had to confront the problem of attracting more capital into Canada.

By 1983, a DEA report broached the idea of sectoral free trade with the U.S.[2] Also in that year, Canada's minister for international trade, Gerald Regan, argued that the Third Option was no longer viable and that, in light of creeping American protectionism, some sort of free trade agreement with the U.S. was necessary.[3] Although this view was not dominant, it indicated that the ideological fabric of the Trudeau government was fraying. In other words, the notions of economic nationalism and diversification of external economic interests seemed to be reaching the end of the line, alongside ever-louder calls for policies of continentalism and harmonization with the U.S. The roots of the upcoming CUSFTA were present in government and in the business community prior to Mulroney's victory.

Nineteen eighty-four marked both the end of the nearly sixteen-year tenure of Prime Minister Trudeau and the victory of a neoconservative agenda under the leadership of Brian Mulroney. Many have suggested that Mulroney's personal background as a native of Baie Comeau, a resource town established by an American newspaper chain in order to provide it with paper, etched an indelible 'coprador' and pro-U.S. mentality into the prime minister.[4] The Mulroney doctrine, as some have termed it, concentrated upon integrating the Canadian economy more closely with that of the U.S., and also advocated a heavier reliance upon foreign investment and the private sector.[5] The Mulroney doctrine and its relationship to CUSFTA will be explored here after first turning to an examination of two reviews of foreign policy conducted by the Progressive Conservative government.

The first major foreign policy review since *FPC* was Joe Clark's *Competitiveness and Security: Directions for Canada's International Relations (CS:DCIR)*, published in 1985. In the opening section, it is noted that 'we are a nation of the Americas, with an interest and an investment in the hemisphere's future.'[6] As shall be seen, however, *CS:DCIR* says precious little regarding Canadian interests in Latin America. A recurring theme was the changing nature of the global political economy, with an emphasis upon international trade, investment, and capital flows.[7] Hence, it was appreciated that the concept of export-led growth in tandem with the growing power of transnational capital were important new influences upon Canadian foreign policy. In a clear reference to the U.S., it was observed that 'for Canada, protectionism poses great dangers'[8] – a view that was instrumental in the eventual success of the pro-free-trade movement. Although the review identified Third World debt as a formidable problem in the global arena,[9] it failed to note that Canada, itself, was well on its way to accumulating one of the world's largest per capita debts. It also omits the crucial observation that in the year it was published, the U.S. descended to the position of a net debtor and began a rapid slide into the position of the world's largest debtor nation – a role which, arguably, undermines its capacity as a hegemon.[10] Disregarding this important fact, *CS:DCIR* argues that the 'United States will remain the world's dominant economic power' as well as the world's foremost power generally.[11] While the Trudeau government opined that U.S. international influence was declining relative to other states, the fact that the Mulroney government saw no sign of wavering American power was an important determinant of its foreign policy.

In its one-page discussion of Latin America, *CS:DCIR* lists a number of points in quick succession.[12] First, it celebrated the wave of democracy that seemed to be sweeping the region, exemplified by Argentina and Brazil. It also recognized the new sense of Latin American solidarity, especially in the wake of the formation of the Contadora Group (which shall be discussed below) and its supporting orbit of states, which it saw as the best hope for conflict resolution in Central America. Furthermore, *CS:DCIR* offered the contentious observation that, although enormous problems associated with debt were plaguing the region, 'the sense of economic despair [had] eased' in the wake of restructuring programs.[13] In retrospect, one can see that the 'despair' had not actually subsided but, in many cases, had carried over into the 1990s.

The Progressive Conservatives' reassessment of foreign policy also pointed out that Latin America was an increasingly important market for Canadian exports, that it was the second largest destination after the U.S. for Canadian investment capital, and that our banks had about $15 billion in outstanding loans to the region. Despite the crises which dotted Latin America, Canada had growing economic interests there. Turning to another prominent topic, although Joe Clark had indicated during his first speech at the U.N. in 1984 that Canada would join the OAS as a full member,[14] the foreign policy review described this issue as an open question.[15] Once again, Canada's relationship to the OAS was shrouded in confusion.

CS:DCIR presented a number of empirical indicators which suggested that Canada faced severe challenges in the global economy. One of these was that Canada spent only 1.39 per cent of its GDP on research and development, compared to nearly twice that amount being spent by the leading economic powers, including the U.S., Japan, the U.K., Germany, and Sweden.[16] During his election campaign, Mulroney indicated that he would raise research and development expenditures to 2.5 per cent of the GDP,[17] although this promise did not appear in the foreign policy review. A commitment which did appear in *CS:DCIR*, however, was a pledge to spend .6 per cent of the GNP on official developmental assistance by 1990 and .7 per cent by 1995.[18] As shall be seen, these turned out to be false promises.

Elsewhere in *CS:DCIR*, the USSR was branded as the most ominous security threat to Canada, and Europe remained the 'most critical military region in the world'[19] – a position that seemed more appropriate to 1945 than to 1985. Although Canada's historical commitment to multilateralism was underscored, the review noted that the influence and credibility of the U.N. were in doubt,[20] though it failed to mention that the U.S. was its most vocal doubter. These and other segments led observers to criticize the review for clinging to an outdated 'realist' assessment of global affairs, and for failing to come to grips with a shifting international distribution of power.[21]

Obviously, the Conservatives' *CS:DCIR* differed radically from the Liberals' *FPC*. As has been noted, *FPC* suggested that the U.S. was being challenged economically by Europe and Japan, and even by some newly industrializing countries. Arguably, this was still the case fifteen years later. From the Trudeau government's perspective, the world was progressing towards multipolarity. In contrast, Clark's document attested to the political, economic, and military strength of the U.S., and beyond that, provided a portrait of a bipolar global climate – an intense contest between the U.S. and the USSR. The contest between the superpowers seemed real enough, especially in the context of the second Cold War, which characterized this period. But *CS:DCIR*'s emphasis upon Europe as the world's most important strategic site, representing baggage from traditional realist and balance-of-power paradigms, seemed to miss the larger point that the warfare between the U.S. and the USSR was expressed not in the North but in the Third World, with Central America being a case in point.

Although both the Liberals and the Conservatives viewed trade as being quite significant for Canada, the paths they pursued for the development of the Canadian export sector were quite distinct from one another. While the Trudeau government, following the Third Option, attempted to diversify trade by channelling it away from the U.S. and towards Western Europe, the Asia-Pacific, and Latin America, the Mulroney government's foreign policy placed more emphasis upon securing the U.S. market against the backdrop of rising protectionism there. What is also striking is that while *FPC* devoted an entire pamphlet to Latin America and its significance to Canada, *CS:DCIR* spent only one page on this topic. This is quite ironic, given that the 1980s witnessed an unprecedented strengthening of Canadian ties to Latin America.

Canada's role in the international arena was, in essence, redefined by the Progressive Conservatives. *CS:DCIR* prompted analysts of Canadian foreign policy to question whether Canada was, or could be, the 'Principal Power' of the Trudeau years, since that status was accorded to a state that was not so heavily influenced by Washington.[22] That is, instead of a power with a distinctive agenda, and which was among the top tier of states in a multipolar world, Clark's document portrayed Canada as a loyal ally of the U.S. in a bipolar global arrangement. Obviously, this sweeping rethinking of Canada's international role had profound effects on its foreign policy.

With the issues raised in *CS:DCIR* as its starting point, a special joint committee of the Senate and of the House of Commons on Canada's international relations was formed in 1985, and it released a major report, *Interdependence and Internationalism (I&I)*, in the following year. Much of *I&I* was purported to be based upon submissions and testimonies from numerous concerned parties regarding specific issues. Notable is the fact that the topic of the Central American crisis was the subject of the largest number of submissions, from both groups and individuals, although it was accorded only three pages in the 196-page document.[23] It is also interesting to observe that topics associated with South America received only one submission,[24] indicating beyond doubt that those in Canada who had interests in Latin America tended to focus upon Central America.

There are two other points worth mentioning with respect to *I&I*. First, it argued that Canada relies too heavily upon information from the U.S. when formulating foreign policy positions. As was observed in Chapter 7, some counter-consensus interest groups strenuously argued precisely this point with respect to the Central American situation. An independent foreign policy requires independent sources of information. Further, Gerald Helleiner, in his submission to the special joint committee, underscored the significance of global stability for Canada:

> The first priority for a country like Canada, so dependent on the stability and predictability of the international economic system, must surely be, overwhelmingly, the stability and order of the international system. This is not of course simply in the sphere of trade, but trade is now in any case inextricably interlinked with financial questions: with money and finance; the entire Bretton Woods system and its capacity to get us through the next recession or get us through to the year 2000 without major breakdown. There can be no higher priority for Canadian foreign policy.[25]

The cultivation of international stability has remained a constant Canadian objective.

Let us now turn to a deeper consideration of the forces behind Canada's economic integration with the U.S., which was a crucial development in the process of hemispheric integration that would occur in the 1990s.[26] For a number of reasons, the Mulroney government was dedicated to developing a free trade agreement with the U.S. As *CS:DCIR* indicated, Ottawa was duly disturbed about American protectionism. Furthermore, some have contended that the Progressive Conservatives believed that if U.S. investment in this country were more easily facilitated, the Americans would become more dependent upon Canada, which in turn would diminish the asymmetric power relations between the two countries. It has also been argued that the Mulroney government saw no necessary linkage between economic and political integration.[27]

The apparent development of trade areas in Europe and Japan was also an important factor behind the Progressive Conservatives' desire for a free trade deal with the U.S. If the world was indeed moving towards introverted trade areas,[28] Canada needed to be guaranteed access to the U.S. market – access that U.S. protectionism seemed to threaten. In September 1985, shortly after the Macdonald Royal Commission released its recommendation in support of a free trade agreement with the U.S., the Mulroney government noted:

> Economics, geography, common sense and the national interest dictate that we try to secure and expand our trade with our closest and largest trade partner, – protectionist measures are always self-defeating. This impulse to protectionism is defensive and negative – yet entirely understandable in human terms. This is what we are up against. The answer to this problem lies in sound agreements, legally binding, between trading partners, to secure and remove barriers to their mutual trade. That is our approach to world trade. And it is obvious that we must find special and direct means of securing and enhancing the annual $155 billion of two-way trade with the United States.[29]

Related to the development of trade blocs was the growing prominence of globalized production and the burgeoning power of transnational corporations (TNCs).[30] TNCs produced for the global market and located their specialized plants wherever labour, resources, and distribution processes were the most efficient. Free trade agreements accommodated the needs of these increasingly potent corporations.

As home to the world's largest TNCs and as the chief perpetrator of the marvels of globalization, the U.S. government appeared more than receptive to a trade agreement with Canada, despite the presence of protectionist noises emanating from some American quarters. In 1984, the U.S. Congress passed a bill which permitted Washington to negotiate bilateral trade liberalization agreements, with Israel and Canada representing the only countries specifically named as prospective participants.[31] No doubt the Reagan administration was pleased with the Mulroney government, a decidedly more pro-business and pro-U.S. administration than had existed under the headstrong Trudeau.

Following the celebrated Shamrock Summit of March 1985, where trade liberalization was high on the agenda, the Reagan administration, in December of that year, notified Congress of its intention to negotiate a free trade agreement with Canada. Successful negotiations were completed in 1987, and the Progressive Conservatives won an election on the issue in 1988. This appeared to be phase one of a process leading towards North American integration in particular (Canada-U.S.-Mexico) and hemispheric integration in general. It would propel Mexican President Carlos Salinas de Gortari to request a similar arrangement with the U.S. in June of 1990, and stimulated President Bush to introduce the Enterprise for the Americas Initiative in the summer of that year.

Canada and the Central American Crisis

During the period 1979-84, as has been seen, Central America took on major significance for Canadian foreign policy.[32] In the 1980s, many had argued that the isthmus was the focal point of Latin American affairs, in effect eclipsing important issues in South America and Mexico. The Central American crisis became an ugly microcosm of the second Cold War, with the U.S. under Ronald Reagan resisting what it perceived to be advances by the Soviet Union in the Third World, particularly in Central America, Southern Africa, Cambodia, and Afghanistan.

This feverish campaign against socialism on the isthmus was part of the Reagan doctrine, which, essentially, turned the Brezhnev doctrine on its head: with the development of strong counter-insurgency efforts, socialist revolutions could revert to 'capitalist democracies.' Strategies for combatting socialism were revamped under the banner of low intensity conflict – a clever, if vicious, concoction that incorporated guerrilla warfare techniques borrowed from successful leftist insurrections, and combined with psychological warfare, diplomatic and economic isolation, and the neutralization of the social progress accomplished by socialist governments. U.S. military assistance to Central America rose from $25 million in 1981 to $188 million in 1986 and fell slightly to $176.5 million in 1987.[33]

In Chapter 7, it was observed that, following the 1984 election of Brian Mulroney, Canada's policy on Central America began to harmonize with U.S. policy. This was especially true with regard to Central American elections, as the Progressive Conservatives failed to follow through on a commitment by the Liberals to send observers to the election in Nicaragua but did send observers to elections in Washington's client states. Another manifestation of this harmonization was the reinstatement of Canadian developmental assistance to two of Washington's hardline client states, El Salvador and Guatemala. It will be remembered that, due to human rights abuses in general and the threat they posed to Canadian personnel in particular, the Trudeau government severed bilateral aid to those countries.

The Progressive Conservatives reinstated bilateral assistance to El Salvador and Guatemala in 1984 and 1987, respectively, citing 'marked improvement in the human rights situation and commitments by the democratically elected government to bring about substantial ... reforms.'[34] Despite this rationale, the human rights situation in those countries deteriorated considerably during the late 1980s. For example, the Washington-based Council on Hemispheric Affairs identified Guatemala, Colombia, and El Salvador (in that order) as the worst human rights violators in the hemisphere.[35] The murder of six Jesuit priests in El Salvador, in late 1989,[36] was but one manifestation of the country's abominable record.[37] It seems plausible that the restoration of Canadian aid to Guatemala and El Salvador was not a result of human rights improvements, but instead was a reflection of the restructuring of Canadian policy to echo that of Washington.

In defence of this aspect of Canadian policy, however, members of the Canadian government have offered two important arguments. Stanley Gooch, former Canadian ambassador to Central America, observed that 'Canada's aid programme to El Salvador is not based on Canada's support for the Duarté initiative [for national reconciliation], but rather is based on the belief that an aid programme, carefully channelled, can alleviate some of the social injustices in that country.'[38] A related position contends that Canadian developmental assistance is designed to help the poorest elements in El Salvador and Guatemala, regardless of human rights abuses that persist there.

A second argument in defence of Canadian aid to Guatemala and El Salvador came from Secretary of State for External Affairs Joe Clark, who told a Calgary audience that

some Canadian NGO's [criticized] Canada's continued relations with El Salvador, Guatemala and Honduras. We have been urged to cut off links, to walk away ... Some European countries have done just that. But when it came time to prepare for peace in Central America, it was not to those countries that the region turned. It was to Canada. For we maintained relations with the entire region – kept doors open, to be in a position to assist when assistance was required.[39]

In other words, by maintaining ties even in countries with grave human rights abuses in Central America, Canada was specially poised to promote peace in the region. I shall elaborate upon this topic below.

In the passage noted above, Clark refers to the strenuous lobbying campaign launched by NGOs and other interest groups focusing on Canadian policy towards Central America. As has been mentioned, their presence as a domestic determinant of Canadian foreign policy was one of the most important developments of the decade with respect to the evolution of Canadian policy in Latin America. Never before had such a well-organized and knowledgeable group worked so hard to have an impact on Canadian policy. Throughout the 1980s, groups such as the

Latin American Working Group, CAPA, OXFAM-Canada, Tools for Peace, an assortment of NGOs, and many others assumed the important role of educating and politicizing the public, defining issues, and having audiences with the government.

Often, lack of adequate government expertise was a problem, with counter-consensus groups calling for a full embassy in Nicaragua, for example, to provide Canadians with information that would not be as reliant on U.S. intelligence sources. The closure of the Canadian Embassy in Guatemala in 1986, explained by Ottawa as a result of budgetary restrictions, only exacerbated the situation. The orchestration of counter-consensus criticism against government policy presumably contributed to Ottawa's appointment of a roving ambassador to Latin America in 1987, whose duties included meeting with, and perhaps placating, Canadian interest groups.

Under the Progressive Conservatives, Canada clearly retracted, to some extent, Trudeau's support for ideological diversity in the hemisphere. This was exemplified in a statement by Joe Clark, following his trip to Central America in 1987: 'The real issue [in Central America] is not Marxism, nor death squads, nor even the abuse of human rights. Those are symptoms.'[40] In Clark's formulation, Marxism – like human rights abuses and death squads – represents a symptom of a problem, not a legitimate ideology or a basis for a political economy. This is hardly an expression of the acceptance of ideological diversity. Similarly, Clark extolled the virtues of free enterprise at the U.N. General Assembly, with no mention of the virtues of ideological pluralism.[41] The point is not to criticize Clark's legitimate preference for market economies, but to emphasize the retraction of Canada's earlier support for ideological diversity. Again, this shows the growing ideological convergence between Washington and Ottawa during the Mulroney era.

While certain components of Canada's policy to Central America changed between 1984 and 1988, others remained constant. Certainly, hemispheric stability remained Ottawa's chief concern with respect to inter-American relations. As has been said, a regional war which became unmanageable, or which spread into Mexico, could preoccupy the U.S. to the extent that it might be unable to adequately perform its global hegemonic responsibilities. This worry served as the central motivation behind Canada's important and genuine contributions to the Contadora Group, which began in 1983. The Contadora Group – consisting of Panama, Mexico, Colombia, and Venezuela – worked to promote peaceful change and conflict resolution. Other countries, such as Canada, supported their endeavours.

The DEA emphasized that 'Canada continues to regard the Contadora initiative ... as the only viable instrument of reconciliation in Central America.'[42] Drafts of the Contadora treaties all focused on the political, economic, and security issues at the base of the Central American crisis. It is in the area of security that Canada was of most assistance. Beginning in 1984, at the request of the Contadora Group, Canada submitted comments to it regarding the establishment of a Control and Verification Commission (CVC). Its role would be to station peacekeeping troops, especially on the Nicaraguan border, which would monitor diplomatic agreements concerning security issues (e.g., the presence of foreign military advisors and troops, border skirmishes, etc.). Canada's consultation regarding the CVC was completed in January 1985, but details were not publicly released due to the 'delicate nature of negotiations.'[43] The CVC was never to reach fruition, but Canada would provide additional consultation for later projects.

Canada's support for the Contadora Group, and the other institutional peace attempts that followed it, clearly distinguished Ottawa's policy from that of the U.S. Along with Canada's continued provision of developmental assistance to Nicaragua, this was one of the key areas in which Canadian policy remained 'independent.' Shortly after the formation of the Contadora Group, it became clear that the U.S. was not at all serious in its rhetorical support of that organization. The escalation in intensity of U.S.-directed Contra forces indicated that Washington preferred a military solution to its differences with Managua, or at least that the Americans were willing to employ military force in an attempt to pressure the Sandinistas into negotiating on purely U.S. terms. It will be recalled that, in September 1984, the U.S. and its allies in Central America, in addition to the four Contadora members, initially backed a draft of the Contadora Treaty. In a surprise move, Managua stated that it was willing to sign the treaty, which prohibited foreign military intervention in Central America and thus had obvious consequences for Soviet and Cuban advisors in Nicaragua. In the aftermath of the Sandinistas' unanticipated willingness to embrace the document, the U.S. and its allies in Central America suddenly found fault with the agreement and refused to sign it unless it was reworked. That was the beginning of the end of the Contadora accord.

Despite Canada's support for the Contadora Group, the government refused to criticize Washington on this issue. The director of the DEA's Central American Division discussed the September 1984 incident but failed to blame the U.S. for sabotaging the treaty. He indicated that 'this is not to criticize those who were anxious to have an agreement at the time, but the provisions of that agreement, particularly of a workable Verification and Control system, had not adequately matured.'[44] Similarly, Joe Clark stated that 'I have seen no evidence that the U.S. is trying to do anything other than make Contadora succeed.' Remarkably, he also noted that Washington's severance of bilateral talks with Nicaragua could be seen 'to strengthen rather than weaken the Contadora process.'[45] That argument was less than convincing.

By the summer of 1986, however, the Canadian government had come to appreciate that prospects for the success of the Contadora initiative were slim indeed. A DEA official concerned with Central American affairs observed: 'If optimism could be a function of the level of negotiating activity, then we should be increasingly confident that the Contadora impasse will be finally broken and the agreement signed on the [6th] of June [1986]. Sadly, the odds are heavily against such an outcome.'[46] Once again, a major reason that a negotiated settlement to the crisis in Central America was impossible was that Washington was bent on militarily overthrowing the Sandinistas. Related to this, shortly after Washington dismissed John Ferch as the U.S. ambassador to Honduras, he observed: 'I always thought we meant what we said. We wanted pressures so we could negotiate. I'm beginning to think I accepted something that wasn't true ... our goal is something different. It's a military goal.'[47]

As has been observed, Ottawa often appeared reluctant to publicly criticize the Reagan administration for stalling the Contadora process. This was paralleled by its hesitance to express its apparent distaste for increased U.S.-sponsored Contra activity in Central America. During his summit meeting with President Reagan in the spring of 1986, Prime Minister Mulroney declined, on a number of occasions, to answer reporters' questions regarding his views on the president's vigorous attempts to gain increased Congressional funding for the Contras. However, in a letter, dated 26 September 1986, to a Canadian interest group involved with Central American affairs, Prime Minister Mulroney stated:

> During my recent visit to Washington, I raised Canada's position on the situation in Central America with President Reagan, Vice President

Bush, Secretary of State Shultz and Congressional leaders. I emphasized to them that we view the problems in Central America as being largely economic and social in origin, and that we believe solutions to these problems must therefore be found in the economic and social sphere. We do not support a military approach; rather, we favour negotiated settlement arranged by the countries of the region themselves.[48]

So, while Mulroney avoided direct public criticism of U.S. policy in Central America at the time of his meeting with officials in Washington, he later offered subtle statements regarding Ottawa's views on the matter. The Progressive Conservative government seemed to be heeding the general advice of the Pearson administration, which, in 1965, suggested that Ottawa should avoid public agreement with the U.S. on sensitive issues.[49]

In addition to its assistance to the Contadora process, Canada also provided support for other attempts at regional conflict resolution. Canada witnessed negotiations between the Sandinista government and Misurasata, a native political organization that experienced difficulty with the Nicaraguan government. Ottawa also offered technical assistance for the proposed Costa Rican-Nicaraguan joint border commission in 1986.[50] Once again, Ottawa remained committed to multilateral attempts at conflict resolution and the cultivation of stability. While the Mulroney government converged ideologically with the Reagan administration to an important extent, it also remained true to Canada's historical commitment to multilateralism and objected to military solutions pursued by the U.S.

As the 1980s wore on, components of the Canadian government became increasingly critical of both the Sandinistas and the U.S. Francis Filleul, Canada's ambassador to Nicaragua, Costa Rica, and El Salvador, commented: 'Nicaragua has been penetrated so badly by Cuba and other countries that it is destabilizing.' In the summer of 1986, he noted:

> Observers from many countries and many backgrounds have said the Sandinistas' direction is Marxist-Leninist. This has not been denied by its leaders, who have on occasion supported that observation. Efforts have been made [by the Sandinistas] to help the poorest in Nicaragua, but there have been no such efforts towards political liberation.[51]

On the other hand, in a boldly significant shift from previous Canadian policy, the government publicly condemned Washington by voting in favour of a U.N. resolution calling on the U.S. to comply with the World Court's decision that it refrain from supporting the Contra invasion of Nicaragua.[52] Britain, France, West Germany, and other traditional American allies abstained from the vote, while only El Salvador and Israel voted with the United States. The U.N. resolution was tabled when it became apparent that the Reagan administration had no intention of heeding the World Court's ruling of 27 June 1986 that

> the United States of America, by training, arming, equipping, financing and supplying the Contra forces or otherwise encouraging, supporting and aiding the military and paramilitary activities in and against Nicaragua, has acted against the Republic of Nicaragua, in breach of its obligations under customary international law not to intervene in the affairs of another state.[53]

One could also interpret Canada's support of the U.N. resolution as a protest against Washington unilaterally attempting to reassert its hegemony. The U.S. had broken international law in Central America, and this was compounded by the 1983 Grenada invasion and the 1986 air strike against Libya.

The Esquipulas II Accord, signed by all five Central American countries in August of 1987, represented a major step towards conflict resolution. It signalled that the Central American countries themselves would lead the peace process. The accord contained a number of stipulations: the disbanding of irregular military forces and the cessation of foreign military assistance; the development of negotiations leading to cease-fires; the resumption of negotiations to develop security provisions outlined in the Contadora initiatives; the creation of national reconciliation commissions; and the establishment of an International Commission for Verification Follow-Up.[54]

Immediately after the signing of the Esquipulas II Accord, Ottawa offered to provide technical advice to promote the peace process, much as it did for the Contadora scheme. In March of 1988, Prime Minister Mulroney stated: 'Canada stands ready to undertake a peace-supervisory role anywhere in the region where it might be helpful, provided the Central American governments themselves desire our involvement and create a framework for effective action.'[55]

In addition to identifying the security threat, Ottawa had other concerns in the Central American crisis. For example, Central American refugees represented a key factor in raising Central America's profile for

Canada.[56] The number of Central American refugees arriving in Canada escalated considerably in 1985, when the DEA estimated that approximately 3,000 regional refugees were allowed to enter the country.[57] Stricter laws against the entrance of refugees in the U.S., implemented in late 1986, prompted a further increase in the rate of Central American arrivals in Canada. The number of such refugees increased fourteenfold during the first few months of 1987.[58]

In 1988, the situation worsened. With regard to the origin of persons claiming refugee status in Canada, Nicaragua ranked first (3,564 refugees), with Panama (1,925) and El Salvador (1,482) sixth and eighth, respectively.[59] In addition to restrictions imposed upon Central Americans fleeing their war-torn homes,[60] in 1988 Ottawa implemented visa requirements for Nicaraguans and Panamanians.[61] While such strategies curbed the flow of refugees from the isthmus, their number was sufficient to generate further Canadian attention towards Central America. It also contributed to the slow process of the hispanicization of Canada.

Summing up Canada's relations with Central America during this period, the region became this country's primary focus in Latin America. Our developmental assistance to Central America more than doubled from $22.1 million in 1981-2 to over $55 million in 1987-8. While it may be true that other states or areas within Latin America were relatively neglected by Ottawa, it is also the case that Canada's involvement in Central America served as the basis to promote a much greater role for Canada in inter-American affairs, as is apparent in the 1990s. The Central American situation demonstrated that Canada possessed a clear interest in the security of the Americas. Ottawa's important contributions towards conflict resolution cemented its closer diplomatic relations with major powers throughout the Americas.

Ideologically, the Mulroney government tilted closer to the U.S. regarding Central American affairs than did the Trudeau government. Since it was intensely interested in cultivating a free trade agreement with the U.S., it is plausible that, particularly after 1985, Canada felt that it must not alienate the U.S. in key foreign policy issues such as Central America.

Despite growing ideological compatibility, however, there were still some important distinctions between U.S. and Canadian policies, including Canada's provision of developmental assistance to Nicaragua, its vote at the U.N. against U.S. policy in Central America, and its important contributions towards peace initiatives which were not supported by the U.S. While Canada and the U.S. shared the objectives of free market economies and democracy for the region, they differed on how to achieve those objectives. These differences were a product of the distinct histories of the two countries, as well as of their different ranks and roles in the global arena.

Regarding the domestic determinants of Canadian policy in Central America, two points are prominent. First, the arrival of significant numbers of Central American refugees to Canada's doorstep crystallized the linkage between inter-American upheavals and tangible domestic concerns. Second, the steady evolution of organized and knowledgeable interest groups concerned with developments in Central America could not be ignored. These organizations were successful at politicizing important issues and critically scrutinized government policy. This was the first time that Canadian interest groups had become so concerned with Latin American affairs, eclipsing even the strong support for Chilean refugees in the 1970s.

Debt, Trade, and Investment
The Third World debt crisis had a profound impact upon Canadian business interests during the late 1980s and, therefore, contributed to Ottawa's intense focus on Latin America. In 1984, aware of a burgeoning assortment of problems, the Canadian inspector general of banks directed lending institutions to set aside reserves of about 10 per cent to 15 per cent of their total bank exposure in the Third World. It was recommended that the figure reach about 18 per cent to 20 per cent by 1989 in order to serve as a cushion against anticipated default.[62] By 1989, Canadian banks had surpassed that target, setting aside reserves of nearly 100 per cent – a figure much higher than that of U.S. banks at the time.[63] Hence, during the period under study here, Canadian banks worked diligently to protect themselves from possible default by Third World countries. The size of these reserves suggests that Canadian banks did not expect to be paid back in full. The creation of reserves also placed lending institutions in the favourable position of being able to sell their loans at a discount 'without incurring further losses on the balance sheets.'[64] Furthermore, Canadian banks made it clear that they were unlikely to make additional loans to Latin American countries for the purpose of servicing existing debt.

Not only did Canadian lending institutions create substantial reserves to protect themselves from possible default by debtors, they also drastically reduced their exposure to Third World loans (to $17 million by early 1989).[65] Much of this was accomplished by selling or 'swapping' loans. The Toronto Dominion Bank, for example, sold $780 million worth of Third World loans in 1988 and swapped $308 million worth of Mexican loans for bonds, the principal of which was backed by U.S. government securities.[66] Similarly, during a six-month period in 1988, the National Bank of Canada sold about $541 million in Third World loans.[67] Additionally, the appreciating value of the Canadian dollar, starting in late 1987 and continuing into 1989, had the effect of reducing Canadian bank exposure in Latin America by approximately $1 billion.[68] It should be noted that Canadian banks were also motivated by a loss of profit, and a decline in investor confidence instigated by the debt crisis. Of the six major Canadian banks, only the Toronto Dominion Bank recorded a profit in 1987; the provisions for Latin American debt, to a significant extent, were responsible for the poor results.[69] During the late 1980s, share prices for Canadian bank stocks fell periodically as a result of a loss of domestic confidence – a loss arising from exposure to Third World loans. For example, Canadian bank stock prices dropped when Brazil declared a moratorium on its debt payments in 1987, and they fell for a brief period at the beginning of 1989 in reaction to riots and instability in Venezuela (where Canadian lending institutions had an estimated $2.2 billion in outstanding loans.)[70]

It is important to emphasize, however, that the effect of the Third World debt crisis on Canada went far beyond the issue of profit margins for Canadian banks. In a 1988 paper entitled 'Canada's Vital Interests in Latin America and How We are Pursuing Them,' the DEA noted that Latin America was Canada's fourth most important export market (after the U.S., the EC, and Japan).[71] In 1983, bilateral trade exceeded $6.7 billion, and 50 per cent of Canadian exports were either manufactured or high-technology goods.[72] Hence, the subsequent decline in Canadian exports to Latin America during the remainder of the decade, which had been triggered by the debt crisis, inflicted significant damage on the sector of the Canadian economy which most observers suggested was in need of strengthening. During the 1980s, Latin America remained the second largest recipient of Canadian direct investment,[73] even though the debt crisis curtailed Canadian commercial relations with the region.

The volume of Canadian exports to the largest Latin American countries dropped from about $3 billion in 1981 to under $2 billion in 1990, with a fall from $2.02 billion in 1984 to $1.9 billion in 1988.[74] Canadian imports from the region declined from $4.3 billion in 1981 to $3.9 billion in 1990, with a fall from $3.8 billion in 1984 to $3.6 billion in

1988.[75] The point is, the Latin American debt crisis, which created the worst economic conditions since the Great Depression of the 1930s, in conjunction with the recession that plagued the northern industrialized countries in the early 1980s, unravelled the important progress the Trudeau government had achieved in expanding Canadian commercial relations with Latin America.

The decline in exports to Latin America naturally resulted in a loss of Canadian jobs. The North/South Institute estimated that roughly 135,000 Canadian jobs were lost between 1982 and 1984 alone due to decreased exports to Latin America.[76] Although the actual number of job losses that can be attributed directly to a decline in trade with Latin America can be vigorously disputed, it remains clear that the effect on employment has been significant.

As noted earlier, Latin America is the second largest recipient of Canadian direct investment after the U.S. In contrast to slumping trade figures between 1984 and 1988, Canada's investment in Latin America increased from $1.65 billion in 1980 to $2.07 billion in 1984 and then to $2.5 billion in 1988.[77] It is interesting to note, however, that Canadian direct investment in Mexico plunged from $270 million in 1984 to $178 million in 1988, and it would decline even further in subsequent years – a point which will be developed in Chapter 9. On the other hand, Canada's direct investment in Brazil rose from $952 million in 1984 to $1.4 billion in 1988.[78]

Placing these figures in perspective, it is important to note that, since much of this investment is in the hands of just a few corporations, the termination or addition of even a single project can account for a relatively significant alteration in the figures. Furthermore, Latin America's share of total Canadian direct investment abroad fell from about 20 per cent in 1975 to about 8 per cent in 1985.[79] This reflected a global phenomenon, in which foreign direct investment by developed countries was directed to other developed states rather than to the sometimes unstable Third World. Nevertheless, as of 1987, about 75 per cent of all Canadian direct foreign investment in developing countries was located in Latin America.[80] The most significant locations for investment at that time were Brazil, Mexico, Argentina, and Venezuela, in that order.[81]

Obviously, there are other crucial points associated with the Third World debt crisis beyond those linked to the issues of trade and investment. During the 1980s, many Latin American countries plagued with dictatorial regimes began to move towards more democratic forms of government. These included: Peru (since 1980), Bolivia (since 1982), Argentina (since 1983), Uruguay (since 1984), Brazil (since 1985), various Central American countries (throughout the 1980s), and Chile (at the end of the decade).[82] These countries, and other Latin American states that already had democratic structures in place, were threatened by the pernicious social and economic effects of the debt crisis.

Restructuring and austerity measures insisted upon by the IMF, which often led to slashes in such basic social services as health and education, acted in conjunction with regional depression to place severe strains on democratic structures throughout Latin America. Obviously, some components of this restructuring were helpful, for example, those which reduced inflation and which promoted eventual economic recovery. It should be noted that, in general, it was military governments which accumulated the regional debt in the 1970s and early 1980s, with the majority of the population receiving few benefits from the lavish borrowing spree. Since it is the masses who overwhelmingly shouldered the brunt of the painful restructuring programs, in many cases the democratic process was paralleled by a rising index of social misery. The implications for rising instability are obvious and have resulted in a trend towards the resumption of military structures in some Latin American countries in the 1990s – a point which will be developed in Chapter 11.

Mexico is a classic example of a country that underwent sweeping IMF-induced changes. Shortly after the debt crisis emerged, President de la Madrid (1982-8) began a radical restructuring process, which included bold moves towards liberalization, especially after 1985. In addition to cuts in social spending, tariffs were dramatically reduced, and, in 1986, Mexico signed the General Agreement on Tariffs and Trade (GATT) – signalling its unequivocal commitment to trade liberalization. A privatization program was begun, and the country embarked upon a path that would eventually encourage ever-greater amounts of foreign investment.

While proponents of the privatization program argue that this process has contributed to the growth and revitalization of the Mexican economy, it has also resulted in greater transnational control. With globalization of production the catch-phrase of the late 1980s and 1990s, the maquiladora sector of Mexico grew dramatically.[83] Thus, it was during this era that the stage was set for the development of the North American Free Trade Agreement and the Enterprise for the Americas Initiative.

Conclusion

From 1984 to 1988 the basis was laid for many of the dramatic changes in the world order that would become manifest in the late 1980s and the 1990s. Following the period of the second Cold War, a new détente between Washington and Moscow commenced around 1985. It was largely a result of the increasingly bankrupt Soviet empire which could no longer assume a strong presence abroad, and which could barely control events within its own borders. This process was assisted by the Reagan administration's rather successful attempts to intensify and accelerate the Soviet decline by pressuring Moscow into costly military competition on a number of fronts.

For Latin America, the withering of Soviet superpowerdom would prompt leftist forces, especially in Central America, to consider an eventual presence at the bargaining table, since it was clear that any support from the Soviet Union or Cuba would shortly evaporate. This is not to suggest that Moscow and Havana were the guiding forces behind revolutionary leftism in the hemisphere, since it was clearly indigenous socio-economic inequities that propelled such movements. But it is no doubt true that the Soviets and Cubans provided materiel and other support which allowed socialist and communist forces to battle the more lavishly bankrolled military proxies of the United States. At any rate, these developments contributed to an emphasis upon peaceful negotiation rather than military excursions in many venues throughout Latin America. As was seen, Canada contributed significantly to the peace process in Central America once changes in the global environment improved prospects for success.

The world order, then, was moving away from a bipolar arrangement to a more uncertain global distribution of power. Accompanying these shifts in military capability was the emergence of a radically new international economic regime. By 1985 the U.S. became the world's largest debtor nation, with Canada and the rest of the hemisphere also deeply in the red. While U.S. military supremacy remained unquestioned during this period, the U.S. and the rest of the Americas seemed more vulnerable economically. Further, the European Community's progression towards the establishment of a trade area in 1992 led others in the system to contemplate a world of three major trade areas: Europe, Asia, and the Americas. The debt crisis and the resultant restructuring/austerity programs would contribute to this process in Latin America by creating some of the requisite conditions for globalized production. Generally, these conditions were already in place in the northern part of the hemisphere, with the Mulroney government's election and the subsequent Free Trade Agreement between Canada and the U.S. This was the precursor for the North American Free Trade negotiations and for the Enterprise for the Americas Initiative, which will be discussed at length in a subsequent chapter.

It has been observed here that ideological changes naturally accompanied these shifts in world order. Certainly the nationalistic economic and political policies of the Trudeau years evaporated during this era, as did similar positions previously assumed by a variety of Latin American states. An ideological convergence in the Americas was apparent, at least on the part of the region's governments (it is not clear that the masses have bought in). Thus there was an ideological component entailed in the process towards hemispheric integration that contributed to its progression economically and politically.

Associated with profound economic and ideological changes was a remodelling of state structures. Widely curtailed state intervention in the economy, deep social welfare cuts, and privatization were the order of the day virtually throughout the hemisphere. This process would accelerate in the late 1980s and into the 1990s. Accompanying these shifts in state structure were changes in state-society relations. Certainly tension was brewing between the state and the populace in many Latin American countries as a result of the sometimes painful restructuring process which most drastically affected the majority of the population. This tension was apparent to a lesser degree in the U.S. and Canada, but neoconservative governments received enough support, especially from the business sectors, to be re-elected.

All these changes signalled the forthcoming emergence of a hegemony in the Americas, that is, a growing convergence between ideology, capabilities, and institutional structures throughout the hemisphere. It was this process that defined the beginning of Canada's unprecedented integration with Latin America. While the focus of this evolution began with the Central American imbroglio and the debt crisis during this period, the foundation was in place for a more varied and intense relationship with the Americas in subsequent years.

9

The North American Free Trade Agreement

The focus of this chapter is on the issues surrounding NAFTA – issues which constitute a truly revolutionary phase in both inter-American affairs and Canadian foreign policy. While it is not clear at the time of this writing that NAFTA will be ratified, the agreement nonetheless represents a bold attempt at an unprecedented integration of the Americas. Emphasis will be placed upon debates surrounding hemispheric integration. As shall be seen, NAFTA has at least as much to do with investment, capital flows, and the role of the state as it does with trade.

Along with those concerns mentioned in Chapter 8 (i.e., Canadian fears of heightened U.S. protectionism, the belief that economic integration did not entail political integration, etc.), the movement towards trade areas in Europe, and to a much lesser extent in Asia, represented an important motivating factor behind the development of CUSFTA. (It is of interest to note that both Canada and the U.S. advised Japan and the Asia Pacific Economic Community not to follow the same course as NAFTA, presumably because they felt threatened by the likelihood of such a development.)[1] If the world was, indeed, moving towards the formation of economic blocs,[2] which, in the darkest scenario, might focus their trade internally, Canada needed to be guaranteed access to the U.S. market.

As the DEA recently pointed out:

Implementation of the FTA marked a significant change in attitude toward foreign direct investment in the Canadian economy. It put an end to a 100-year strategy of encouraging investment in Canada to serve the Canadian market. Time has eroded the relevance of such a strategy. Instead, Canada now competes for investment to serve the North

American market and even the global market, a trend which will accelerate following negotiations of the NAFTA.[3]

The successful negotiation of CUSFTA in 1987 propelled Mexican president Carlos Salinas de Gortari to request a similar agreement with the U.S. in June of 1990.[4]

Implications of the NAFTA Negotiations

A North American free trade area in one form or another, and the implications which flow from it, are obviously among the major issues facing Canada with regard to inter-American affairs. It has redefined Canada's role in the Western Hemisphere. As the DEA has observed: 'Liberalization, deregulation and privatization in Latin America provides an historic opportunity for Canada to assume a role in the Americas. The NAFTA negotiations with the U.S.A. and Mexico mark only the first stage of what could become a hemispheric free trade area.'[5] Even if there is no official agreement among the countries involved, however, it is important to note that de facto integration is already occurring and is likely to proceed into the foreseeable future.[6]

If successful, NAFTA would comprise a population of 360 million people with a total GDP of about $6 trillion (U.S.).[7] This compares with the European Economic Area, which has a total population of 380 million people and a GDP of $3.4 trillion (U.S.). North American integration would be a revolutionary development in that it would entail a free trade area between a developing and two developed countries. There are a plethora of indicators which demonstrate the gap between Canada and the U.S., on the one hand, and Mexico on the other. Among these, it may be of interest to note that, while Mexico's per capita income was $2,930 in 1992, the figure for both the U.S. and Canada was over $21,400. And, while infant mortality was measured at 40 for 1,000 live births in Mexico, it was 9.2 for the U.S. and 7.2 for Canada.[8] It is estimated that 26 per cent of the Mexican population do not have access to potable water, 20 per cent lack access to health services, and 29 per cent are unemployed or underemployed.[9] Roughly one-third of the Mexican population is under the age of 11; two-thirds of the population are under 25.[10]

Beyond the developmental chasm, one is struck by the power differentials apparent within NAFTA countries versus, for example, the EC. Within the NAFTA region, the U.S. is responsible for 85 per cent of regional economic output and for 70 per cent of the area's population. By contrast, Germany accounts for 25 per cent of the European Community-European Free Trade Area (EC-EFTA) output and 22 per cent of its combined population.[11] Furthermore, all three North American countries are major debtors. The U.S. is the world's largest debtor nation, Canada holds the title for the highest per capita public debt as well as the largest foreign debt relative to GNP in the world, and Mexico has one of the highest debt burdens of the developing countries.[12] Although these points are useful for a cursory comparison of the EC and NAFTA countries, they will later be related to specific features of the latter.

While U.S. president Bush and Mexican president Salinas enthusiastically announced on 10 June 1990 that they shared the objective of creating a comprehensive free trade agreement, debate continued during the summer of that year regarding whether or not Canada was willing (or welcome) to join them. In September 1990, then Canadian minister for international trade, John C. Crosbie, announced that Canada was considering entering into negotiations with Mexico and the U.S., but it was not until 5 February 1991 that Ottawa formally announced that it would join the trilateral talks. One ramification of this is that Canada's participation in the trilateral talks has lent a degree of legitimacy to the process.[13] That is, Canada's presence mitigated against perceptions of the U.S. having imperialistic designs on a hemispheric trade area, especially from the Mexican perspective.

The Agreement

While an exhaustive treatment of the nearly 2000-page NAFTA document is beyond the scope of this study, a consideration of the text's highlights is in order. The agreement includes a phase-out of almost all tariffs affecting trade among the three member nations. Some tariffs will be eliminated immediately. Others, in particularly sensitive or vulnerable areas, will be phased out over a ten- to fifteen-year period. For Canada, the protracted phase-out pertains to apparel, most footwear, toys, plastics, and certain manufactured goods.

Major changes from CUSFTA are apparent in NAFTA, specifically with respect to the auto industry. Rules of origin under CUSFTA for North American content were 50 per cent for cars and light trucks, but NAFTA boosted this figure to 62.5 per cent.[14] It appears that the motivation for this significant alteration came from pressure exerted upon Washington by the 'Big Three' U.S. auto-makers, in their attempt to discourage Asian and other foreign auto-makers from utilizing Mexico as a conduit for sales to the North American market.[15] This should be viewed in the context that, in 1992, General Motors and Ford posted the largest corporate losses in U.S. business history.[16] Mexico and Canada opposed the hikes in rules of origin, fearing this would discourage badly needed Asian investment. Overall, higher rules of origin amount to a new form of protectionism – a form that is bloc-based rather than state-based.

Turning to the agricultural sector, it is here that Mexico is the most vulnerable. About 26 per cent of the Mexican population works in agriculture. The agreement would make 2.7 million workers in agricultural collectives, as well as a million small landowners, compete with transnational agribusiness.[17] Mexican corn producers are especially vulnerable.[18] However, the central worry is that a considerable number of agricultural workers will be displaced as a result of NAFTA, prompting them to move to large cities and exacerbating the horrific urban problems which already exist. As well, concern has been raised that liberalization of the agricultural sector will lead to Mexico being dependent on foreign food.[19]

With respect to the Canadian agricultural sector, CUSFTA continues to hold for Canada-U.S. trade, while NAFTA provides a separate agreement for Canada-Mexico trade.[20] Ottawa has expressed hope that certain Canadian exports will benefit from the agreement, especially grains, pork, fish, potatoes, and processed foods. Exempt from the agreement are Canadian import quotas for supply-managed egg, poultry, and dairy products.

With regard to textiles and apparel, NAFTA includes new rules of origin which specify that, in order to qualify under the agreement, not only must garments be manufactured in North America but so must the yarns and fabrics used to make those garments.[21] These rules are designed to protect Mexican and U.S. producers from their Caribbean competitors.[22] Once again, trade is only free if you live in North America – otherwise parts of the agreement can be considered protectionist.

From the Canadian perspective, the outcome of negotiations in the energy sector is particularly controversial. Critics of CUSFTA have argued that Canada gave up too much in allowing greater foreign ownership of Canadian energy, as well as in granting security of supply provisions coupled with special pricing arrangements to the U.S.[23] While it was widely expected that the Mexicans would buckle under U.S. pressure to accept the arrangement set in the CUSFTA precedent, Mexico held firm and refused the liberalization of foreign ownership in the energy sector and also rejected security of supply provisions.[24]

Mexican officials claimed that to do otherwise would violate their country's constitution. Canadian critics of the energy component of CUSFTA wonder why Canadians did not bargain as effectively as the Mexicans.

The service sector is also dealt with in NAFTA, which widens the provisions set under CUSFTA. Under the agreement, transportation services will be liberalized, affording the trucking industry greater freedom for international travel within NAFTA region. Further, Mexico has agreed to open its market to business and professional services and has also provided full access to its financial service sector. Ottawa suggests that this will mean a boon for Canadian banks, trust companies, security brokers, and insurance companies wishing to invest in Mexico.[25]

Ottawa also claimed that Canada may benefit from NAFTA's government procurement provisions, which raise the ceiling for government contract opportunities from $20 billion under CUSFTA and GATT to $70 billion under NAFTA.[26] Thus, there is the hope that Canadian firms will be successful in securing government contracts in Mexico as that country develops. Article 1015 of NAFTA, in an attempt to diminish corruption, stipulates greater transparency in the handling of government contract bids.

NAFTA also includes the most comprehensive rules regarding intellectual property rights ever negotiated in a major international trade agreement.[27] This is particularly significant in the context of global economic restructuring and transnational production.[28] If Canada commits substantial funds for research and development in a move to restructure its domestic economy towards knowledge-intensive and high-tech industries, rules for intellectual property rights will provide a greater degree of security than in the past. It is important to note that, in 1988, the U.S. International Trade Commission ranked Mexico as the planet's fourth-worst violator of intellectual property rights.[29]

A major weakness of NAFTA is its environmental provisions. The agreement states only that member countries 'should not' relax environmental standards in efforts to attract foreign investment. The only recourse is the following: 'If a Party considers that another Party has offered such an encouragement, it may request consultations with the other Party and the two Parties shall consult with a view to avoiding any such encouragement.'[30] It is worth underscoring that throughout the NAFTA negotiations, Canada attempted to secure tougher environmental regulations than those that were eventually agreed upon.[31] The Clinton administration believed the environmental component of

NAFTA to be unacceptable and indicated its commitment to establish a parallel accord which would both toughen environmental regulations and ensure their enforcement.

Not included in NAFTA are cultural industries, health and welfare services, and the large-scale exportation of water. Article 2204, the accession clause, permits any country to join NAFTA following the appropriate approval process. The interesting point here is that membership is not limited to countries of the Americas. New Zealand and Australia, for example, which have expressed interest in joining NAFTA, would be eligible to do so.

Turning to other aspects of NAFTA, it is important to emphasize that the agreement is subject to interpretation. An important consideration in this regard is the fact that subsidies remain largely undefined, as is the case in CUSFTA. One effect of this is that the U.S. relationship between the state and business would likely be replicated among other NAFTA members. A probable scenario, then, is a floating standard of allowable government intervention in the economy – a standard largely dependent upon the situation in NAFTA's most powerful signatory, the U.S. Within this context of U.S. dominance, some have suggested that NAFTA might provide both Canada and Mexico with more predictability regarding commercial affairs.[32]

Other implications of the agreement include its 'seal of approval' effect upon NAFTA members, especially with respect to developing countries. In relation to the accession clause, as Patricio Meller observes: 'By joining NAFTA, a country gives out a positive signal to investors in general regarding the degree of maturity and stability of economic reforms, in a manner that is similar to the "seal of approval" granted by the IMF to a country's macroeconomic policies.'[33]

It is striking that the NAFTA affords virtually no attention to Mexico as a developing country. Unlike the EC, NAFTA provides no developmental funds for its poorest members. Implicitly, NAFTA advocates a 'trade not aid' developmental model – a policy made more explicitly in the Enterprise for the Americas Initiative (EAI), as shall be seen.

Finally, there are two other specific components of NAFTA that are worthy of mention. First, throughout the text, NAFTA defers to GATT on numerous issues, especially in highly sensitive areas such as with regard to certain agricultural subsidies. It also suggests that the U.S. is interested in seeing GATT succeed, that is, that Washington does, indeed, favour liberalized global trade rather than introverted trade blocs – a point to which I shall return. Second, article 1021 of the agreement provides, in principle, for government assistance to small- and medium-sized businesses in order to help them cope with international economic restructuring. Such programs are to be developed on a national level.

The Debate

Let us briefly examine some contextual points before considering the arguments for and against NAFTA and, more generally, hemispheric economic integration. While the Mulroney government was eager to solidify a free trade agreement with the U.S., Ottawa was decidedly less zealous regarding the notion of a trilateral arrangement. Gordon Ritchie, who served as the deputy chief negotiator of the 1988 CUSFTA, observed in the spring of 1992 that, with respect to NAFTA, 'I've never seen much in it for Canada.'[34] The government, at least initially, seemed more motivated by what it had to lose than by what it had to gain by entering the talks.

It is also important to recognize that Canadian trade and investment in Mexico has been rather small. Canada's exports to Mexico represented less than 1 per cent of Canada's total export market during the late 1980s and early 1990s, and their level actually declined from $638 million in 1989, to $608 million in 1990, and to $460 million in 1991 (they are dominated by grain, oilseeds, and pulp and paper products).[35] An important turnaround occurred in 1992, when Canadian exports to Mexico rose to $770.6 million.[36] Conversely, imports from Mexico to Canada have grown steadily since 1986, when they represented $1.16 billion, to $2.75 billion in 1992. These were dominated by automotive products, computers, and crude oil. Overall, the current volume of Canadian trade with Mexico has been meagre but growing, and Canada has begun to appreciate the increasing significance of Mexico as a trading partner.

Despite the booming maquiladora sector (which will be discussed below), Canadian direct investment in Mexico decreased from $207 million in 1986 to $175 million in 1990. But, as with exports, levels of Canadian direct investment have risen substantially in the early 1990s, to an unofficial figure (used by the DEA) of $575 million in 1992.[37] Furthermore, a record level of 4,500 potential Canadian exporters visited the Canadian embassy in Mexico City in 1992 to signal their interest in tapping the Mexican market (compared to 2,200 in 1991 and 193 in 1989).[38]

While Canada has belatedly appreciated Mexico as an important venue for investment, other countries moved in more quickly. Foreign direct investment in Mexico doubled to $30 billion between 1985 and 1990, with two-thirds of the increase originating from U.S. corporations.[39] The limited Canadian investment that does exist is concentrated in the mining sector.[40] There is also a contingent of Canadian auto parts manufacturers that has located in Mexico as well as a couple of Canadian firms that went there and then returned.[41] Ottawa is providing further encouragement for Canada to catch up with the investment boom in Mexico. 'Direct investment allows Canadian companies to concentrate low value-added manufacturing and assembly operations in Mexico to improve the competitiveness of the high value-added production and services centred in Canada.'[42] The same report, however, goes on to warn that, 'politically it may be difficult to encourage such investment,'[43] since it may entail job losses in this country – an issue which is addressed below.

Let us now proceed to discuss a number of debates surrounding the NAFTA negotiations, beginning with those in favour of the agreement. A deeply controversial issue concerns the effect of NAFTA upon Canadian employment. Supporters of NAFTA have suggested that Canada will witness a net creation of between 5,000 and 6,000 quality employment positions by 1995 if the agreement is implemented. These jobs would appear primarily in banking and construction as well as in Ontario's auto factories, according to a report from the Institute for International Economics in the U.S.[44] Greater access to the Mexican market would be responsible for most of this new employment. Additional Canadian jobs could also be created to assist in the process of building Mexico's infrastructure, thus contributing to its future growth.

When questioned about potential job losses in Canada and the U.S. as a result of NAFTA, Mexican president Salinas responded: 'Those are jobs that would be lost ... anyway, if not to Mexico then to the Asian Tigers or other newly industrializing countries.'[45] It is argued that Canadian industry must remain competitive in order to maintain current employment levels and/or to create new employment opportunities. Related to this argument is the belief that a NAFTA would press Canadian industry to become globally competitive, thus creating new jobs. It is an argument that conforms to the policy recommendations delineated by Michael Porter, who was commissioned by the government and the Business Council on National Issues (BCNI) to perform an analysis of Canada's competitive position. Porter contends that globalization of production can stimulate Canadian competitiveness, providing that Ottawa is prepared to make the necessary structural adjustments.[46]

A crucial debate has emerged regarding whether North American integration will push social standards and programs in an upward or downward direction. Proponents of NAFTA maintain that if the agreement is ratified, the resultant increase in Canadian competitiveness and productivity would bode well for higher government revenue, which would support Canada's social programs. This is quite significant, since, as was noted earlier, the Canadian government is the world's largest per capita debtor. Ottawa has found it difficult to fund existing social welfare programs, let alone new ones (such as a long-promised federal daycare system). It is also possible that social programs would harmonize upwards, for example, by promoting development in Mexico, thus raising its social standards towards the level of those enjoyed by the U.S. and Canada. Furthermore, one could argue that the Clinton administration's revised view of the U.S. health care system is an example of American social programs harmonizing upwards towards the Canadian level.

Another important controversy concerns ecological issues. Proponents of NAFTA have suggested that the economic development that would be created by North American free trade would lead to a greater respect for environmental concerns. With regard to the Mexican case, if existing environmental regulations were vigorously enforced, and if NAFTA promoted economic growth in Mexico, then actual ecological standards could rise. Ottawa claims to be dedicated to environmental protection in any agreement reached with Mexico, and, in 1992, it provided that country with $1 million to assist it in upgrading its environmental monitoring and enforcement activities.[47] Once again, in order for NAFTA to lead to environmental improvements, TNCs must stop using developing countries as a means of cutting costs through ecocide, and local governments must start creating and enforcing green policies.

Another point of contention centres around the issue that the U.S. and Mexico seemed prepared to cut a deal whether or not Canada was involved. If Ottawa chose not to join the integration process, that could motivate some investors to shun this country and instead locate in the U.S., exacerbating a process already under way. As well, if Ottawa avoided the talks, Washington would be in a position to negotiate a better deal for U.S. traders and investors in Mexico. A crucial point, then, is that the hub-and-spoke model, with the U.S. at the centre of bilateral arrangements with other hemispheric states, would seem to benefit the U.S. more than the others. But as one observer has pointed out, one should not exaggerate the hub-and-spoke effect. Potentially more significant determinants of investment location include cheaper costs of production, levels of education and infrastructure, government regulations and assistance, environmental policies, etc.[48]

If being party to the new continentalism can save Canada from the perils of the hub-and-spoke model, one must also look at the potential pitfalls that could be encountered along the NAFTA path, particularly with regard to employment. It is estimated that Canada has lost 461,000 manufacturing jobs in the period between the establishment of CUSFTA and January 1992.[49] Although one can quibble with the figures, there is no question that a significant number of jobs have indeed disappeared. While the recession no doubt accounts for much of this loss, many of the positions are expected to be lost forever as a result of the transfer of manufacturing production in Canada mainly to the United States (the average Canadian manufacturing wage is 37 per cent higher than in the seven states of the U.S. southeast[50]) and, to a lesser extent, to Mexico (where wages may be 10 per cent of those in Canada). In other words, against the context of important job losses in Canada, the prospect of even deeper cuts resulting from NAFTA represents a major worry.

Compounding this concern, if unemployment worsens in the U.S. as a result of industry moving to Mexico, Canada's exports to the U.S. could drop as a result of this, eventually placing in peril additional Canadian jobs.[51] More broadly, even if Canadian jobs are created in certain areas while losses occur in others, it may be unrealistic to expect displaced workers to secure jobs in other sectors, due to different training requirements. A related complication includes the cost of retraining programs, estimated to be around $8,000 (U.S.) per worker,[52] at a time of fiscal crisis resulting from the Canadian debt. As well, Canada's record of job retraining is not a stellar one. The Economic Council of Canada, for example, ranked Canada ninth out of eighteen countries for job training and education.[53] In contrast to the general support for NAFTA on the part of Mexican unions, Canadian unions naturally oppose the deal.[54]

Further, it has been observed that many of the manufactured products that Mexico exports to the United States are in sectors identical to those exported by Canada.[55] A recent study indicated that the similarity index of Mexican and Canadian exports to the U.S. more than doubled from 16 per cent in 1971 to 34 per cent in 1987.[56] Statistics Canada reports that this competition is particularly acute with respect to automobile production, where Mexican productivity rates are rising, as well as with respect to tele-electronic products.[57] In early 1992, the Mexican Automobile Industry Association (MAIA) reported that they had experienced 'the best year for the automobile industry in the country's history,'[58] with productivity in auto parts assembly plants reaching about 80 per cent of U.S. levels and with wages hovering at about 10 per cent of U.S. levels.[59] More generally, in 1989, Canadian productivity was estimated to be 6.5 times higher than Mexican productivity, although Mexican wages were about 10 per cent of Canadian wages.[60] It should be noted that Canada and Mexico compete in sales of crude oil to the U.S.,[61] and that Canada's textile and printing sectors, in addition to some fruit and vegetable growers, also fear losses if NAFTA is successful.[62] Overall, a major concern is that NAFTA, and/or hemispheric economic integration generally, will accelerate the process of deindustrialization and disinvestment in Canada that commenced with CUSFTA.

Critics are also concerned about NAFTA's benefit to large corporations at the expense of small- and medium-sized enterprises (SMEs). Recent work has suggested that, while large TNCs may be poised to take advantage of hemispheric economic integration, SMEs lack the capacity to do so.[63] Thus, some SMEs have expressed their reservations regarding NAFTA and have also suggested that state policies more closely reflect the interests of large corporations than those of smaller firms.[64] While those concerns are legitimate, it is important to emphasize that Article 1021 of NAFTA outlines special programs for small businesses, including access to government procurement and the creation of a network of small businesses.[65]

Critics worry about the possible downwards harmonization of social welfare programs. If job losses and movement of capital out of Canada to either the U.S. or Mexico are a product of NAFTA, then the debt-ridden government coffers will be hard-pressed to finance existing programs. Furthermore, Canadian taxation levels, which are generally higher than those in either the U.S. or Mexico, may discourage capital from either locating or remaining in Canada. This may pressure Ottawa to lower tax rates to the U.S. level in order to remain competitive, thus causing a probable decrease in funding for social welfare programs, which will begin to harmonize with those south of the border.[66] Canada has already experienced the restructuring of family allowance benefits and unemployment insurance, while a federal daycare program has been shelved.

Another concern lies within the realm of environmental issues. Critics of NAFTA raise the spectre of TNCs moving to Mexico not only to take advantage of cheap labour, but also because Mexican environmental standards tend to be more lax than those in the U.S. or Canada, and its existing regulations are often not enforced.[67] It has been argued that NAFTA does not ensure environmental protection, and that a strong parallel accord is required. There is legitimate concern that the ecocide apparent in Mexico's maquiladora region will be exacerbated by NAFTA. Obviously, ecological damage in Mexico has the potential to affect the atmosphere of the entire planet. For this reason, Canada's House of Commons Standing Committee for External Affairs and International Trade urged that 'human rights, social policy and the environment should be taken into account as Canada develops its trade relations with Mexico.'[68] Beyond this, there is the fear that lower environmental standards and practices in Mexico may exert pressure on Ottawa to harmonize its environmental policies downwards. In 1993, it was reported that Ottawa was considering reducing environmental controls if they adversely affected Canada's economic competitiveness.[69]

A final debate concerns the issue of whether or not NAFTA will actually promote development in Mexico. While a thorough analysis of this question is beyond the scope of this study, it is worth considering some related points. If NAFTA does not promote Mexican development, there will be negative consequences for all member countries. Within the NAFTA framework, in order for the Canadian economy to flourish, Mexico must develop and provide a growing market for Canadian exports. And, as it develops, it is hoped that Canadian firms will win government procurement contracts in Mexico. If, instead, NAFTA results in sub-development, Canada will be left with the painful consequences associated with economic restructuring but with few of the alleged benefits. NAFTA gone awry could also result in security problems in Mexico – problems that Canada might find itself increasingly obligated to resolve.

Finally, it is interesting to note that, in 1993, Canada's two largest provinces were split regarding support for NAFTA. Ontario, under the NDP government of Bob Rae, opposed NAFTA on the grounds that it would exacerbate the job losses and plant closures that have been apparent since the implementation of CUSFTA. Quebec, on the other hand, supported the agreement, as it did CUSFTA. In 1993, Gerald Tremblay, the province's industry minister, noted: 'Quebec is one of the only provinces that is ready to open its doors to the world.'[70] Not only does Quebec support NAFTA, but, as was seen in Chapter 1, French Canada has a legacy of appreciating the link between its own Latin culture and those in Latin America.

Now that some of the most salient debates regarding the implications of NAFTA have been presented, let us now turn to a very brief summation of U.S. and Mexican motivations for a North American free trade agreement – motivations which may be similar to those propelling the more general process of hemispheric economic integration. Beginning with the U.S., proponents of NAFTA argue that the creation of a North American trade area, perhaps as a precursor to a hemispheric trade area, would enable the U.S. to compete more effectively with the EC and an Asian trade area led by Japan. A U.S. official recently observed that NAFTA would promote U.S. economic strength and global influence.[71] Moreover, as the world's largest debtor nation, with its total debt approaching $4.4 trillion by September 1993,[72] the U.S. badly needs to increase its exports not only to service its debt but, ultimately, to maintain its global power.

American TNCs are especially keen on NAFTA as a means of increasing their competitiveness with global rivals. It is the U.S.-based transnational sector that is the most competitive sector of the economy, with national capital generally more vulnerable.[73] Thus, transnational capital and, especially, U.S. firms constitute the driving force behind NAFTA. To reiterate, one can surmise that rules of origin stipulations within NAFTA are designed to exclude or discourage Japanese and other foreign firms from utilizing Mexico as a conduit for the export of products to the U.S.[74] In other words, NAFTA is designed, in part, to keep Mexican production advantages within the purview of North American TNCs. To this extent, then, transnational capital appears to be fractured along bloc lines.

The Bush administration supported NAFTA on the assumption that it would entail job creation in Mexico, which, in turn, would diminish potential security problems and, at the same time, help stem the level of illegal Mexican immigration to the U.S.[75] As well, NAFTA (with parallel accords) has won support during the Clinton administration, partly on the premise that even if some American jobs are lost to Mexico, the U.S. has a better chance of reaping benefits from job creation there than if TNCs moved to Asia. Opposition to the deal in the U.S., as in Canada, comes from those who fear job losses, social polarization,[76] environmental degradation, and a deterioration in social programs and standards.

From the Mexican perspective, that country had been gearing up for more liberalized trade since shortly after 1982, when it announced it could no longer borrow enough funds to meet its loan payments. A sweeping restructuring of the economy soon followed. Encouragement for foreign investment, reduction of tariffs, privatization of state-owned corporations, cuts in social spending, and the like were among the radically new policies pursued by the Mexican government. Moreover, Mexico's 1986 entry into GATT signalled that it was on the road to economic liberalism. As well, the successful 1987 CUSFTA negotiations prompted Mexico to seek similar access to the U.S. market, since it, too, feared rising American protectionism.[77] Structural adjustment policies (SAPs) insisted upon by the IMF should also be counted as among the crucial factors which contributed to Mexico's restructuring of its economy.[78] By early 1993, this restructuring prompted about one-third of the total capital flight from Mexico in the early 1980s to re-enter the country.[79] It is important to note that the boom of the maquiladora sector in the late 1980s accompanied SAPs, and that revenue from this export processing zone has provided Mexico with the foreign exchange required to service its debt.

The maquiladora sector of Mexico has been flourishing since the late 1980s and, after oil, constitutes its largest source of hard currency. Its success has been responsible for encouraging President Salinas to liberalize Mexico's economy in an attempt to assist the process of national development. This component of the economy delivers 90 per cent of Mexico's products to the U.S. and accounts for 65 per cent of its total manufactured exports. Most of the maquiladora companies are owned by U.S. parents,[80] although Japanese and German corporations are an increasingly strong presence. The maquiladora zone has enticed investors with cheap labour, low taxes, a subsidized infrastructure, a relatively unregulated atmosphere in such realms as safety standards and environmental protection, as well as commercial access to the U.S. – the world's biggest national market.

Mexican labour unions, with strong links to the government, are generally supportive of NAFTA, as are most large corporations. Some smaller, indigenous enterprises, however, may be driven out of business due to their inability to compete with transnationals. In 1992, a leading financial newspaper in Mexico predicted that 340,000 jobs would be lost for this reason.[81] Local farming would be particularly vulnerable under NAFTA, with 700,000 farm employees expected to be out of work over the next fifteen years as a result of a phase-out of agricultural duties.[82] These sorts of considerations raise the question of whether, or to what extent, NAFTA will promote economic and social development in Mexico. Almost certainly it will provide additional hard currency, although estimates of net job creation vary considerably. An optimistic estimate is that a net gain of 600,000 jobs will occur by 1995.[83] But nearly 1 million potential workers enter the economy each year (it is important to note that, currently, the maquiladora sector employs only about 600,000 people). In other words, even if 600,000 jobs are created over the next couple of years, unemployment levels will remain exorbitant.

Alternatives

Very broadly there are two sets of alternatives: one which opposes hemispheric economic integration and another which aims to operate within the integration process but with some important amendments. These alternatives and critiques may apply as much to the general process of economic hemispheric integration as they do to NAFTA. Those who assume a highly critical view of NAFTA tend to share some common criticisms of the integration process, many of which were mentioned above. In addition to feared job losses and a downward harmonization of social and environmental policies, many critics resent the obviously increasing power of transnational corporations and the related threats to Canadian economic and political sovereignty which may accompany the process of economic integration.[84] Underpinning this concern is the power that TNCs possess to play one country off against another, through their ability to shift operations internationally based upon considerations of labour wages, exchange rate distinctions, government regulations, etc. Thus, states may lose power to control their economic and political destiny in such a global environment, especially in the context of an international capital shortage.[85]

The economic sovereignty issue is particularly pertinent in the Canadian case, where 40 per cent of the manufacturing sector is controlled by U.S. corporations, and another 25 per cent is controlled by other foreigners.[86] Some believe that CUSFTA, NAFTA, and the EAI, as well as other processes of economic integration in the hemisphere are propelled by the historic principle of U.S. 'Manifest Destiny.'[87] Other criticisms focus upon ethical considerations associated with the doctrine of com-

petitiveness, where the quest for efficiency and productivity may supersede social considerations.[88] What options are available to cope with
such difficulties?

One set of alternatives, proposed by the Action Canada Network, has
suggested a process which commences with the destruction of the
Canada-U.S. Free Trade Agreement, a view which is shared by Canadian
nationalists such as Mel Hurtig.[89] Other components of this alternative
include the following: the careful screening of all foreign investment to
ensure Canadian control over the political economy; the pursuit of
global trade through GATT, rather than regional schemes; the insistence
that product manufacturing must be done in the country where product
sales occur; severely limited foreign investment in key services such as
those associated with culture, finance, and the media; and an equal-pay-
for-equal-work policy throughout the continent and the hemisphere.[90]

With respect to the Action Canada proposal, while it is true that
CUSFTA is unpopular in parts of Canada, one probable result of simply
abrogating the agreement would be retaliation by sectors of the national
and international business community, through such tactics as disinvestment. In all likelihood this would be accompanied by severe punitive measures on the part of the United States, the destination of over
three-quarters of Canadian exports. Thus, an alternative which incor-
porates such an approach would, on the face of it, seem to defy the
interests of TNCs as well as the U.S., and would also demonstrate a more
vigorous Canadian control over the country's political economy. But it
would no doubt exacerbate existing economic and social problems.

If some version of NAFTA does not reach fruition, a likely result would
be the bolstering of the maquiladora sector. TNCs would continue to
locate there, but Canada would not be provided with a more preferential
access to the domestic Mexican market. Also, if NAFTA was rejected and
the maquila sector grew, both Canada and the U.S. would have less input
regarding environmental concerns, human rights, and other issues
associated with the Mexican context. Further, given Quebec's support
for CUSFTA and NAFTA, abrogation and rejection would likely exacerbate tensions among Canada's provinces.

There exist other promising alternatives worthy of consideration
which would keep this country in step with hemispheric and global
economic trends, and which, presumably, would not entail as many
pernicious consequences. In essence, this set of alternatives would
accept the prevalence of an open economy and export-led growth, the
movement towards hemispheric free trade, as well as the virtues of the

market. One such prospect concerns a redefinition of the role of the state, as noted above. While a minimalist state model predominated in this hemisphere from the early 1980s until the arrival of the Clinton administration, it is worth underscoring that this was not the case in other successful market-driven economies, such as Japan, Germany, and South Korea. The old North American view clung to the premise that the less state intervention in the economy the better. Rather than arguing in quantitative terms, however, there has been a recent shift towards the adaptation of what one might call a qualitative line of thought, where the focus is upon the quality of state policies and actions which may advance productivity and competitiveness.[91]

A strong state which promotes research and development as well as innovative retraining programs for displaced workers, and one which provides an industrial plan to coordinate the efforts of business, labour, and academia, would exemplify positive government intervention.[92] Further, the state would have to have a direct interest in providing social adjustment programs for those displaced by the integration process, otherwise political opposition to free trade arrangements would likely intensify and government revenues would shrink. Special programs need to be developed for unskilled workers, particulary women and immigrant groups, since they 'appear to be disproportionately employed in the labour-intensive industries facing increased competition from developing countries.'[93] Hence, a remodelling of the role of the state to cope with new global realities may be an important, positive, and feasible alternative to consider.

Other renovations of state policies will naturally accompany hemispheric economic integration. As integration proceeds, for example, there already is an observable tendency towards the formation of hemispheric sub-regions within an overall free trade agreement based upon such factors as proximity and complementarity of production. We are witnessing the dawn of numerous sub-regions – one which encompasses Ontario, Quebec, and the U.S. Northeast, another involving the western provinces and northwestern U.S. states (the Cascadia region), and perhaps yet another may develop which involves the western regions of Canada, the U.S., and Mexico. Such arrangements presumably would entail the creation of political institutions to deal with new economic realities. If this were to occur, it would necessarily involve a decentralization of some functions currently performed by the federal government. But again, this would not necessarily mean a weaker central state, if it were accompanied by the enhancement of other duties performed by Ottawa, such as the promotion of research and development, the coordination of various sectors of the political economy to achieve higher productivity and competitiveness, etc.

Further, traditional concerns regarding the level of foreign ownership in Canada require some rethinking. At issue is the type of investment in question. As Robert Reich has observed, as it relates to the U.S. context, more important than who owns the firm is the issue of how many people are employed by the firm in the host country in knowledge-intensive jobs.[94] From this perspective and extrapolated to the Canadian case, what may be significant is that Canada needs to possess a highly skilled workforce and first-class infrastructure capable of attracting knowledge-intensive and high-tech industry. A chief concern is that Canadians are employed in cutting-edge and well-paying industries, to the extent that increasingly lower-paying manufacturing jobs, which are lost to the southern U.S. and Mexico, will be balanced by the creation of better jobs. Obviously the Canadian case is distinct from the U.S. one regarding the issue of repatriation of capital by TNCs, since much more of the Canadian economy is foreign controlled. Nevertheless, what may be increasingly important, at least in some sectors, is not necessarily who owns the firm, but who is employed by the firm to perform research and development as well as strategic problem-solving tasks. High levels of employment in such areas will help Canada retain its high standard of living.

The scenario described above requires a strong state with a coherent industrial policy. A niche in the world economy needs to be established; education and training will require restructuring. Government assistance could be provided for technological development performed by any corporation – foreign or local – which hires Canadians for knowledge-intensive positions (in research and development, engineering, for example).[95] Once again, a revamping of state policies is crucial for Canada to cope with globalized production.

The Clinton administration's introduction of parallel accords to deal with environmental and labour issues with respect to NAFTA suggests that NAFTA alone is inadequate.[96] While accepting the thrust of hemispheric economic integration, then, Washington under Clinton has chosen the alternative to amend various components of the project. Beyond the labour and environmental issues, another worthy option, suggested by Edward Broadbent in his capacity as president of the International Centre for Human Rights and Democratic Development, would be to incorporate a clear human rights component into any free trade agreement between Canada and Latin American states. With regard to NAFTA negotiations, Broadbent has suggested a monitoring agency for human rights in Mexico, which would be concerned with both economic and political rights.[97] As well, there is no good reason to rush into NAFTA by 1994 if the agreement remains plagued with problems.

Canadian Bilateral Relations with Mexico

With some exceptions, Canada's inter-American relations in the 1980s were dominated by the Central American issue. By 1989, when it became clear that Mexico was interested in entering a North American free trade agreement, Canadian bilateral relations with that country expanded considerably. Both Canada and Mexico appreciated that a new global and hemispheric reality dictated closer contacts between them, and so attempts were made to revive, or even to supersede, the strong bilateral relations fostered in the 1970s. By late 1989 and early 1990, Canada and Mexico placed each other on their respective priority lists.

A series of ministerial meetings in 1990 represented a key turning point.[98] In January of that year, a major delegation from Mexico, including the president, arrived in Canada to begin work on establishing a number of agreements, ranging from trade issues to controlling illicit narcotic trafficking. In March, Prime Minister Mulroney led a delegation to Mexico, where the aforementioned agreements were signed. Attempts were made to initiate more intimate relations not only between the federal governments, but also between the Mexican states and the Canadian provinces, especially Ontario, Quebec, British Columbia and Alberta. Thus, stronger bilateral relations have accompanied developments in the multilateral realm under the NAFTA negotiations. There were also suggestions on the part of the Mexicans that Mexico and Canada utilize one another as counterweights to the enormous power of the U.S. during NAFTA negotiations, resurrecting memories of the Trudeau government's attempt to foster a similar arrangement in an endeavour to offset the towering presence of the United States.[99] The issue of common ground between Canada and Mexico is one which should be explored more fully in the future.

A development in Mexico which is likely to affect Canadian-Mexican bilateral relations is the creation of Mexican president Carlos Salinas Gortari's 'social liberalism.' While it is beyond the scope of our purpose to delineate the entirety of that philosophy (which was announced in

1992), components of it are relevant to Canadian foreign policy. Particularly relevant is Mexico's position on sovereignty.

> In the view of our social liberalism, sovereignty is fundamental. It is the reason for our survival and the only objective that gives meaning to the goals we pursue, because we truly want to attain them. Mexico's geographical position cannot be ignored and leaves no room for doubt: the nation must ensure its strength at all times in order to remain a sovereign entity as a neighbor to the world's strongest power.[100]

If this proclamation is serious, the notion of Canada and Mexico strengthening their bilateral ties in order to maintain their respective sovereignties vis-à-vis the U.S. deserves Ottawa's serious attention.

Another facet of the Mexican commitment to social liberalism is the role it defines for the state.

> In the economic sphere, social liberalism assumes that a market without State regulation foments monopoly, increases injustice and in the end nullifies growth itself ... Social liberalism therefore proposes a State that promotes and encourages private initiative, but has the capability to firmly regulate economic activity and thus prevent the few from taking advantage of the many; a State that channels attention and resources toward meeting Mexicans' basic needs, is respectful of labor rights and union autonomy, and protects the environment.[101]

Earlier, in the discussion of policy alternatives for hemispheric economic integration, it was suggested that Canada renovate state institutions and policies in order to cope with new hemispheric and global realities. What is required is a strong state – a state which will intervene to foster growth and justice. This is a view which appears to converge with the model provided by the Mexican president.

Canada and the Enterprise for the Americas Initiative

NAFTA may represent phase one in the development of a hemispheric free trade area. On 27 June 1990, President Bush announced the EAI, which envisages free trade from pole to pole. Michael Wilson, Canada's minister of international trade and minister of science and technology, indicated that Canada was 'certainly supportive' of the initiative. He also observed: 'We have seen the pressures that [the EAI] has put on other countries in Latin America to form trading blocs to allow easier negotiation into a broader free-trade agreement, and I would think it is a natural flow.'[102] This is a fresh orientation for Canada, especially since, in the past, it had feared regional integration schemes in Latin America.

While the topic of Latin American integration is much too broad and complex to be dealt with thoroughly in this endeavour, a cursory discussion of the EAI is in order. The EAI consists of three major components: (1) expanded inter-American trade; (2) increased investment for Latin America; and (3) reduction of Latin American debt. The first goal involves the successful completion of the Uruguay Round of GATT, the establishment of greater bilateral economic relationships among hemispheric countries, and, of course, the establishment of a free trade zone in the Americas.[103] Certain elements of this goal seemed to have been reached by 1993. A plethora of bilateral agreements have been signed between the U.S. and Latin America, while sub-regional trade areas became a popular notion immediately after Bush's announcement of the EAI. But GATT talks, and the prospects for internationally liberalized trade, were in jeopardy by mid-1993.

The second objective, increased investment for Latin America, centres on the creation of funds (administered by the IADB and the World Bank) which would be utilized to provide loans and grants to Latin American countries to initiate reforms which would promote international investment. Up to $300 million annually would be provided in the form of grants, with the U.S. contributing $100 million and with Europe and Japan providing the rest. But by late 1992, the U.S. Congress had approved only a fraction of the $100 million proposed for market-oriented investment reforms in Latin America. However, it is difficult to imagine that, even if the U.S. came up with its full share of the funding, this would be matched by Europe and Japan. Hence, by early 1993, this pillar of the EAI appeared to be on shaky ground.

The third goal, Latin American debt reduction, deserves serious consideration. This proposal entails the reduction of debt to commercial banks and to the U.S. government – a reduction linked to market reform in Latin American countries. An important and progressive component of this plan entails the development of an environmental trust fund, which would consist of diverted interest payments owed on outstanding debts to the U.S. Since, in the case of NAFTA, environmental welfare has received considerable support from the Clinton administration, this aspect of the EAI may reach fruition.

The EAI, as enunciated by Bush, has important implications for developmental assistance to Latin America. Upon announcing the initiative, President Bush made the following observation: 'All signs point to the fact that we must shift the focus of our economic interaction towards a new economic partnership because prosperity in our hemisphere depends on trade, not aid.'[104] This point deserves some rethinking. While one may accept the premise that market reforms and free trade will assist in the development of Latin America, any reduction of developmental assistance to that region is quite unwise. Aid reductions will, presumably, result in increased social tensions in Latin America, especially at a time of 'adjustment fatigue.' Any resultant instability created or exacerbated by aid reductions would not bode well either for market reform or for free trade.

Finally, there is the related question as to whether hemispheric integration, and the movement towards trade areas in Europe and Asia, will result in highly introverted commerce within blocs rather than in liberalized global trading arrangements. In Europe, a remarkable 71 per cent of total exports remain within the region. By contrast, in the Americas and Asia the amount of exports remaining within each of these regions is 46 per cent and 44 per cent, respectively.[105] Thus, while the European trade area suggests the possibility of introverted global trade blocs, the other two areas do not.

Within the Western Hemisphere, over three-quarters of Canadian exports and 43 per cent of Latin American exports go to the U.S.[106] Furthermore, Canada's trade to the Pacific Rim has decreased from $17.1 billion in 1988 to $15.7 billion in 1990, and, in those same years, its trade to the EC has risen only slightly from $11.2 billion to $12.2 billion. Canadian trade with Latin America as a whole rose in the early 1990s (see Tables A.1 and A.2 in Appendix). U.S. exports to Latin America in 1992 exceeded those destined for Germany or Japan, while the rate of increase of U.S. exports to Latin America during 1991 and 1992 was three times as great as was that for all other regions.[107] U.S. commerce with Japan (number 2), West Germany (number 8), and Great Britain (number 10) were among the world's top ten bilateral trading relationships in 1989.[108] Clearly, Washington has more of an interest in preserving global trade than in pursuing an introverted trade bloc.

Canada, too, along with its commitment to hemispheric free trade, seems devoted to liberalized international commerce. As a highly placed official at the DEA recently observed, 'We would not and should not loosen our other ties across the Atlantic and the Pacific. The object is not an exclusive trade bloc but rather a building block for further international cooperation.'[109] Overall, while the intention of both Canada and the U.S. is to work for the establishment of global trade, developments in other areas, particularly Europe, mitigate against this.

Conclusion

Two primary changes in the global arena characterize the world order in the post-Cold War era. The first is the dissolution of the Soviet Union. Second, and equally significant, are the sweeping shifts in the realm of international production. These include the hegemony of the market economy, globalized production, and the apparent formation of a triad of economic regions. The evolution of NAFTA must be viewed in such a context.

Let us begin by considering the global economic scenario. NAFTA is a manifestation of a trend towards globalized production. The agreement reflects the increasingly dominant position of transnational capital. North American TNCs, faced with increasingly stiff competition from European and, in particular, Asian rivals, are generally enamoured of the notion of a trade area with sources of cheap Mexican labour in close proximity to the U.S. market. Beginning in the late 1980s, a rich literature has appeared which debates the existence and prospects of an international transnational class.[110] Rules of origin in NAFTA, particularly in the automotive sector, suggest, however, that transnational capital may be fractured along bloc lines. There is no question that U.S.-based TNCs are dominant within the NAFTA region.

While TNCs are arguably the chief beneficiaries of NAFTA, it must be underscored that the governments of both the U.S. and Canada have supported the agreement at least partially as a result of their political fear of being shut out of Europe. That is, beyond economic concerns, if the European Community evolves into an important global political power and if internal squabbling and Central European turmoil are overcome, the political focus of the U.S. and Canada may be increasingly upon Latin America. Here is where the EAI may become increasingly significant.

The dissolution of the Soviet Union is also important with respect to the creation of NAFTA. With the disappearance of the 'Evil Empire,' as President Reagan was fond of calling it, the U.S. has concentrated its energies upon economic restructuring in the face of global shifts that were noted above.[111] NAFTA represents a product of this refocus, as does the EAI. Further, the absence of the Soviet Union will reveal that the political instability which is present in the developing countries of this hemisphere is rooted in domestic social and economic inequities, and is not the product of foreign subversion – a point which will be expanded upon in the chapter concerning security issues.

The shifts in international production and security arrangements go hand in hand with profound ideological changes. These take an economic form in the hegemony of the market economy, globalized production, the focus upon exports and competitiveness, and so on, which are embodied in both NAFTA and the EAI. What is interesting is that while support for democracy, widely defined, would also appear to be a pervasive idea globally, NAFTA has sidestepped the issue of Mexican authoritarianism.

Changes in the world order discussed above represent an important determinant for alterations in state policies and institutions. Governments in Canada and the United States must now cope with the prospect of high unemployment amidst economic restructuring. What's good for General Motors, in the form of moving plants to Mexico, may not necessarily be perceived as good for the U.S. or Canada, at least in the short term. Ottawa, then, must devise an industrial policy capable of reinvigorating the domestic economy and thus satisfying social demands.

10

Canada and the Organization of American States

If the NAFTA negotiations marked a rejuvenation in Canadian-Mexican relations, the multilateral dimension of Canada's new Latin American strategy accelerated sharply after it entered the OAS as a full member in 1990. Canada's decision to enter the organization correlated with a new international distribution of power – an arrangement which included a stronger Canadian role in Latin America.

Background
In previous chapters Canada's relationship with the PAU and the OAS was traced, and will be summarized here. Prior to the termination of the Second World War, Canada, at times, wished to join the PAU but was prevented from doing so by U.S. opposition. Resurrecting the assumptions that underpinned the Monroe Doctrine, the U.S. viewed Canada as a conduit for British interests in Latin America, with Washington, in effect, threatened by the naval and economic power of the U.K. (despite that country's precipitous decline on both counts).

It was not until after the Second World War, with Britain devastated and with unprecedented U.S. hegemony in Latin America, that the U.S. was comfortable with Canadian participation in an inter-American political institution. With the emergence of the OAS in 1948, Washington wanted Canada to join the new organization to assist in its crusade against socialism in Latin America. Correctly viewing the new institution as a vehicle for the U.S. Cold War agenda, Canada refused to join, fearing it would become mired in military conflicts throughout the hemisphere. This fear was not unreasonable, especially considering the pressure Canada would have been under to sign the Rio Treaty.

Canada kept its distance with respect to the OAS until the election of the Trudeau government in 1968. The Liberal government's attempt to diversify trade, channelling it away from the U.S. and towards regions such as Latin America, served as the basis for a more significant Canadian position in inter-American relations. Still, tension between an increasingly nationalistic Latin America and a beleaguered U.S. meant that, if it joined the OAS as a full member, Canada would be caught in their crossfire. Instead, Canada decided to seek membership in the OAS as a permanent observer. This move signalled to Latin America that Canada was moving towards a more serious relationship with it, but, at the same time, Ottawa managed to sidestep being trapped in the midst of sniping between the U.S. and Latin America, because Canada's position as permanent observer did not entail voting rights.

The weakness of the OAS in the late 1970s and into the 1980s – exemplified by its failure to address successfully the debt crisis, the Central American imbroglio, and the Falklands/Malvinas war – did not encourage Canada to consider upgrading its position to that of full member. As late as 1988, only one year prior to Canada's announcement that it would, indeed, become a full member, a discussion paper was circulated in the DEA which was highly critical of the OAS. It quoted views expressed by the foreign minister of Barbados at a 1985 OAS General Assembly meeting:

> The symptoms of the crisis are everywhere: widespread public apathy and cynicism about the usefulness of the Organization and its failure in the past five years to tackle, let alone resolve, any of the major political and economic problems besetting the hemisphere ... Powerless to avert a tragic war in the South Pacific, a mere spectator of the conflicts in Central America, helpless in the face of the Latin American debt crisis, unable to meet the security needs of the micro states of the Caribbean, marginal to the development needs of the region, and now, like the proverbial last straw, facing a financial situation so desperate that it may soon verge on bankruptcy, the OAS seems consigned to total irrelevance and inaction.[1]

By 1988, the Canadian government was well aware of the apparent weakness of the OAS, but it also indicated that Canada was committed to revitalizing it.[2]

The Post-Cold War Era, Canada, and the OAS
Economic restructuring and the possible emergence of trade blocs represented an important backdrop for Canada's entrance as a full member into the OAS. Beyond dramatic economic shifts, international

security arrangements were also undergoing radical changes. The retraction of the USSR from global military and strategic commitments, against what appeared to be its imminent collapse, ushered in a new reality in the late 1980s. The western Cold War agenda of fighting communism suddenly dissipated. That is, it now seemed likely that Canada's full membership in the OAS would not threaten to immerse the country in crusades against communism or other military adventures, especially since a precedent had been set that full members of the OAS were not obligated to become signatories to the Rio Treaty.

Accompanying this new economic and strategic reality was the ideological convergence of the vast majority of Latin American governments. This meant that, at least in the short term, there would be less likelihood of Canada being caught between frequent battles with Latin America on the one side and the U.S. on the other. This, too, fostered an atmosphere which contributed to Canada's new role in the OAS, as did Latin America's movement towards democracy.

The DEA conducted a major foreign policy review with respect to Latin America in 1988-9, in the context of pivotal global shifts. Key policymakers responsible for a stronger orientation towards Latin America included Louise Frechette, the assistant deputy minister for Latin America, and, especially, Richard Gorham, who wore two hats as Canada's roving ambassador to Latin America and Canada's permanent observer at the OAS. While Gorham had harboured some doubt regarding full Canadian membership in the OAS earlier in 1988, by the end of the year he was convinced that Ottawa should seek full membership in the organization. His decision was influenced by rapid global and hemispheric shifts.

By early 1989, Frechette and Gorham proposed the idea of full OAS membership to Secretary of State for External Affairs Joe Clark, whose role was crucial. It will be recalled that he had been a key player throughout the 1980s regarding Canadian foreign policy towards Central America. In attempting to broker a diplomatic resolution to the Central American crisis, Clark established solid relationships with numerous Latin American heads of state. In other words, Canada's focus upon the Central American crisis of the 1980s provided the stepping stone for its greater appreciation of Latin America in general. Thus, Clark accepted the recommendation for full Canadian membership at the OAS.

The next step was to convince Prime Minister Mulroney of the soundness of the idea, a task which proved to be rather easy. During his

June 1989 visit to Europe, Mulroney had been impressed with Mexican president Salinas de Gortari and Venezuelan president Carlos Andrés Perez. A few months earlier, the Mexican foreign minister had urged that Canada take up full membership at the OAS.[3] All this added up to Ottawa's decision by late summer of 1989 to join the Organization of American States as a full member.

In a speech before the General Assembly in 1989, Clark announced that Canada's decision to become a full member of the OAS 'represents not so much a decision to become a member of an organization as it does a decision to become a partner in the hemisphere.'[4] Canada's full membership commenced, officially, in January 1990, and, significantly, Ottawa refused to sign the Rio Treaty. According to Clark, the key issues in inter-American affairs included: illicit narcotics flows, environmental degradation, human rights, debt, trade, and an emerging and redefined dialogue between developed and developing countries.[5]

Canadian Policy at the OAS

Any hopeful euphoria that accompanied Canada's momentous decision to adopt a new role at the OAS was quickly dispelled during events surrounding the U.S. invasion of Panama in December 1989. Canada was the only country in the hemisphere, besides the staunch U.S. client state of El Salvador, to support Washington's globally unpopular position. Ottawa's stance was expressed by Prime Minister Mulroney, but, since Canada was not officially a member of the OAS until 1990, it was spared having to vote on the issue (the vote was twenty to one against the U.S.). It is interesting to note that rumours in Ottawa suggested that DEA officials stayed up all night to prepare a careful and cautious text that was critical of the U.S. invasion of Panama, but that Prime Minister Mulroney uttered his opinion of the Panamanian situation to reporters prior to receiving their advice.

At any rate, as was observed in earlier chapters, this was exactly the kind of episode that Ottawa had feared OAS membership would entail: having to side either with the U.S. or an overwhelming majority of Latin American states on highly contentious issues. Canadian critics pointed out that Canada's position in the OAS merely echoed Washington's[6] and, perhaps, left Latin Americans with a similar perception. The episode seemed to lend credence to the view expressed by Alfred Pick, Canada's first ambassador-observer to the OAS (1972-5), just prior to the Panamanian invasion: 'The current government has neither the will nor the capacity to pursue a responsible, independent policy in the OAS.

We are bound to disappoint the Latin American and Caribbean Commonwealth members.'[7]

While Canada weathered a rather embarrassing beginning in the world's oldest regional international organization, the situation appears to have improved steadily since then. On 8 January 1990, the same day that Canada's new ambassador to the OAS presented his credentials, he voted with the majority of Latin American countries in condemning the illegal incursion of U.S. military personnel into the Nicaraguan Embassy in Panama during the invasion.[8] This represented a well-meaning but ultimately lame attempt by Canada to balance its previously expressed support for the U.S. military adventure.

While the Panamanian storm was dissipating, Ottawa identified a number of objectives during its first year of full membership in the organization, and made concrete progress towards their achievement.[9] First, Canada would participate in revitalizing the institution. In addition to contributing to the Program of Action for Strengthening the OAS, Canada was also successful at launching an annual hemispheric summit of Heads of State to strengthen communication and to establish personal ties among the Americas' leaders. Second, this country's effort to strengthen democratic development was manifested in the OAS's acceptance of Canada's important proposal for the establishment of the Unit for the Promotion of Democracy (UPD) in the fall of 1990. The UPD would initially focus upon election monitoring, but as the 1990s progressed, would concern itself with the threat to democracy posed by emerging militarism in the hemisphere – a point which shall be returned to later.

A third Canadian objective was to fortify specialized agencies within the OAS which focused on so-called non-traditional issues. In addition to efforts to raise hemispheric consciousness with respect to environmental issues, Canada also applied, effective January 1991, to join the Inter-American Drug Abuse Control Commission (this will be elaborated upon in Chapter 11). Another goal was to facilitate understanding between Canada and Latin America through support for the creation of the Canada-Latin America Forum (FOCAL), superbly directed by Edgar Dosman. FOCAL has been instrumental in fostering linkages between Canadian business, cultural, and academic groups.

Balancing Canada's successes in the OAS were a number of stinging rebukes by Canadian critics. New Democratic Party leader Edward Broadbent chastised the government for spending about $6 million in annual dues at the OAS while Canada had recently curtailed diplomatic relations with Ecuador, Guatemala, and Brazil. John Turner, as Liberal leader of the Opposition, suggested the government was being hypocritical in pretending to immerse itself in inter-American affairs through full membership at the OAS while reducing developmental assistance to the region by $20 million during the previous year.[10] A further 10 per cent cut in Canadian developmental assistance to Latin America for the fiscal years 1993-4 and 1994-5 would provoke similar criticisms.

Compounding John Turner's critique of Canada's performance during its first year as a full member of the OAS, the Liberal party released a scathing 'Report Card' regarding Canada's record in the organization. The assessment indicated that the party fully supported a new and expanded role for Canada in the hemisphere, but it charged that the Progressive Conservatives had mismanaged affairs at the OAS and had bungled Canada's general policy in Latin America. The assessment rightfully chastised Canada's performance regarding the U.S. invasion of Panama and suggested that Ottawa failed to delineate a clear and coherent foreign policy with respect to inter-American affairs.

The Liberals also attacked Ottawa for an insufficient performance with respect to human rights and democratic development, but perhaps this was unfair given Canada's role in establishing the Unit for the Promotion of Democracy (UPD). On this count the Liberals focused not so much on Ottawa's policy within the OAS as upon its provision of developmental assistance to human rights abusers in Guatemala and El Salvador. The Report Card also attacked the slashing of Canadian developmental assistance to Latin America, Ottawa's weak policy on Latin American debt, and the lack of programs to inspire increased Canadian trade with the region. This evaluation of Canadian policy demonstrated that there was a lack of coherence between certain aspects of Canada's policy in Latin America and what it was doing in the OAS. Although it offered important criticisms of Canadian policy in Latin America, the Liberal report card was weakened by not focusing more clearly upon Canada's actual performance at the OAS.

Turning to the second and third years of Canada's membership at the OAS, in 1991 External Affairs identified five objectives for Canada within the institution that were similar to those expressed during the previous year: implementation of the Unit for the Promotion of Democracy (UPD) (proposed by Canada in 1990); ratification of inter-American human rights agreements; promotion of Canadians for elected posts in the OAS; participation in environmental, developmental, and drug agencies; and the lowering of trade and investment barriers.[11] Thus the policies outlined a year earlier in 1990 seemed to represent a policy agenda which Canada was prepared to pursue in subsequent years.

Canada has also supported the Inter-American Commission of Women, an agency within the OAS, by providing it with expertise as well as a $150,000 grant.[12] In the realm of human rights, Canada has worked with a variety of commissions associated with the OAS regarding indigenous peoples' rights as well as 'disappearances,' or politically motivated murders. The challenge remains, however, to achieve consensus on what actually constitutes human rights in the hemisphere. Human rights is a topic that can have multifaceted meanings, linking political, economic, and legal structures. Hence, there is space for varying interpretations which render the development of a single definition of human rights difficult to achieve. Obviously this stifles the development of effective policies on the subject.

By 1993, many of the government's objectives for Canada's role in the OAS have met with progress. With regard to Canadians assuming significant posts within the OAS, lawyer Jonathan Fried was elected to the Inter-American Juridical Committee. The body provides advice to the OAS on legal matters pertaining to inter-American affairs. Examples of the committee's work include the provision of advice with respect to the legal ramifications of NAFTA, as well as a statement to Washington condemning the U.S.-directed kidnapping in Mexico of a Mexican national implicated for drug-trafficking and murder. Further, a Canadian, Sonia Saumier-Finch, assumed the directorship of the Science and Technology department at the OAS.

Regarding the objective of promoting democracy and human rights in Latin America, the UPD initially tended to focus upon election monitoring.[13] Beginning in late 1991 and through to 1993, however, Canada has spearheaded an attempt to expand that mandate, with its strong interest in re-establishing democratic structures following the coups in Haiti and Peru. Prior to this, it is of interest to note that John Graham, former Canadian ambassador to Venezuela, was appointed as head of the Unit for the Protection of Democracy. His appointment presumably reflects the strong Canadian concern demonstrated at the OAS for the restoration of democracy in Haiti and Peru.

Canada was among the most outspoken critics of the Haitian coup both within and without the OAS. Shortly after Haitian President Aristide was deposed, Secretary of State for External Affairs Barbara McDougall issued the following announcement: 'We are bitterly disappointed with developments in Port au Prince. Canada believes the OAS can make a difference, and at the meeting tomorrow I will be seeking ways we can achieve the immediate restoration of Haiti's legitimate government.'[14] Canada provided a plane for an OAS mission to restore democracy in Haiti, and joined in an economic boycott of the island. This was followed by the suspension of Canada's official developmental assistance. By late 1992, however, the island maintained its resolve to defy the wishes of its hemispheric partners. The blockade, limited to OAS members, was porous to goods from non-member countries and from smugglers. As well, there were disputes among OAS members regarding what kind of punitive measures should be taken against Haiti. By the end of 1992, the organization's policy was obviously failing.

On 27 December 1992, Prime Minister Mulroney boldly suggested a possible naval blockade of Haiti, which would include forces from Canada, Venezuela, France, and the U.S. While the naval blockade never materialized, the threat of such a development seemed to initiate progress in resolving the Haitian debacle. In December 1992, the OAS joined ranks with the U.N. in an attempt to resolve the crisis. The inclusion of the U.N. meant that OAS policies, such as an economic boycott, could be expanded globally, thus turning up the heat on the leaders of the Haitian coup. The OAS and the U.N. appointed a joint special envoy, Dante Caputo, the former Argentine foreign minister, to deal with the situation. Under Caputo's leadership, a joint OAS/U.N. civilian mission of about 300 members was established in efforts to accelerate the return of a constitutional government in Haiti. Canada has pledged $2.35 million in support of this mission.

Thus, Canada assumed a commendable leadership role in efforts to restore democracy in Haiti – a role which was distinguished from that of the U.S. both by Ottawa's activism and by its sense of urgency. From Washington's perspective, the real crisis did not hit until huge numbers of Haitian refugees attempted to flee to the U.S. in early 1993 under the newly elected Clinton administration. The strong Canadian policy can be explained, in part, by the pressure exerted upon Ottawa by Canada's Haitian community, but considerable emphasis must also be placed upon the government's resolve to uphold democratic structures in Latin America during the 1990s.

Canada has voiced similar support for the return of democracy to Peru, following the coup led by President Fujimori in April 1992 which dissolved both the Peruvian Congress and the country's constitution. Secretary of State for External Affairs Barbara McDougall told the OAS: 'Let's face this issue squarely – regardless of any rationalization, his

[Fujimori's] conduct was unconstitutional – illegal – and unacceptable. If that is not clearly recognized, then no effective action is possible.'[15] McDougall proceeded to threaten to implement economic sanctions if democracy was not restored. In contrast to the Haitian situation, President Fujimori took the OAS position seriously. He addressed OAS members, promising the election of a constituent assembly by the end of 1992. This body would be responsible for redrawing a Peruvian Constitution that would be ratified through a referendum.

An OAS observer force, including eleven Canadians, attended the Peruvian elections and deemed them to be free and fair. But by March 1993, the DEA still harboured concerns regarding President Fujimori's promised road to democracy. Among these was the 'ambiguity' surrounding the constituent assembly's supposed responsibilities. Originally, the assembly's mandate was not to exceed six months, but this was extended through 1995, the end of President Fujimori's first term. In 1993 it appeared that the constituent assembly would perform the duties of the Congress, which was wiped out during Fujimori's coup. This, according to Canada, was not part of the original agreement between Fujimori and the OAS.[16] Also, the Peruvian situation is complicated by the Andean Drug War (an issue which will be discussed in Chapter 11).

Finally, it is important to situate Canada's work in the OAS within the social and economic context of the particular countries involved. With respect to both Peru and Haiti, widespread human rights abuses in conjunction with desperately weak economies and highly inequitable distributions of wealth did not bode well for the durability of democratic structures. In other words, reliable democratic development will only occur in concert with strong economies and the establishment of social and economic justice.

Future Challenges

One of the OAS's major challenges is to construct a sufficient consensus in order to achieve clear and meaningful objectives. The question is how to harmonize the interests of the organization's very diverse thirty-four members and still arrive at a potent policy. This is especially important at a time when the OAS must prove itself to be an effective institution, particularly in light of its pronounced failure to deal effectively with the numerous crises facing Latin America in the 1980s. If consensus can be achieved, the OAS could become a powerful and effective body for aiding with conflict resolution. But if no consensus prevails, the organization may prove to be of little utility. Polarization between the enormously powerful U.S. and the rest of its members also poses a potential problem for the OAS, as the Panamanian episode demonstrates. By mid-1993, while some degree of consensus has been reached on a number of issues among government leaders throughout the Americas, there is still deep Latin-American resentment against U.S. power and policy.[17]

More generally, an issue likely to dominate the OAS is the re-emergence of the military in Latin America, after a process of democratization seemed to sweep the region in the 1980s. I have already noted the successful coups in Haiti and Peru, which are among the poorest countries in Latin America. However, the almost-successful 1992 coup attempt in Venezuela, one of Latin America's richest countries which enjoyed a 9 per cent growth in GDP in 1991, plainly illustrates the important correlation between income equity and political stability. The failed coup in Guatemala in 1993 underscored the frailty of democratic structures in that country, although here the OAS was successful in restoring a semblance of democracy. With respect to the entire region, heightened instability, produced by increasing poverty and, in some countries, by IMF-directed policies of painful structural adjustment, render it difficult for North American-style democracy to flourish.

Canada, Cuba, and the OAS

The Cuban situation remains an important diplomatic and security issue. With the Castro government more isolated than ever, and with social tensions potentially set to rise as a result of the dramatic termination of trade and aid relations with the former USSR, the government in Havana is under severe stress. Canada's special historical ties with Cuba, epitomized by its triple-decade commercial relationship with the island despite a nearly hemispheric-wide boycott, suggests that Canadians should assume a leading role in reintegrating Cuba into hemispheric politics. This is especially true given Canada's new position in the OAS.

But the prospects for Canada assuming a leadership role in the process of Cuban reintegration seem mixed. On the one hand, Secretary of State for External Affairs Barbara McDougall offered some encouraging remarks on the matter at the OAS General Assembly in Chile in 1991. 'We look forward to the time when the vision of the founders of the OAS for a universal hemispheric forum can be realized and Cuba will retake its place in the Organization as a full member of the hemispheric family.'[18] On the other hand, however, Canada's ambassador to the OAS compared 'the Cuban regime to a rotten apple tree and Canada, he stated, could be counted on not to shake the trunk (as others were wont to do) but rather stand by and let the decayed growth fall.'[19] Thus, there was a division between Canada's ambassador to the OAS and the secretary of state for external affairs – a division that would have to be resolved before Canada could take effective measures to help integrate Cuba into mainstream hemispheric politics. Despite any internal Canadian disagreements over what to do about Cuba, it is the U.S. position that matters most. President Clinton's embrace of a policy that restricts even further U.S. trade with Cuba seems to suggest that Washington is not at all ready to initiate more cordial diplomatic relations with Havana.

Conclusion

Shifts in the world order represent the central factor behind Canada's new role at the OAS.[20] Since the formation of the organization in 1948, Canada viewed it as a vehicle for the United States' Cold War agenda. By 1989, however, the Cold War was over and a fresh world order was emerging. The meaning of the OAS as an institution was changing. In this new situation, Canada's full membership at the OAS no longer entailed pressure from the U.S. to join in Washington's vigorous crusades against communism in the hemisphere. This does not imply, of course, that the U.S. will no longer engage in military adventures in Latin America, as the Panamanian and Andean episodes demonstrate, but that the intensity of U.S. participation in military conflict in the hemisphere is likely to diminish. Thus, the OAS may now be seen as the political institution of the Americas during a process of integration, rather than as an instrument for U.S. contestation against international communism. As such, it has provided a more inviting venue for full Canadian membership.

A crucial factor which contributed to Canada's full role at the OAS has been hemispheric economic integration. With the move towards greater inter-American economic partnership after the successful completion of CUSFTA, and with the possibility of the world economy moving towards global trade areas, it was clear in 1989 that this country's position in inter-American affairs was on the rise. With respect to particular OAS functions, beyond its devotion to security affairs, it has formed a special working group on the EAI, which Canada has been invited to join.[21]

In addition to increased hemispheric economic integration, the changing nature of the Latin American state has contributed to Canada's new role at the OAS. The acceptance of the democratic ideal throughout most of Latin America is apparent. This is not to say that this ideal has necessarily been achieved in many parts of the region, given the presence of coups and attempted coups, and the emergence of so-called 'low intensity democracy.'[22] The point is that Canada never felt comfortable with the military governments that presided over Latin America in past decades, and the embrace of the democratic ideal throughout most of the region assists in the task of inter-American integration.

Accompanying the aforementioned changes in the world order, in both economic and security realms, has been an ideological hegemony reflected in government policies throughout most of the Americas. This ideological common ground presumably has contributed to Canada's new position as a full member in the OAS. The ideological convergence throughout most of the Americas has meant that the OAS would be much less likely to represent an arena of acerbic contestation between the U.S. and Latin America, a feature which previously contributed to Canada's reluctance to join the institution as a full member.

A central point, then, is that a changing world order has carved out a new role for the OAS. During the post-Cold War era, we are witnessing the formation of a U.S.-led hegemony in the Americas, one more potent than any arrangement in the past. Robert Cox has observed that institutions provide a forum that can diminish the likelihood of the use of force, and so there is a strong relationship between institutionalization and Gramsci's definition of hegemony.[23] Conceptualized in this way, institutions such as the OAS represent a means of stabilizing and perpetuating a particular order.[24] Although the inter-American system is not without its problems, an emerging hegemony is apparent in the increasing fit between ideological consensus, integration through economic and security arrangements, and institutionalization through such vehicles as the OAS. Conceptually, then, the OAS may be seen to represent the institutionalization of an emerging hegemony in the Americas.

A number of challenges remain for the OAS to fulfil that role. While a broad ideological consensus exists in the early 1990s among governments in the Americas, it is no small feat to achieve agreement among the organization's thirty-four members on particular policy issues. As was mentioned, there is also a simmering resentment among many Latin American policymakers towards the uses of U.S. power. Related to this, in order for the OAS to work effectively, the immense power differential between the U.S. and other hemispheric states must not impede the objectives of consensus and compromise. Conceptually, if the weaker states of the hemisphere are to consent to a new order in the Americas, and if the OAS is to represent the effective institutionalization of a new hegemony, it is necessary for the strong in the system, particularly the U.S., and to a much lesser extent Canada, to play a proper leadership role. That is, the strong states of the Americas must assume a hegemonic rather than a dictatorial stance, and be willing to offer concessions to ensure the weak's acquiescence to their leadership.[25]

Related to the discussion of the formation of inter-American hegemony and institutionalization is Canada's potential role as the hemispheric 'bridge.' As we have seen in previous chapters, Latin Americans for decades have invited Canada to play a bridging role between the region and the United States. This has been particularly true regarding developmental issues and security concerns. Ottawa's close relations with Washington, along with Canada's record of recognizing that indigenous socio-economic inequities are generally at the root of security problems in the Americas, leave Ottawa perfectly poised for such a role. The Americas do not yet represent a community, but the region seems to be moving towards the establishment of one. Ottawa could assist in that process.

11

Security and Conflict Resolution

Along with major shifts in global and hemispheric economic structures, the security arrangement in the Americas is also being redefined. With the USSR gone and the Cold War over, who or what is the enemy in Latin America? A central contention is that Canada, especially through its new position at the OAS, can help to identify the real enemies in Latin America. These include: poverty and the inequitable distribution of wealth; the sometimes pernicious effects of structural adjustment policies; resurging militarism, civil war, and arms proliferation; sexism; racism; and environmental degradation. Canada's path-breaking role in conflict resolution in Central America, as well as the implications of Latin American immigration, will also be addressed. And, since the Andean Drug War is among the hemisphere's most outstanding strategic issues in the early 1990s, beyond the general task of redefining security, considerable attention will be devoted to it.

Redefining Security
The post-Cold War era has ushered in a new reality for hemispheric security. The movement towards hemispheric economic integration, alongside what appears to be the emergence of global tripolarity, has rendered inter-American security more important to the U.S. and Canada than ever. Not only are Canada's economic stakes in the hemisphere growing by leaps and bounds, but Ottawa's political commitment to the hemisphere, as manifested in its full membership in the OAS, means that Canada has a new responsibility for defining and resolving inter-American security problems. From the Canadian perspective, it may be an unfortunate truth that Washington will largely define the security agenda for the Western Hemisphere. The task for Canada is to work in

concert with its Latin American sister states to encourage Washington to assume a progressive stance with respect to inter-American security.

Obviously, there is a relationship between a strong economy with a relatively equitable division of wealth, on the one hand, and stability and security, on the other. A clear example in this regard is Venezuela, a country which witnessed fabulous growth rates in the early 1990s but which has suffered major coup attempts, apparently with some support from the populace. The point is that a relatively equitable distribution of wealth, in conjunction with some restoration of social programs (which were curtailed in structural adjustment policies), need to be in place in order to provide the stability required for the development of democratic structures. Closely related to this is the problem of civil war in Latin America. It has largely been civil wars (sometimes overlapped with international manipulation), rather than wars between Latin American states, which have plagued the region since 1945.[1] In the early 1990s, Colombia, Peru, and certain Central American countries are among those facing catastrophic internal conflict. In all these cases, poverty and a highly unequal distribution of income are fuelling domestic warfare. Beyond the fundamental and monumental feat of promoting development and socio-economic justice, the Central American case has demonstrated that institutional conflict resolution can be an important tool for defusing civil warfare – a point to which I shall return.

The issue of reducing the size of armies and arms purchases in developing countries has become an important feature of post-Cold War politics. With proxy wars between the superpowers being things of the past, the North has grown less enthusiastic in its endeavour to militarize the South. This has been underscored in the wake of the Gulf War, which shocked developed Western nations into appreciating the consequences of arming undeveloped nations to the teeth. The former president of the World Bank, Robert McNamara, suggested a 50 per cent reduction in arms purchases by all developing countries by the year 2000.[2]

In Latin America, reducing military personnel and hardware could assist in minimizing the monstrous consequences of civil warfare. Funds previously utilized for military purposes could be diverted to more productive uses, alleviating somewhat the social tensions which contribute to civil strife in the first place. This is especially significant in the context of social repercussions emanating from the 'adjustment fatigue' associated with economic restructuring in the face of Third World debt. Military reduction policies could be tied to debt restructuring and aid programs, and through policies promoted by the Organization of American States. The likelihood for the success of such endeavours is enhanced by the prevalence of civilian rather than military governments throughout Latin America. But this will be no easy task, as countries such as Colombia have increased their military budget in the early 1990s. With regard to the nuclear dimension, Argentina and Brazil are the two most likely candidates for developing such programs, but the momentum for these projects has been diminished by the friendly and cooperative relationship which has existed between them since the 1980s.[3]

Racial tension is also an important source of conflict throughout the Americas. Testimony to this has been the historic oppression of Aboriginal people in Canada and the related Mohawk crisis which erupted in 1990. The Los Angeles riots of 1992 demonstrated the enormity of racial problems in the richest and most powerful country in the hemisphere. Claims, such as those made by Mario Vargas Llosa (Peruvian novelist and former presidential candidate), that Peru can modernize with the 'complete assimilation' of indigenous peoples compounds the civil strife in that country. One could go on citing examples of racial tension and its relationship to instability. The point is that at a time when security is being redefined, racial conflict needs to be addressed at both the national and hemispheric levels. Defining the scope of the problem, and constructing common policies aimed at defusing potential crises, should be considered top OAS priorities.

Gender considerations should also be prominent when redefining hemispheric security. While the study of international relations can be traced back as far as the writings of Thucydides almost 2,500 years ago, it is striking that the relationship between gender and international power relations has only begun to receive considerable attention since the late 1980s.[4] While it is beyond the scope of this book to offer a comprehensive analysis of gender and inter-American security, a number of themes are apparent in this regard. Violence against women, in peace as well as in war, should be viewed as a serious security matter. Feminist analyses often advocate redefining violence as something more than the infliction of pain by the use of force. From a feminist viewpoint, violence can be conceived as the infliction of pain, whether it be through the use of force, through economic and social structures, etc. From this perspective, such issues as sex tourism, structural adjustment policies which promote disproportionate suffering by women, and the pernicious effects of the feminization of labour, should be considered when redefining hemispheric security concerns.[5]

Turning to another prominent issue, environmental sustainability is key to inter-American security. Security is a matter of protecting our economic, social, and political way of life. In the Cold War era, it was the communists who were touted as the biggest threats to the Western lifestyle. We are belatedly coming to see that reproduction of human life is fundamentally dependent upon having an environment capable of sustaining it. Ecological destruction due to assaults from economic production or warfare threatens the core of human existence and, thus, represents a profound security concern.

As well, any economic union reached through NAFTA or EAI introduces Canada to a new security agenda. While much has been written regarding the economic consequences of hemispheric integration, little has been published regarding the effect it will have on inter-American security. Obviously, this is a topic that requires further research. Suffice it to say, however, that if NAFTA, or a wider hemispheric economic integration agreement, is ratified, Canada will have to devote more attention to hemispheric security than ever before.

Finally, a major debate concerns the relationship between the military and new security issues discussed above. Previously, mainstream analysis tied the military directly to security affairs. Military issues and security issues were viewed as one and the same. The contention here, however, is that while it may be possible for the military to expand its scope in relation to some possible new security concerns mentioned earlier, clearly some security issues should not be viewed as within the domain of the military. As a crucial political actor, if not the major one, in many Latin American countries, one would expect the military to vigorously resist any reduction to its size or role.

This discussion is not meant to provide an exhaustive list of elements which need to be considered when redefining hemispheric security. Rather, it is meant to provide, albeit in a cursory fashion, points of departure for the long but urgent process of defining and coming to grips with the real threats to stability and human welfare in the Western Hemisphere. Canada has the potential to be a key player in this process.

Central America

With the collapse, or at least the severe weakening, of the USSR being obvious to most observers by the late 1980s, the security situation in Central America seemed bound to change. Indigenous inequities were at the root of the Sandinista revolution in 1979 and were also the basis for guerrilla insurrections in El Salvador and Guatemala throughout the

1980s. But the Central American Left read the writing on the wall: the USSR's imminent demise meant that any support from Moscow would evaporate, leaving them more vulnerable than ever to lavishly financed U.S.-supported attacks.

In Nicaragua, the relentless U.S. military pressure exerted upon the Sandinistas through the illegal Contra insurgency, in addition to other aspects of low intensity conflict (including psychological warfare, diplomatic and economic isolation, and the like), served to wear down the majority of the Nicaraguan population. If charting a nationalistic and democratic-socialist course through the support of the Sandinistas meant perpetual warfare and deprivation, the local population wearily and desperately began to consider other options. Similarly, in El Salvador and Guatemala, entrenched polarization coupled with mounting years of bloodshed also led the populations and governments to consider more peaceful approaches to conflict resolution.

The House of Commons Special Committee on the Peace Process in Central America released a report in 1988 which suggested a greater commitment of Canadian resources to the isthmus countries, and which urged Ottawa's increasing support for conflict resolution mechanisms.[6] This advice, along with Canada's history of endorsing such measures, was instrumental in its 1989 participation in the United Nations Observer Mission in Central America (ONUCA). ONUCA, with participation from Canada, Spain, and West Germany, became 'the first truly international peacekeeping operation in Latin America.'[7] One function of ONUCA was to verify that Nicaragua was not supporting leftist guerrillas in El Salvador, and that neither Honduras nor Costa Rica was assisting the Contras. It was also in charge of verifying Contra demobilization.[8]

Canada's contribution to ONUCA (the majority of its peacekeeping forces were made up of Canadians) has won the respect of Latin American countries, and has underscored Ottawa's historical commitment to multilateralism and conflict resolution. Beyond the significance of attempting to defuse one of the ugliest conflicts in the Americas, ONUCA has a wider meaning. It may be considered an important test case for U.N. peacekeeping missions, in an era in which both the role of the U.N. and security in general are being redefined. In other words, the value of ONUCA is both regional and global.

Also in 1989, Ottawa came under fire from Canadian critics for praising U.S. 'humanitarian assistance' to the Contras, which violated the Esquipulas II Accord.[9] In addition, such critics were unhappy with continued Canadian support for Honduras, El Salvador and Guatemala, especially given their human rights abuses and their support for anti-Sandinista activity. In 1990, Secretary of State for External Affairs Joe Clark told a Calgary audience:

> Some Canadian NGOs criticize Canada's continued relations with El Salvador, Guatemala and Honduras. We have been urged to cut off links, to walk away ... Some European countries have done just that. But when it came time to prepare for peace in Central America, it was not to those countries that the region turned. It was to Canada. For we maintained relations with the entire region – kept doors and borders open, to be in a position [to help] when assistance was required.[10]

Thus, the government asserted that, by maintaining ties even with human rights abusers, Canada was poised to promote peace in Central America. Appeasing critics, Canada's 1990 decision to upgrade the consulate in Guatemala to embassy status effectively provided Ottawa with a better source of regional information, though some NGOs and other critics would have preferred an embassy in Nicaragua.

A major turning point occurred in 1990. Through an electoral process, Nicaraguans chose to oust the Sandinistas and to elect the pro-U.S. Chamorro Government. The U.S. contributed at least $9 million to the campaign of Violeta Barrios de Chamorro, editor of the CIA-supported newspaper *La Prensa*, and the election was characterized by heavy U.S. intervention. Canada contributed $700,000 to the electoral process as a whole.[11] It will be recalled that Canada failed to send observers to the Nicaraguan elections of 1984.

The electoral victory of a pro-U.S. government in Nicaragua, coupled with the demise of the Soviet Union as a superpower and the increasing isolation of Cuba, meant that Washington would no longer consider Central America to be the venue of strategic significance that it represented throughout most of the 1980s (except for Panama, as will be seen). Although it was no longer the site of superpower contestation, the same problems which have always plagued the region remain. Poverty, an inequitable distribution of wealth (especially in Honduras, Guatemala, and El Salvador), and human rights abuses (particularly in El Salvador and Guatemala), persist. Compounding the situation is the intense political polarization apparent in Nicaragua, El Salvador, and Guatemala. Thus, uprisings may likely erupt once again. The demise of the Soviet Union has also made it clear that conflict in Central America is fundamentally a result of indigenous poverty and socio-economic injustice, rather than a product of international communist subversion.

Canada's role in Central America has grown considerably since 1979. Early on in this period it will be recalled that key Canadian foreign policymakers were content with assuming 'quiet acquiescence' with respect to the Reagan administration's bellicose ambitions during the Second Cold War. But steadily, Ottawa increased its role in the Central American crisis. This is not to say that Canada's policies have been unblemished. But, in the main, Ottawa gradually pursued conflict resolution and peacekeeping mechanisms that have helped Central Americans. Canada also came to see that it has a responsibility for security problems in the Americas.

It is crucial to emphasize that this metamorphosis has largely been a product of the tireless efforts of Canadian interest groups, church groups, and NGOs which have prodded Ottawa into action. There is little doubt that if it were not for such groups, the 'quiet acquiescence' would have predominated. This is not to say that the policies Ottawa actually pursued were identical or even similar to many of those advocated by counter-consensus interest groups. The point is that these groups helped define Central America as an important issue for Canadian foreign policy. The lesson is that organized interest groups can make a huge difference to Canada's foreign relations.

Panama, although not part of Central America proper, also presents a major security issue in the early 1990s due to the scheduled transfer of the Panama Canal to the Panamanians by the end of the decade. A central issue is who should defend the canal once the transfer takes place. As Robert Pastor notes, although recent polls suggest that 70 per cent of Panamanians would prefer that the U.S. remain to defend the canal, this could re-ignite tension in the country.[12] A better idea is the composition of an inter-American force designed especially for the task, perhaps under the auspices of the OAS. There is no question that the Panama question will become more significant as the year 2000 approaches.

The Andean Drug War

Aside from the broad project of redefining inter-American security relations, the Andean Drug War is probably the most salient strategic issue facing the Americas in the early 1990s.[13] The Andean region, by 1992, was receiving more U.S. military assistance than was any other region of the hemisphere.[14] The U.S. provided $104.1 million in military assistance to Bolivia, Colombia, Ecuador, and Peru in Federal Year (FY) 1991, $146.9 million in FY 1992, and over $56 million in each of those years to assist police with narcotics control training.[15] By the early 1990s, Colombia replaced El Salvador as the largest recipient of U.S. military assistance in Latin America.[16] This has created a situation that some have called the 'Central Americanization' of the Andean countries. The significance of this is compounded by the fact that cocaine trafficking is considered to be Latin America's largest multinational industry.[17]

The Andean crisis is extraordinarily complex. Within a context of economic despair, indigenous populations engage in cocaine production, in a situation that has been exacerbated by the implementation of the most extreme 'hyperliberal' shock policies Latin America has witnessed. Compounding the issue is the presence of a variety of guerrilla groups and drug lords, who add a dimension of violence to countries whose governments are already engaged in immense human rights violations and political corruption. This sinister concoction is further complicated by Washington's militarization of the region since 1989, with the U.S. (at least until early 1993) focusing upon curtailing the international supply of cocaine rather than on dealing with forces within American society which promote drug consumption. Before analyzing Canada's interest in the drug war, it is necessary to provide a discussion of the situations in Peru, Bolivia, and Colombia.

Most of the production of coca leaves occurs in Peru's Huallaga Valley, where it is estimated that 60,000 to 300,000 families make a living cultivating coca leaves.[18] Those families cultivating one or two hectares have incomes estimated to range upwards from $5,000 (U.S.) annually[19] in a country where the per capita income is $960 per year. It is estimated that 250,000 hectares are being utilized for coca production in the early 1990s.[20]

By 1993, there was a pronounced migration from the Upper to the Lower Huallaga region. Vast pollution caused by the herbicide Spike, which was used in the Upper Huallaga during the García presidency, combined with the presence of a crop-destroying fungus (fusarium oxysparun), caused an exodus to the Lower Huallaga. This tendency has strengthened as legitimate crops such as coffee have reached record low prices, rendering cocaine production as perhaps the only viable alternative.[21]

In order to reach an adequate understanding of the momentum behind the influx of peasant families into the Huallaga Valley to engage in coca cultivation, one must appreciate the devastation of the Peruvian political economy. The context of extreme poverty that characterizes Peru is responsible for the huge numbers of Peruvians who make a living from the drug trade, which, in turn, promotes profound corruption and demoralization.[22]

A long list of statistics attests to the economic and social misery suffered by Peruvians. Between 1980 and 1985, inflation in Peru was measured at 3,000 per cent.[23] Between 1985 and 1990, during the presidency of Alan García, prices rose an incredible 2 million per cent.[24] Inflation in 1989 was 2,775 per cent, jumped to an astonishing 7,749.7 per cent in 1990,[25] and simmered down to 139 per cent in 1991[26] as a result of 'Fujishock' (a phenomenon which will be discussed shortly). The average monthly salary of Peruvians, however, remained at $35 (U.S.) during the early 1990s.[27] In mid-1993, three-quarters of the population were classified as undernourished and were either underemployed or unemployed.[28] Roughly 70 per cent of the population work in the 'informal sector,' selling whatever services or products they could in a desperate attempt to survive.

The IMF prescribed austerity measures which were imposed in the summer of 1990 by newly elected President Fujimori, dubbed by the local media to be the 'Fujishock.' This restructuring resulted in the price of gasoline rising from 13 cents a gallon (U.S.) to $4 per gallon in tandem with food prices increasing by 400 per cent.[29] A state of siege was declared in Lima in an attempt to suppress anticipated public violence in the wake of the 'shock' policies.

Amidst economic devastation, the cocaine industry has represented a 'safety valve' of survival.[30] The drug, worth about $1 billion (U.S.) annually to the Peruvian economy in the early 1990s, has been Peru's biggest export,[31] representing about 30 per cent of the value of its total legal exports and composing 18 per cent of its GDP in 1987.[32] It is estimated that production of the narcotic has employed up to 15 per cent, directly or indirectly, of the country's workforce.[33] Realistic attempts to eradicate coca production in Peru, then, must come to grips with a political economy that strongly encourages its participation in the international cocaine industry.

Related to this is the revolutionary activity in Peru which is dominated by Sendero Luminoso and, to a lesser extent, by the Movimiento Revolucionario Tupac Amarú (MRTA). Both groups have been competing for influence in the Huallaga Valley, the hotbed of coca growth, although Sendero Luminoso is by far the strongest. Reports in the early 1990s indicated that Sendero Luminoso 'may be planning to set up an independent state in the country's central jungle – the heartland of Peru's lucrative coca trade,' although the strength of this group has been diminished in 1992-3, a point to which I shall return.[34] Coca production in the region has been the rebel movement's principal source of funding; it is estimated that it has received $20 to $30 million annually from its role in producing cocaine.[35]

There appear to be significant ties between the coca growers and either Sendero Luminoso or the MRTA – ties which presumably have to do less with ideology than with material necessity. The rebel groups have striven to represent the interests of the growers and to protect them from the intimidation of traffickers. Furthermore, the guerrilla groups have opposed the U.S. proposal for the aerial spraying of the Huallaga Valley with chemical defoliants and have also opposed the use of biological defoliants.[36] In other words, the revolutionary groups have protected the coca farmers from attempts by the Peruvian government and by the U.S. to eradicate crop production. A major strategic problem for Lima and Washington has been that the local population perceives Peruvian/U.S. military forces to be working against their economic interests.

The civil war between the government and Sendero Luminoso has resulted in the deaths of at least 25,000 Peruvians since 1980, the creation of at least 200,000 internal refugees, and a bill of damage totalling more than $21 billion.[37] With the capture on 12 September 1992 of Abimael Guzmán, Sendero Luminoso's leader, and other top members of the guerrilla organization has come speculation that its power may be waning. Supporting this view is the fact that the 'Red October' offensive, threatened by the Sendero Luminoso in the wake of Guzmán's capture, has failed to materialize. Since then, President Fujimori has decreed that 10,000 shotguns be distributed to peasant self-defence groups known as Rondas Campesinas. By the middle of 1993, the government had captured Sendero's technical experts, and subsequently a series of the group's car bombs failed to detonate properly. Frequent pictures in the Peruvian press of the imprisoned Guzmán, previously thought of by Sendero followers as 'the last Inca,' has detracted from his previous charismatic aura. It has been rumoured that Sendero will diminish its terrorist activity, and instead will focus on political work by infiltrating organizations representing the interests of the poor.[38]

The government's impressive capture of Guzmán and other Senderistas has strengthened enormously the position of President Fujimori, who, with the backing of the Peruvian military, launched a coup in April 1992. Fujimori assumed absolute power by suspending the Constitution and dissolving Congress. Thus, it is possible that Guzmán's capture is strengthening Fujimori's hand at the expense of democracy. Some believe the situation in Peru to be an example of 'Low Intensity Democracy' – a situation in which an initial electoral mandate can provide governments with almost dictatorial powers.[39]

At the beginning of this discussion it was stated that, in the name of the war against drugs, the Andean region has become the object of U.S. militarization. It is important to realize, however, that Washington, under the Bush administration, indicated that this militarization process would also be used to combat local leftist rebel movements.[40] To this extent, at least until early 1993, the 'Drug War' has also been a U.S.-sponsored war against the guerrilla Left in Peru and, as shall be seen, in Colombia as well.

It has been observed that the governments of Latin America, especially Peru and Bolivia, were reluctant to accept Washington's militarization plans.[41] Equally worrisome is that militarization has been occurring against the backdrop of enormous human rights abuses. Amnesty International released a report in Lima in July 1990, which indicated that Peru had the worst record of disappearances and illegal detentions on the planet[42] – a position it has held since the late 1980s. Reports in 1992 indicated that the human rights situation in Peru was worsening.[43] Thus, the militarization of the drug problem appears to exacerbate an already disastrous human rights situation. President Fujimori's response to this chaotic environment, especially regarding the corruption of government institutions, was to impose a dictatorship.

Bolivia, South America's poorest country, has been caught in a similar crisis. Suffering economic impoverishment and low global demand for legitimate exports such as tin and coffee,[44] about 50,000 Bolivians were estimated to be involved in coca-leaf production in 1993, with many more indirectly profiting from the drug trade. Estimates suggest that, by mid-1993, about 30,000 hectares were cultivated for this purpose.[45] Bolivia's estimated $3 billion in annual coca revenues in 1991 exceeded the value of all its other exports combined, though other estimates are much lower, projecting that Bolivia received only $375 million (U.S.) from drug trafficking in 1993.[46] Furthermore, some have estimated that narcotics trafficking directly or indirectly involves up to 20 per cent of the adult workforce.[47] Some economists have argued that the 'economic miracle' achieved by Bolivia since hyperliberal shock policies were implemented in 1985 has had less to do with those policies than it has to do with 'cocaine stabilization.'[48] Hence, there is a strong link between Bolivian debt, U.S. hegemony through such avenues as financial manipulation of the IMF, and the drug war.

Associated problems in Bolivia have included increasing drug addiction among the local population, environmental degradation resulting from coca production and processing, corruption of local authorities, and massive regional disparities related to the influx of narcodollars. U.S. military assistance to the country increased 50 times between FY 1988 and FY 1990.[49] Washington's pressuring of the Paz Zamora government to allow U.S. training of the Bolivian army has created considerable tension. Once the agreement was reached in April 1991, massive protests by labour groups, opposition parties, and the Catholic Church began to threaten Bolivia's stability. A scandal emerged in mid-1992, when 122 U.S. soldiers appeared in Bolivia, ostensibly to build schools, and then proceeded to accelerate the militarization of the drug war.[50] There are also profound doubts regarding the Bolivian government's commitment to the military project devised by the U.S.[51]

As with Peru and Bolivia, narcotrafficking and narcoterrorism in Colombia need to be placed in the context of the country's political economy. It is useful to note that, while in the 1980s Latin America in general suffered its worst economic disaster since the Great Depression, Colombia's economy has grown an average of 5 per cent annually throughout the decade.[52] But the wealth that has been recently created in Colombia has been skewed overwhelmingly towards the economic elite. In 1987, for example, business profits increased by 120 per cent, while real salaries in the industrial sector decreased by 4 per cent.[53] Moreover, the Colombian government provides statistics which reveal that 58 per cent of the population lives in poverty.[54] America's Watch reported that in the late 1980s the top 10 per cent of Colombia's population received 40 per cent of the national income, while the bottom 20 per cent received only 5 per cent.[55] In the countryside, the top 3 per cent of the landed elite owned 70 per cent of the arable land, while 57 per cent of the regional farmers owned 2.8 per cent. The situation has been exacerbated by the effects of narcoterrorism, since peasants unable to cope with the effects of such terrorism resort to leaving their land for what is usually an even less prosperous urban existence.

The central point, then, is that the majority of Colombians remains poor despite the infusion of narcodollars into the economy. In a context of general impoverishment, approximately $1 billion (U.S.) to $1.5

billion in cocaine profits has been repatriated into Colombia annually in the late 1980s, representing about 3 per cent of its yearly GNP.[56] (Most of the profit is made not in Latin America but by retailers in the North.)[57] The Medellín cartel, Colombia's most prominent group of traffickers, has been listed in Fortune 500, while cartel-leader Pablo Escobar, prior to his imprisonment in 1991, has been hailed as one of the wealthiest people in the world.

While their wealth has provided narcotraffickers with significant political power, the extent of this power is limited, as they generally are not afforded legitimacy by important sectors of the Colombian economic and political elite. The most blatant sign of this, of course, is that their means of livelihood is illegal and, until recently, was punishable by extradition to the U.S. Hence, narcotraffickers have resorted to terrorism in an attempt to force the Colombian state to provide them with the legitimacy they desire.[58]

Political violence launched by narcotraffickers reached a crescendo in 1990 and the early part of 1991. Tactics shifted from targeting socially prominent figures opposed to narcotrafficking to terrorizing the public at large. According to General Miquel Maza, the former director of the Departamento Administrativo de Seguridad (DAS) (the central agency in Colombia battling the drug crisis), this was carried out through placing bombs in public areas such as shopping malls.[59]

Superimposed upon narcoterrorism has been intense guerrilla warfare on the part of numerous and competing leftist rebel groups. The alliance network in Colombia is significantly more complex than is the network in Peru. It is of interest to note, for example, that in some important areas the narcotraffickers have shared an ideological overlap with the state in Colombia. The cocaine cartels are fiercely committed to free enterprise and are vehemently anti-communist.[60] Ideologically, then, the cartels find themselves aligned with a generally pro-capitalist government, which, at times, has viewed the guerrilla-left as a greater threat than the narcotraffickers.[61] Furthermore, the narcotraffickers share an ideological alignment with the landed elite in the countryside, who are opposed to socialist guerrillas because of the latter's commitment to a more equitable distribution of resources. Hence, the support for right-wing paramilitary groups has been the product of an ideological alignment among narcotraffickers, the landed elite, and moonlighting members of the police and/or army.

But this ideological alignment has been complicated and limited by other factors. It has been a shaky alliance, embraced by only fractions of the state and the economic elite, as weightier elements of both refused to accept the legitimacy of the narcotraffickers, despite their ideological convergence. Against this backdrop, violence emanating from narcoterrorists, from the guerrilla-left, from the state in its war against both, and from criminal elements in Colombia reached horrific proportions in the late 1980s and early 1990s. Assassination has been the leading cause of death among males between the ages of 15 and 44.[62]

This brings us to the important topic of human rights. There exists a range of abuses in Colombia, including those committed by guerrillas, narcoterrorists, and the state itself. The state's involvement in human rights abuses has taken the form of military participation in illegal detentions, tortures, and massacres,[63] as well as aerial bombardments of villages suspected of sympathizing with the guerrilla Left.[64] In other cases, members of the armed forces have participated in paramilitary groups which engage in violent human rights abuses, or such groups are permitted to carry out their activities with the complicity of the state. In 1988, the Andean Commission of Jurists noted

> that the general opinion – except among government authorities who were careful in addressing the issue – is that the military justice system is not only partial in its judgment, but its actions provided a true guarantee for impunity for paramilitary groups, which are, at least in part according to various sources, comprised of members of the military.[65]

Colombia seemed to reach its saturation point, with respect to the tolerance of violence, by mid-1991. Attempts by traffickers to terrorize the population into accepting their legitimacy proved unsuccessful. Moreover, President Gaviria's tough stance of combining a substantially reinforced military/police force with the threat to extradite traffickers to the U.S. if they did not surrender within a specified period, turned out to be effective. Leading cartel traffickers, such as Pablo Escobar, surrendered. Militarily exhausted by escalating government attacks, the majority of the guerrilla Left came to the bargaining table in the period 1990-2 under an umbrella-group called the Coordinadora Nacional Guerrillera Simón Bolívar (CNGSB). Both events led to the hope that the cycle of violence and chaos in Colombia had come to an end.

By early 1992, despite the presence of some positive developments, there were some increasingly worrisome signals. The Cali cartel was reported to have absorbed the market dominated by the Medellín cartel prior to Escobar's incarceration. Narcotrafficking in the early part of 1992 was as bad as ever, and there were reports that Colombia was becoming increasingly engaged in the cultivation of opium poppies and the heroin trade.[66] By mid-1993, there was estimated to be 86,500 acres of poppies under cultivation in Colombia.[67] And not only is the cocaine trade being supplemented by the heroin trade, but the spraying of defoliants in efforts to eradicate drug-crop production has resulted in widespread environmental protests.[68]

By mid-1992, any remaining hope for peace in Colombia was shattered. On 22 July 1992 Pablo Escobar escaped from his luxury 'prison.' It would appear that Escobar had the power to stay or leave as he pleased. For Colombians and the world, then, it became clear that President Gaviria and the Colombian government were not in control. A wave of terror has rocked Colombia since Escobar's escape. By 1993, the posting of extravagant rewards for Escobar's capture, totalling $19.5 million (U.S.),[69] in tandem with the growing strength of rival cartel leaders, suggests that Escobar's days are numbered. What it does not suggest is that the Colombian government is winning the war against narcotrafficking and terrorism.

A resurfacing of the guerrilla war has also served to highlight the apparent weakness of the Colombian state. Commencing with stalemates in late 1991 and early 1992 in negotiations between the government and the Coordinadora Nacional Guerrillera Simón Bolívar (CNGSB), an umbrella group for the guerrilla Left, the situation slid into the depths of frequent and violent confrontation by the summer of 1992. As a result of the government's virtual 'declaration of total war,' the CNGSB launched a major offensive in late October 1992 throughout the countryside as well as on the outskirts of Bogotá.[70] The guerrillas explained their offensive as a show of force meant to bolster their position in any imminent negotiations with the government.

More than 100 people were killed between October and November 1992 amidst a wave of violence, including twenty-two police in Medellín, who were murdered in retaliation for the shooting death of the Medellín cartel's second in command.[71] Bogotá's *El Tiempo* newspaper indicated that 17,465 Colombians died between 1987 and 1991 as a result of guerrilla attacks.[72] But, in 1993, the Andean Commission of Jurists argued that 74 per cent of the political killings in 1992 were not committed by drug traffickers or guerrillas but by the government itself.

The commission suggested that military-sponsored massacres in the Colombian countryside in 1992 claimed more lives than were lost during the entire sixteen-year Pinochet dictatorship in Chile.[73]

Before turning to Canada's role in the drug crisis, let us focus on some points regarding the so-called Andean Drug War. Bolivia, succumbing, as it did, to severe IMF-directed shock policies after 1985, serves as a classic example of a country in the grasp of U.S. financial power. In contrast, both Peru and Colombia, in some important ways, defied the norm. A recalcitrant Peru under Alan García refused to submit to certain IMF directives, with Lima attempting to define its own terms for refinancing its substantial debt. Ultimately, however, that policy proved unsuccessful. Peru's Sendero Luminoso should also be granted maverick status, as, rather than engaging in peace talks with the government (a policy pursued throughout Central America and even in Colombia), it and the MRTA demonstrated the resolve to grow stronger and more militant than ever. 'Cholera in the time of hyperliberalism' is an appropriate metaphor for this rather stark period.

With respect to Colombia, while some components of the country's guerrilla groups converted to mainstream politics, other factions continued to pursue subversive strategies. Colombia was less vulnerable to manipulation by the U.S. and the IMF than were other Latin American states because it had the best record vis-à-vis debt repayment. This was a result not only of Colombia's entrepreneurial spirit but also of the presence of hefty amounts of narcodollars, which found their way into government coffers.

While, since 1982, U.S. dominance over Latin America may be stronger than ever, some immense contradictions remain. These are clearly visible with respect to the current crisis in the Andes. The region has suffered from debt adjustment fatigue, causing the misery index to rise precipitously for the majority of the population. In the Andean case, at least until 1993, U.S. assistance has tended to be in the form of relief from debt payment rather than in the form of developmental aid. This situation has encouraged the drug trade, luring increasing elements of the population, in the absence of any viable alternatives, into cocaine production.

Not only does the drug trade absorb an increasing proportion of the population, but restructuring policies which worsen the plight of the majority serve to delegitimize the state and to foster support for guerrilla movements. In other words, the policies which are supposed to strengthen U.S. dominance in Latin America are the same policies which undermine state and regional stability, which, in turn, weakens U.S. dominance.

If these policies have contributed to the flourishing cocaine trade and to guerrilla insurrections in the Andes, the U.S.-led drug war from 1989 on has also had disastrous results. First, the U.S.-led militarization of the Andean region has not been successful in combatting narcotrafficking. By 1992, more cocaine has been produced in more places than ever before.[74] Alarmingly, but predictably, militarization of the Andes has resulted in the 'balloon effect,' whereby cocaine production and distribution have been pushed into Brazil, Argentina, and Venezuela.

It is estimated that 85 per cent of the profits associated with the cocaine trade accrue to distributors and pushers in rich northern countries.[75] Thus, the profit motive in the North, combined with the hunger for drugs there, propels the illicit narcotics trade. A crucial point is that, under the Bush administration, the U.S. spent roughly 70 per cent of its narcotic-control funds on interdiction and eradication, with only 30 per cent of the budget being devoted to reducing consumption. By early 1993, critics have suggested that those percentages be reversed. Furthermore, while some have noted that, in theory, legalization of the drug trade could defuse the crisis,[76] there is little political will in either the North or in the Andean countries to support such an approach. The only exception is Bolivia, where President Gonzalo Sanchez de Lozada has suggested that cocaine legalization be discussed as a viable alternative to the crisis.

Canada and the Andean Drug War

I shall begin with a discussion of cocaine use in Canada and will then turn to the issue of Canadian foreign policy and the Andean Drug War. In 1990, it was estimated that 3.5 per cent of the Canadian adult population had used cocaine at some point in their lives, while 1.4 per cent (280,000) were current users of the drug. By 1993, it was estimated that fewer people used cocaine for recreational purposes than during previous years, but that there were more chronic users. The highest rate of use has tended to be among those in the age range of 25 to 34.[77] In the early 1990s, there was estimated to be between 50,000 and 100,000 'crack' cocaine addicts in the metro Toronto area alone.[78]

Remarkably, cocaine-related offenses under the Federal Drugs Act rose from 3,275 in 1983 to 13,249 in 1990 for adults,[79] and they rose from 93 in 1986 to 258 in 1990 for juveniles.[80] Statistics in 1991 from the Royal Canadian Mounted Police (RCMP) indicate that cocaine is more available than ever, and that prices were falling.[81] It is clear that the cocaine problem in Canada has worsened considerably over the last decade, and there is debate as to whether or not the problem has peaked. It is worth noting that the preceding figures neither indicate the relationship between cocaine use and other crimes nor do they convey the social tragedies associated with cocaine addiction.

Cocaine seizures in Canada have skyrocketed from 170,082 kilograms (kg) in 1985 to 1,249,000 kg in 1991.[82] Naturally, this has led to speculation that some of the cocaine entering Canada may be destined for other locales, particularly in the U.S. Since 1988, Colombian traffickers have been devising plans to transport cocaine directly into Canada from South America.[83] Canada's sparsely populated Atlantic coast remains a favourite point of entry for vessels loaded with illicit drugs. Since 1987, there has been an agreement between the RCMP and the Department of National Defence, whereby the police are entitled to request the assistance of the military in drug interdiction efforts.[84] It is also worth noting that Canada spends approximately 70 per cent of its narcotic- control budget on dealing with consumption and about 30 per cent on interdiction (this is the reverse of the U.S. allotment of funds during the Bush era).

Canada's cocaine epidemic has affected Ottawa's policy in Latin America in a number of significant ways. Canada concluded a $2 million program (1990-1) with Colombia to provide its anti-drug forces with intelligence and surveillance equipment as well as with bomb detectors.[85] Following the termination of the project in 1991, it was decided not to renew it (the possible motivations behind this decision will be addressed below). It had been combined with an on-going arrangement with the RCMP to assist in training the security forces of Colombia, Peru, and other countries in the region. By the early 1990s, the RCMP had representatives in Bogotá, Lima, and Caracas.

There exist a number of concerns and implications regarding the provision of Canadian security assistance to Colombia and Peru. A primary worry is that Canada's assistance to the security apparati of Andean nations may be utilized beyond its intended use, which is to combat the forces of narcoterrorism. It was demonstrated above that both Colombia and Peru have exceedingly poor records regarding the role of the state in human rights violations, and that the state in both countries has been engaged in a civil war with leftist guerrillas. Canadian assistance, in the forms of bomb detectors to Colombia, for example, is obviously quite beneficial in that it contributes to saving lives, rather than destroying them. But other types of assistance, such as the provision of training for security personnel in Colombia and Peru, or supplying intelligence-gathering equipment, may be used by the Andean governments to combat the Left and/or indirectly support human rights abuses by the state. Thus, there is nothing to stop the Colombian or Peruvian governments from utilizing Canadian assistance, beyond its intended purpose.

While Canada's contribution was rather meagre, it piggybacked with U.S. militarization of the region, which, as was noted, amounted to $142.3 million in the fiscal year 1991. This militarization was exacerbated by the Bush administration, which threatened to withhold other forms of assistance unless the regional governments cooperated with U.S. objectives.

At issue, then, is that the timing of the Canadian security assistance paralleled the U.S. military buildup in the region. Interest groups and concerned individuals raised the question as to whether Canadian policy converged with Washington's apparent attempt to exert ever greater influence in Latin America. Against this backdrop, a major Colombian newsmagazine in June 1990 criticized growing U.S. intervention in Colombia and in Latin America generally, and also suggested that Canada was working with the U.S. in its hegemonic project.[86] This episode, then, raised the serious question regarding the independence of Canadian policy in inter-American affairs.

In the context of criticism by Canadian interest groups and individuals regarding Canada's $2 million program to Colombia, as well as by Colombian journalists who charged that Ottawa was supporting U.S. interests in the region, Canada decided to terminate the program. But there were presumably other reasons behind the decision not to renew the project, not the least of which were severe fiscal constraints faced by Ottawa. In addition, high-placed officials in the Latin American section of the Department of External Affairs (DEA) insist that External is generally critical of U.S. militarization of the Andean countries in the name of fighting drugs, and thus components within the Canadian government may have urged the termination of the project.[87] What is clearly required is an evaluation of that program. Did it serve Canadian interests? Did this element of Canadian policy contribute to the problem of militarization and conflict perpetuation?

The central question becomes: How can Canada assist in promoting conflict resolution and demilitarization as it relates to narcotrafficking/terrorism in the Andean countries? There is a definite connection in this case between conflict resolution, prospects for demilitarization, and developmental strategies. It is worth noting that Peru received the largest amount of Canadian developmental assistance to any country in Latin America ($120 million in 1990), with Bolivia and Colombia also near the top of the list, receiving $50 million and $64 million, respectively.

Canadian officials in Bogotá have indicated that the climate of human rights abuses in Colombia has made it difficult to implement aid. By the early 1990s, in the interest of the safety of Canadian personnel, Ottawa preferred to train Colombians in Canada or to have a minimum number of Canadians direct them in their fieldwork.[88] A representative from a Canadian NGO working with the poor in Colombia suggested that violence in the field is primarily committed by the state and/or by paramilitary groups. Regardless of the source of the violence, however, its presence has had a clear and negative impact upon Canadian developmental assistance to Colombia.

Canada's ambassador to Peru has indicated that the delivery of aid has become an ever-greater problem. She noted that, in the early 1990s, the only projects which could be implemented were those which were short term or which were staged over a period of time so that results could be obtained in the likely event that it became necessary to leave quickly.[89] As well, in 1992, DEA officials reported that the situation had deteriorated due to Sendero Luminoso guerrillas targeting foreign aid workers.[90]

Another issue concerns the targeting of Canadians by narcoterrorists. As a result of the autumn 1989 capture, in the Maritimes, of a cocaine-laden Colombian plane, Colombian narcotraffickers informed the Canadian embassy in Bogotá that Canada would be the object of retaliation due to its persecution of their confrères. Thus, Canadians in general were threatened by narcoterrorism. Consequently, security at the Canadian embassy was bolstered substantially, and the spouses and children of embassy officials were told to leave Colombia. In late 1991, as a result of calmer conditions in Colombia, the families of Canadian diplomatic personnel were permitted to return to Bogotá.

Canadian commercial opportunities have also been negatively affected by narcoterrorism. The unwillingness of Canadian businesspeople, for example, to travel to Colombia to pander their wares has contributed to sagging Canadian exports over the late 1980s (a fall from $224 million in 1987 to $164 million in 1989).[91] By 1992, exports to Colombia rose back to 1987 levels – perhaps as a result of the temporary lull in terrorism during late 1991 and early 1992. However, officials in Bogotá note that Canadian investment in Colombia has been cut sharply in the late 1980s and early 1990s due to the instability generated by narcoterrorism.

Similarly, Canadian exports to Peru have fallen from $120 million (Cdn) in 1987 to $56 million in 1989.[92] But factors other than instability resulting from narcoterrorism are also responsible for this decline in Canadian exports, such as Peru's drastic shortage of capital. While the large picture suggests a further drop in Canadian commercial opportunities, a Canadian government fact sheet listed the defence requirements of Peru as a 'main sector of interest for Canadian companies.'[93]

Clearly, there must be a multilateral solution to the severe problems discussed above. That is, there must be active cooperation between the drug-producing South and the drug-consuming North. The OAS could be very useful in mediating a negotiated solution to the drug wars, particularly through its Inter-American Drug Abuse Control Commission (CICAD). Canada became a member of CICAD in 1991 and offered a one-time contribution of $800,000 for the period 1991-2. Since then, Canada has continued to work within this agency to promote a multilateral solution to the problems of narcotrafficking and narcoterrorism.

CICAD, formed in 1986, has adopted a program that subscribes to the following points: (1) there is a relationship between socioeconomic development in the South and the phenomenon of narcoterrorism and trafficking; (2) policies must be pursued to reduce consumption of drugs, that is, to reduce the market for narcotics; (3) actions taken globally to combat narcotrafficking and terrorism must not impinge upon the sovereignty of target producing countries; and (4) 'multilateral cooperation is becoming increasingly vital to the effectiveness of efforts to reduce the demand for drugs, prevent drug abuse and combat unlawful trafficking in drugs.'[94] Hence, the argument advanced in this book is the same as that advanced by CICAD, especially with respect to the need for increasing economic development in the South, reducing consumption in the North, and developing a multilateral approach to narcotrafficking.

CICAD should be the central arena in which Canada formulates, in concert with other countries, its domestic and global narcotics policies. Working within CICAD, Canada would be following its historical propensity to seek multilateral solutions to global crises and would be less susceptible to the charge that Ottawa is in collusion with Washington. Canadian officials could also improve CICAD through advocating greater scrutiny of program proposals (both to be certain of their financial consequences and to avoid duplication of programs), and better evaluation of existing projects.[95]

It is significant to note that a general rethinking of the U.S. war on drugs, which began in 1989, emerged in Congress during the last months of the Bush administration. A hopeful sign came in October 1992, when Congress voted to prohibit military assistance to Peru in FY 1993, though military aid persisted for Colombia and Bolivia during that year.

CICAD may find that its policies are more in tune with the Clinton government than they were with the Bush government. Reports in early 1993 suggested that the Clinton administration was strongly considering reversing the Bush administration's 70-30 funding split, which was skewed towards drug interdiction and eradication rather than towards curbing consumption.[96] The March 1993 announcement by the Clinton administration of the appointment of Alexander Watson to the position of assistant secretary of state for inter-American affairs is a good sign for the Andean region. Watson's background as U.S. ambassador to Peru, Bolivia, and Colombia from the late 1970s until 1989 suggests that more attention may be devoted to the Andean crisis. Clinton's appointment of John Shattuck to the post of assistant secretary of state for human rights is also a positive signal, since he formerly headed the U.S. branch of Amnesty International – which has been quite critical of human rights abuses in the Andes. Thus, it may be that a more sensible approach to the Andean drug crisis will emerge in the mid-1990s.

There are at least six general questions that Canadian policymakers should ponder within CICAD. First, how can Canada work in concert with other countries in the Americas to reduce drug consumption? This would entail a debate regarding the amount of funding and attention that should be devoted to drug interdiction, education, and eradication. Also pertinent is the question of the harmonization of drug laws throughout the Western Hemisphere.

Second, what policies can be implemented in the short term to help alleviate the disastrous effects of narcoterrorism in Latin America? Is Canada's provision of security assistance to Colombia, discussed above, a wise path to follow? What kind of security assistance can combat narcoterrorism and trafficking without contributing to human rights violations and/or civil warfare?

Third, what role does Canada play as a transit point for the flow of drugs elsewhere? Related to this is the issue of Canada's role in drug interdiction. Current efforts by the RCMP could be explored and evaluated, and NORAD's role in drug interdiction should also be probed.[97] Multilateral efforts at controlling the flow of narcotics will prove more effective than will unilateral efforts.

Fourth, to what extent does Canada ship drug-producing chemicals to Latin America? Statistics Canada indicated, for example, that Canada sold 1,334 kg of acetone to Colombia in 1989.[98] The question is raised as to what extent Canadian exports of such chemicals as acetone, sulphuric acid, kerosene, and so on are being utilized in drug production in Latin America. CICAD must promote careful scrutiny of these sorts of transactions.

Fifth, to what extent is Canada involved in money-laundering, and what can be done to prevent it? The Colombian security agency DAS noted that narcotraffickers utilize Canada as a venue for money-laundering, but the extent of this remains unclear.[99]

Sixth, what types of aid policies can be formulated so that Canada can effectively assist in the long-term economic development of drug-producing countries? The executive secretary of CICAD suggests that long-term income-substitution policies are crucial, and that recent crop-substitution programs have been short-sighted and ineffectual.[100] In a similar vein, Canada's ambassador to Peru suggested that rather than programs of crop substitution, other projects should be explored, such as improving the infrastructure required for the shipment of local produce.[101] Canada also has programs in place to strengthen judicial agencies in Andean countries – programs which require further evaluation in a multilateral context. Coordinated inter-American assistance holds the most promise for successfully addressing the complex relationship between development and the drug war. Hemispheric trade, investment schemes, debt-repackaging or cancellation, and the establishment of reasonable prices for legitimate regional commodities should also be probed in an effort to promote development in the Andean region.

Immigration
When poverty and/or security problems reach desperate proportions in Latin America, there is a tendency for the local population to seek refuge elsewhere. An increasing number of Peruvians and Colombians, for example, have attempted to take refuge in Canada, joining the Central Americans as one of the leading groups of immigrants from Latin America to Canada.[102] Recent tension in Haiti and Venezuela may mean

a wave of immigration from those countries. The number of new landed immigrants in Canada from Latin America in the period January-September 1989-91[103] was 19,112 in 1989, 21,319 in 1990, and 25,210 in 1991. Expressed as a percentage of all immigrants, this rose from 13.1 per cent in 1989 to 15.6 per cent in 1991.[104] Hence, immigration will likely continue to be a prominent issue in the 1990s, especially given progress towards hemispheric integration. It will contribute to the slow process of the hispanicization of Canada, with this country's hispanic population now estimated to be near 150,000 people.

Conclusion

The new hemispheric reality has precipitated a focused dédication to economic integration on the part of virtually all states in the Americas. The prospects for an economic union, in the context of general ideological harmonization, spark fresh concern for security arrangements in the inter-American system. While the implications for economic integration are becoming clearer, power shifts surrounding the emergence of the post-Cold War era have resulted in a rather blurry strategic agenda for inter-American affairs. The redefinition of security represents the broadest and most significant challenge for the hemisphere. Who or what is the enemy in Latin America in the post-Cold War era? Through its full membership at the OAS, Canada can assist in the process of delineating the real threats to inter-American security at this critical historical juncture.

Certainly, highly inequitable distributions of wealth can threaten both stability and democracy, as the 1992 attempted coup in Venezuela demonstrated. A related security threat for the 1990s is resurgent militarism, often born of economic inequity and/or the proliferation of chaos associated with poverty, underdevelopment, and the effects of structural adjustment policies. Hence, there is a clear relationship between strategic and economic problems. The increasingly popular notion of downsizing the military throughout Latin America is further testimony to this. Environmental degradation has also been rightly defined by Canada as a non-traditional but, nonetheless, crucial security threat.[105] Sexism and racism pose significant security problems in the hemisphere, as do narcotrafficking and narcoterrorism.

Conclusion

Changing hegemonic structures have been crucial in the preceding analysis of the evolution of Canadian foreign policy towards Latin America. Hegemony has been defined as a fit between material power, ideas, and institutions. If 'dominance' can be employed as a synonym for hegemony in the realist sense, 'consent' is its synonym from the critical theory perspective.[1] Within these changing hegemonic structures, of crucial importance are production arrangements, security regimes, ideological proclivities, institutional mechanisms, and models of the state. While there has been considerable discussion of the influence of domestic actors upon Canadian foreign policy towards Latin America, the focus here has been upon the changing international context in which they have operated. The actions of policymakers and interest groups have had significant influence, but they are limited by the opportunities present in any given world order.

Canada's role in inter-American affairs has evolved from that of distant observer, albeit with some important economic interests, to that of full partnership in the Americas. Prior to the Second World War, Canada had important economic interests in Latin America, particularly near the turn of the century. But Ottawa's political relations with the region were quite limited. Certainly, the lack of Canadian autonomy in foreign policy until the 1926-31 period was a significant factor in this regard. But there were other constraints as well. Generally, the pre-Second World War situation was symbolized by Canada's relations with the PAU. The PAU was not particularly important in itself, but Canada's relationship to it was an important barometer of Ottawa's political dealings with Latin America as a whole. The same would later hold true with respect to Canada's relationship with the OAS.

It was shown, for example, that the vast majority of Latin American countries were always quite eager to have Canada join the PAU, in the hope that Ottawa would offset growing U.S. power. Canada wished to join, but Washington's fear that Ottawa would function as a conduit for British interests in the Western Hemisphere prevented this. By so doing, the U.S. resurrected the essence of the Monroe Doctrine. This signalled to Ottawa that political relations with Latin America were going to be quite complicated during this era. Moreover, Canada's focus in foreign policy was solidly upon the North Atlantic.

Hence, hegemonic structures conditioned Canadian policy in Latin America. As a loyal ally to the declining U.K., and amid growing relations with the rising hegemon, Ottawa found that any objective for expanded political relations with Latin America faced certain barriers. Foremost among these, Washington seemed unprepared to permit a greater Canadian presence in Latin America until British power completely collapsed. The Second World War, entailing the crumbling of an old world order and the introduction of a new global reality, ultimately resulted in a more profound Canadian relationship with Latin America, both diplomatically and economically. Latin America served as a venue for Canadian surplus exports, and as a source of badly needed dollars, against the backdrop of a war-torn Europe that would soon be unable to purchase Canadian products. This was an important phenomenon, given the increasingly formidable capacity of Canadian industry during this period.

Along with growing economic relations came the establishment of solid diplomatic contact with Latin America. Ideologically, the obvious enemy during the Second World War was the fascist project launched by the Axis powers. This found expression, for example, in Canadian concerns with respect to the philosophical underpinnings of the government of Argentina. As the first country in the Western Hemisphere to immerse itself in the war effort, Canada was also perturbed by the apparent complacency displayed by other hemispheric states during the initial phase of the war.

With the end of the Second World War, a new hegemonic era arose, as did a fresh contestation between international capitalism and international communism – the Cold War. A prominent component of this 'Great Contest' was the rivalry between two different systems of production, especially in developing regions such as Latin America. To the extent that Canada was concerned with political developments in Latin America, Ottawa took exception to U.S. analyses which emphasized international communist subversion as being at the root of Latin American instability. Instead, Canadians generally maintained that indigenous problems, particularly inequitable distributions of wealth and widespread social injustice, were responsible for regional turmoil. According to Canada, it was socio-economic inequities which led portions of the population in Latin America to consider socialism or communism, which promised the poverty-stricken majority a bigger slice of the pie. For Canada, then, production arrangements in the region raised questions regarding the power relations associated with how, and for whose interest, production occurs. Hence, while Ottawa and Washington converged with respect to their preferences for capitalism and democracy in Latin America, they differed with respect to the appropriate methods of attaining those objectives.

Reflecting drastic global shifts and a new hegemonic arrangement, new international institutions were created. Canada supported the U.N., viewing it as the most appropriate forum for a foreign policy which had multilateralism as its centrepiece. For Ottawa, a less satisfactory institution was the OAS, developed in 1948 as the Cold War congealed. Canada viewed this organization as a vehicle for Washington's anti-communist agenda, and as an arena which was hopelessly dominated by the U.S. (in contrast to the more balanced U.N.). When the tables had turned and the U.S. wished to have Canada on board at the OAS, after years of rejecting its presence at the PAU, Ottawa responded with a resounding 'No.' Compounding Canada's doubts regarding the OAS was Ottawa's contention that the organization represented regionalism at a time when globalism was the most appropriate course for preventing a rerun of the great wars which had plagued the first half of the century.

It is ironic that, while this era marked the dawning of Pax Americana (i.e., the heyday of global U.S. hegemony), from a critical theory perspective, it is doubtful whether hegemony existed in the inter-American system. While there is no doubt that U.S. dominance in the hemisphere was stronger than ever, what is questionable is the level of consent for this arrangement emanating from other countries in the Americas. As was noted, the U.S. relied on force to discipline its Latin American partners throughout the Cold War, while many Latin American states were themselves led by military governments. Added to this was Canada's growing concern of falling under the U.S. shadow. With regard to hemispheric relations, this was manifested in Ottawa's refusal to immerse itself more fully in inter-American affairs for fear of being bullied by Washington. Hegemony as consent, and as a fit between ideas, institutions, and material power, did not appear to be present in the Americas during the Cold War. Certainly, the OAS did not represent the successful institutionalization of hegemony.

Ottawa's disinterest in the OAS paralleled a disengagement from Latin America during the early postwar years. Rather than build upon the economic basis established by elevated levels of Canadian trade with the region during the war, Ottawa chose to reinforce its already intense focus upon the North Atlantic and, especially, to secure a place in the lucrative business of reconstructing Europe. Canada also found unappealing the state structures, that is, the military dictatorships, which generally predominated in Latin America. Still, Ottawa maintained diplomatic relations with the region and, on a very modest level, attempted to take advantage of commercial opportunities.

By the late 1950s, Canadians began to have considerable doubts regarding their economic relationship with the U.S., doubts which would have an impact upon Ottawa's policy towards Latin America. The 1957 Gordon Report set alarm bells ringing with regard to U.S. economic influence in Canada, which, many feared, posed a threat to Canadian sovereignty. There was considerable distrust of the U.S. Canadian diplomats indicated that this distrust should foster a greater degree of understanding on the part of Canada regarding similar predicaments faced by Latin Americans. Such an understanding would underpin Canada's future potential for acting as a bridge between Latin America and the U.S.

This era also witnessed some important distinctions between Canada and the U.S. regarding their policies towards leftist movements in the Western Hemisphere, differences which stemmed from their varying ranks in the global arena as well as their unique histories of economic and political development. While the U.S. viewed military intervention as the appropriate policy in Guatemala in 1954, in Cuba during the 1960s, in the Dominican Republic in 1965, and so on, Ottawa viewed it as a heavy-handed, superficial, and misplaced response to profound social and economic inequities.

The international situation was significantly redefined in the late 1960s, when Pax Americana began to wane. The U.S. was engaged in a losing battle in Vietnam – a battle which rendered the U.S. globally unpopular. The OPEC crisis of the early 1970s posed another challenge to Pax Americana. Furthermore, the U.S. faced increasing economic challenges from Europe and Asia, and, with the collapse of Bretton Woods, it abandoned its global economic leadership role. The U.S.

found itself in a world which appeared to be shifting towards political and economic multipolarity as opposed to bipolarity.

Canada, like much of Latin America during this period, grew increasingly nationalistic and was critical of American policy on a number of fronts. In Canada this development meant, among other things, a stronger role for the state in the economy coupled with acerbic criticisms of U.S. foreign policy. For Latin America this generally spelled the acceleration of import substitution models and, in certain quarters, the adoption of dependency theory. Although always appreciating U.S. strength even in its depleted form, neither Canada nor Latin America placed much faith in consenting to U.S. leadership in hemispheric affairs, and to this extent hegemony was not present in the inter-American system.

In an attempt to address the altered global environment, the new Trudeau government boldly refashioned Canadian foreign policy. Trudeau's Third Option formula, designed to bolster Canadian sovereignty and power by diverting trade away from the U.S., specified Latin America as a new target for Canadian economic and political interests. The 1970s were marked by enormous progress in the establishment of closer Canadian ties to Latin America. While its primary focus was upon fostering more intimate bilateral relations with the major Latin American political and economic powers, Ottawa chose to join the OAS as a permanent observer. This was a symbolic move, demonstrating that Canada wished to raise its profile in Latin America. But the pronounced tension between the U.S. and Latin America meant that the time for full Canadian membership in the OAS had not yet arrived.

Several visits by Prime Minister Trudeau to Latin America, including his celebrated meeting with Castro, as well as numerous Canadian trade missions, characterized Ottawa's new penchant for bilateral relations. Canada's support for ideological diversity in Latin America was displayed with respect to the Cuban issue as well as in the Canadian decision to accept nearly 7,000 Chilean refugees, mostly leftists, displaced by the U.S.-supported Pinochet dictatorship. Related to this, the era witnessed the birth of Canadian interest groups which focused upon inter-American affairs. They were particularly interested in the Chilean situation, as well as in the sale of CANDU nuclear reactors to Argentina.

The brief reign of Prime Minister Joe Clark (1979-80) foreshadowed changes that would take place during the Mulroney era, including a Canadian policy towards Central America that was closer to that of the U.S., as well as a rethinking of economic structures which affected

Ottawa's policy to the region. The return of the Liberals to power in 1980 was followed by some bold initiatives, such as FIRA and NEP, which signalled that Canada did not accept the new economic and political agenda characteristic of the neoconservative revolution already in place in Reagan's U.S. and Thatcher's England. At this point, then, Canada was out of step with the emerging New Right agenda which would solidify in the 1980s and early 1990s.

While the nationalistic views of Trudeau were shared by Latin American powers such as Mexico at the beginning of the decade, Latin American political and economic nationalism was truly detonated by the debt crisis, which emerged in 1982. This crisis resulted in the imposition of neoconservative structures by the U.S.-dominated IMF. That is, international finance capital, through institutions such as the IMF and the World Bank, altered Latin American state structures to conform with the U.S.'s 'hyperliberal' project. The debt crisis set the stage for an emerging hegemonic structure in the Americas – a structure which was underpinned by the power of transnational production and which was dominated by the U.S.

The debt crisis exposed Canada's economic vulnerability in Latin America. The unwillingness of Canadian banks to loan additional funds to the region, coupled with Canadian business's fear of Latin American instability, signalled a temporary Canadian withdrawal from the region. That is, Canada's progress towards fortifying commercial links with Latin America in the 1970s stopped in the 1980s, largely as a result of the Latin American debt and the Canadian recession.

Also important during this era was the Central American crisis, which emerged with the Sandinista revolution in 1979 and the subsequent resolve on the part of the Reagan administration to do whatever it took to rid the isthmus of socialism. The formation of well-organized and well-informed Canadian interest groups motivated the government to take a fairly strong role during the crisis. Clearly, political and security problems in Latin America had become an important Canadian concern. Ottawa, during the Trudeau years, formulated an independent policy in Latin America, which included some important support for Nicaragua. While Canadian relations towards Central America would move closer to U.S. policy during the Mulroney years, Canada's quite significant role in conflict resolution and peacekeeping in the isthmus solidified a relationship with the major Latin American powers which helped form a basis for Canada's new partnership with the Americas in the 1990s.

A new era emerged with the election of Prime Minister Mulroney in 1984, signalling harmonization of the Canadian political economy with that of the United States on a number of levels. These included the alteration of government structures and policies, which was exemplified by a more inviting environment for foreign investment (especially U.S. investment), a process of privatization, and generally strong support for U.S. foreign policy initiatives. Importantly, by 1984, both Canada and Latin America seemed to be in step with the neoconservative hegemonic project launched by Washington at the beginning of the decade. This provided the foundation for an integration process which would occur in the late 1980s and into the 1990s.

With the exception of Central America, the Canadian government (as well as the U.S.) more or less neglected the rest of Latin America during this period. Interest groups, as well, focused almost solely upon the isthmus with little attention afforded to the rest of the Americas. So, too, did academics, who in the main did not bother, for example, to devote significant attention to Mexico. And, as was noted, the Canadian business community largely pulled back from the region in light of the debt crisis and anticipated instability, while the major Canadian business lobby group, CALA, disbanded in disgrace in the early part of the decade.

The post-1988 period witnessed further progress towards a new hegemonic era and an emerging Canadian partnership with Latin America. The successful CUSFTA signalled a new production arrangement, which perhaps represented a prototype of sorts for the rest of the hemisphere. It precipitated progress towards possible North American and hemispheric integration, entailing revolutionary economic and political restructuring throughout the Americas. This was a product of global shifts, including the emerging dominance of globalized production and the concomitant growth in power of transnational corporations, the possible movement towards global trade areas, as well as the hegemony of the market economy and the doctrine of competitiveness. Thus, economic changes globally and hemispherically have been a crucial determinant of Canada's new partnership with Latin America. It is of interest to note that Ottawa's important attempt to solidify Canadian relations with Latin America during the Trudeau government's tenure occurred in the context of challenges to U.S. hegemony, while deeper relations between Canada and the region which characterize the post-1989 period have occurred during a period of inter-American integration fostered by progress towards a U.S.-led hegemony.

If globalized production and the growing power of transnational capital are primary characteristics of the post-Cold War era, so are the collapse of the USSR and the accompanying shifts in global security. The process of political integration with the Americas, characterized by full Canadian membership in the OAS, was facilitated by an atmosphere in which Ottawa was not pressured to support Washington's campaigns against communism or socialism in Latin America. Movement towards ideological conformity in the Americas also meant that full membership in the OAS would be unlikely to place Canada in the crossfire between Latin America and the U.S. (although the Panamanian, Haitian, and Andean episodes demonstrate that contentious issues could still arise). More generally, shifts in both production arrangements and strategic concerns in the post-Cold War era may suggest a new capacity – as yet unrealized – for the OAS to represent the institutionalization of an emerging hegemony in the Americas.

While there appears to be a dawning hegemony in the hemisphere – in terms of ideological convergence, institutional rejuvenation, as well as a clearly accepted model of economic relations and a hierarchy of politico-military power – distinct alternatives exist within that parameter. Canada and its inter-American sister states should consider abandoning the minimalist state, for example, in efforts to cope with new production arrangements. Economic integration in the Americas, as was noted, has largely reflected global economic restructuring and the rising power of transnational capital. Given that context, considerable caution and care are required to ensure that any free trade agreements with hemispheric partners are well negotiated, to promote the protection of inter-American labour, resources, and culture, to protect against environmental degradation, to prevent the downward harmonization of social standards, and to protect human rights. Only when the potential pitfalls of free trade agreements are fully confronted can procedures be developed to avoid them.

Through its new full membership in the OAS, Ottawa can help to define the real enemies in the hemisphere: inequitable distribution of wealth, resurgent militarism, ecocide, sexism, racism, and so on. Further, Canada can work with its hemispheric colleagues to promote conflict resolution with respect to the Andean drug war. Finally, this country can play the crucial bridging role which Latin Americans historically have hoped that Canada would assume. Obviously this will require political will, courage and independence on the part of Ottawa. In the early 1990s there exists considerable resentment among Latin

Americans vis-à-vis the U.S.[2] Considerable work needs to be done in the hemisphere in order to achieve a true inter-American community.

Beyond the difficulties noted above, in addition to other problems noted elsewhere in the book, a major contradiction is present which may have a negative impact upon inter-American integration. That is, the integration process was launched alongside major economic restructuring at a time of recession. Components of the population in the Americas who have been, or may be, dislocated and/or disempowered during this process will likely resist hemispheric integration. While governments virtually throughout the Americas have converged ideologically, these governments may find themselves presiding over populations which do not share an enthusiasm for an inter-American bloc.

Although certain local groups and individuals did have some effect, it has been international determinants which have ordained Canada's changing role in inter-American affairs. Through its commitment to NAFTA and hemispheric economic integration in general, its resolve to fortify bilateral relations with key countries in Latin America, and its new role in the OAS, Canada is now a full member of the Americas.

One hopes that the Canadian government will devote additional resources to the Latin American Division of the DEA, that it will provide greater funding for Latin American projects through CIDA, and that it will create more programs to promote Canadian commercial, cultural, and educational initiatives, and so on. Regrettably, by early 1993, due to cutbacks and fiscal crisis, precisely the opposite has occurred. One hopes those decisions will be reversed. Beyond the realm of government, the Canadian private sector must also focus more intensely upon Latin America. Canadian academics should continue to develop research projects to grapple with the new hemispheric reality, and should have funds made available to them for such endeavours. Presumably, Canadian NGOs will continue to define new ways of looking at Latin American and inter-American development.[3]

In retrospect, one can see that there were a number of periods in the twentieth century when Canada seemed to be on the threshold of deeper relations with Latin America but then pulled back. In the post-Cold War era, are we on the brink of establishing an entrenched relationship with Latin America? What if NAFTA never reaches fruition? What if the recent wave of militarization in Latin America spreads to a large state, through, for example, a bloody coup in Brazil? What if hemispheric economic integration produces disastrous results for Canada?

Those are real possibilities, and the volatile and alarming global political events in the recent past require that any predictions regarding the future of inter-American affairs be made with the utmost caution. Projecting from available evidence at this juncture, however, it seems reasonable to predict that Canada's relations with the Americas will continue to grow, largely because changing international structures and what appears to be an emerging hegemony in the Americas provide the context for true Canadian entrenchment in hemispheric affairs. Certainly the world seems to be moving towards the establishment of trade areas, which means Canada's place in this hemisphere will assume greater significance. Further, even if a NAFTA is not implemented, de facto integration is already occurring through CUSFTA and the maquiladora program in Mexico. In the strategic realm, as well, the North Atlantic focus assumed by Canada and the U.S. may be slowly shifting. While Europe will always be important for North America, Washington and Ottawa seem more willing lately to let Europeans assume a greater share of handling their own affairs. Ever since the Central American crisis, Canada certainly has appeared more dedicated to resolving strategic issues in the Americas than it ever has in the past.

For better or worse, then, it would appear that the new global reality has dictated a larger Canadian role in hemispheric affairs. The challenge for Ottawa is to develop the vision necessary to formulate policies which help it and its hemispheric partners to steer clear of painful potentialities. It is worth reiterating that Canada's new relationship with the region is one of partnership. This is defined by a common stake in hemispheric economic prosperity and security. Challenges remain, not the least of which is the necessity for a timely reorientation by Canada to its new place in inter-American affairs.

Appendix

Table A.1

Canadian exports to Latin America (millions $Cdn.), 1945-92

Country	1945	1950	1955	1960	1965	1970
Argentina	6.0	13.4	6.8	19.4	32.7	59.1
Bolivia	0.3	2.3	1.1	0.3	1.7	2.2
Brazil	16.7	15.8	11.5	19.8	17.5	87.4
Chile	2.6	6.9	3.8	6.6	10.5	22.9
Colombia	5.0	14.8	22.7	16.6	17.4	24.6
Costa Rica	0.5	2.3	3.6	3.0	5.4	6.0
Cuba	4.5	18.0	17.5	13.0	52.6	58.9
Dom. Rep.	0.7	3.0	4.3	5.1	6.2	20.5
Ecuador	0.4	1.4	5.0	3.9	4.7	3.5
El Salvador	–	1.5	1.8	0.8	2.7	3.4
Guatemala	0.4	1.5	2.5	2.1	4.0	3.6
Haiti	0.6	2.5	2.4	1.5	1.3	4.9
Honduras	0.2	0.6	0.6	1.4	1.0	2.8
Mexico	8.2	17.6	37.1	38.0	51.0	91.7
Nicaragua	0.3	0.8	1.8	1.3	2.8	2.2
Panama	1.0	9.0	2.8	3.7	4.6	7.7
Paraguay	0.04	0.1	0.1	0.1	0.2	0.2
Peru	4.0	3.7	6.0	8.9	21.9	35.9
Uruguay	1.9	1.9	2.4	2.4	3.3	4.4
Venezuela	4.1	25.5	30.8	35.3	73.0	111.4
Total exports to Latin America	57	142	164	183	314	500
Total global exports	3,218	3,118	4,282	5,256	8,525	–
Exports to Latin America as percentage of total exports	1.8	4.5	3.8	3.5	3.7	–

Table A.1 (continued)

Canadian exports to Latin America (millions $Cdn.), 1945-92

Country	1972	1975	1978	1980	1982
Argentina	67.8	58.8	98.1	232.1	92.0
Bolivia	1.7	5.6	7.0	7.3	9.0
Brazil	87.9	202.9	419.8	900.4	546.0
Chile	10.8	30.8	56.9	112.4	68.0
Colombia	28.7	38.9	83.4	236.0	225.0
Costa Rica	7.1	11.8	21.0	30.3	16.0
Cuba	58.9	228.9	219.4	421.8	324.0
Dom. Rep.	14.8	28.3	22.1	53.7	51.0
Ecuador	5.3	22.8	47.6	84.5	65.0
El Salvador	4.0	8.2	17.4	15.6	15.0
Guatemala	4.7	11.2	22.9	22.2	34.0
Haiti	5.1	12.6	19.7	26.8	23.0
Honduras	3.0	8.1	15.9	24.2	15.0
Mexico	100.1	222.4	232.3	494.0	455.0
Nicaragua	2.1	4.0	9.5	15.1	15.0
Panama	7.8	17.8	23.1	55.6	47.0
Paraguay	.2	.4	.5	4.1	–
Peru	60.5	82.5	44.5	56.7	110.0
Uruguay	3.1	6.6	8.0	17.8	13.0
Venezuela	154.9	348.0	689.9	682.0	672.0
Total exports to Latin America	635	1,950	2,059	3,493	2,795
Total global exports	20,140	33,367	52,842	75,964	84,530
Exports to Latin America as a percentage of total exports	3.2	5.8	3.9	4.6	3.3

Table A.1 (continued)

Canadian exports to Latin America (millions $Cdn.), 1945-92

Country	1985	1988	1990	1991	1992
Argentina	67.8	62	48	64	101
Bolivia	2.0	5	5	5	15
Brazil	685.0	521	502	617	621
Chile	82.0	141	200	150	145
Colombia	163.0	250	213	153	229
Costa Rica	21.0	29	27	22	24
Cuba	330.0	230	176	131	113
Dom. Rep.	36.0	60	57	59	66
Ecuador	50.0	44	37	47	68
El Salvador	15.0	20	16	13	11
Guatemala	17.0	18	28	18	23
Haiti	25.0	18	15	15	8
Honduras	14.0	19	10	5	13
Mexico	398.0	500	608	460	771
Nicaragua	18.0	23	11	13	10
Panama	54.0	37	16	19	18
Paraguay	2.0	2	2	2	4
Peru	48.0	65	58	77	89
Uruguay	5.0	11	20	13	12
Venezuela	332.0	392	274	418	325
Total exports to Latin America	2,360	2,447	2,323	2,303	2,666
Total global exports	119,474	138,498	148,664	–	–
Exports to Latin America as percentage of total exports	2.0	1.8	1.6	–	–

Source: Statistics Canada, *Exports: Merchandise Trade*, cat. 65-202, various years; *Canada Year Book Minister of Industry Trade and Commerce*, various years

Table A.2

Canadian imports from Latin America (millions $Cdn.), 1945-92

Country	1945	1950	1955	1960	1965	1970
Argentina	7.3	10.9	4.4	19.4	5.4	9.0
Bolivia	0.03	2.4	0.02	20.3	0.4	0.1
Brazil	7.6	28.2	30.7	19.8	35.6	49.3
Chile	0.6	1.4	0.3	6.6	1.7	2.8
Colombia	11.7	13.3	22.2	16.6	16.8	26.6
Costa Rica	0.6	3.4	5.9	3.0	6.7	12.1
Cuba	7.5	4.1	10.0	13.0	5.3	9.5
Dom. Rep.	6.2	1.2	1.5	5.1	2.1	1.9
Ecuador	2.0	1.5	5.2	3.9	8.5	10.5
El Salvador	–	0.8	3.0	2.4	2.7	4.0
Guatemala	1.8	5.8	4.5	2.1	2.9	6.0
Haiti	0.5	1.8	1.6	1.5	1.1	0.8
Honduras	8.0	5.6	1.7	1.4	10.2	13.1
Mexico	13.5	33.0	28.8	38.0	27.2	47.3
Nicaragua	0.001	0.3	1.4	1.3	0.2	1.1
Panama	0.03	5.5	9.0	3.7	19.4	7.7
Paraguay	0.2	0.4	0.2	0.1	0.5	0.7
Peru	0.1	4.0	0.9	8.9	9.1	4.3
Uruguay	0.1	2.8	0.5	2.4	1.0	0.2
Venezuela	17.3	87.3	187.3	35.3	254.7	339.2
Total imports from Latin America	79	214	319	185	411	546
Total global imports	1,586	3,174	4,712	5,256	8,633	–
Imports from Latin America as a percentage of total imports	5.0	6.7	6.7	3.5	4.8	–

Table A.2 (continued)

Canadian imports from Latin America (millions $Cdn.), 1945-92

Country	1972	1975	1978	1980	1982
Argentina	11.7	13.2	48.0	36.1	53.0
Bolivia	0.9	5.3	15.1	16.7	8.0
Brazil	61.9	170.2	248.4	348.1	497.0
Chile	6.5	50.0	51.4	97.1	119.0
Colombia	30.4	32.2	82.0	101.6	92.0
Costa Rica	10.3	18.6	29.3	35.2	32.0
Cuba	11.1	81.5	60.6	163.5	94.0
Dom. Rep.	4.5	24.3	25.7	17.5	17.0
Ecuador	10.7	21.1	105.0	40.6	50.0
El Salvador	3.8	3.1	12.5	26.9	21.0
Guatemala	6.8	19.5	24.4	25.1	22.0
Haiti	1.7	3.6	6.0	6.6	8.0
Honduras	19.4	11.8	31.8	39.6	28.0
Mexico	53.0	95.4	184.5	345.5	999.0
Nicaragua	2.6	13.0	13.0	31.5	26.0
Panama	3.7	6.3	18.9	45.7	17.0
Paraguay	1.4	1.2	4.0	4.5	1.0
Peru	9.2	11.5	49.6	94.5	32.0
Uruguay	0.5	1.5	5.4	14.2	10.0
Venezuela	410.9	1,111.0	1,249.0	2,216.8	1,802.0
Total imports from Latin America	661	1,699	2,275	3,707	3,928
Total global imports	18,669	34,805	50,102	69,128	67,855
Latin American imports as a percentage of all imports	3.5	4.9	4.5	5.4	5.5

Table A.2 (continued)

Canadian imports from Latin America (millions $Cdn.), 1945-92

Country	1985	1988	1990	1991	1992
Argentina	91	123	139	130	112
Bolivia	8	22	22	5	5
Brazil	808	1,192	798	706	715
Chile	130	160	180	184	202
Colombia	89	138	132	136	131
Costa Rica	41	50	57	88	132
Cuba	44	87	130	153	256
Dom. Rep.	18	36	39	37	33
Ecuador	72	85	147	150	108
El Salvador	36	41	18	16	13
Guatemala	26	38	37	40	42
Haiti	10	7	14	11	1
Honduras	21	27	13	15	22
Mexico	1,331	1,327	1,748	2,574	2,751
Nicaragua	26	64	63	46	32
Panama	23	30	4	14	6
Paraguay	3	–	1	–	1
Peru	68	86	128	72	95
Uruguay	8	11	45	21	21
Venezuela	1,092	459	577	482	325
Total imports from Latin America	3,945	3,983	4,292	–	5,013
Total global imports	104,914	131,171	136,224	–	–
Imports from Latin America as a percentage of all imports	3.1	3.0	3.2	–	–

Source: Statistics Canada, *Imports: Merchandise Trade* cat. 65-203, various years; *Canada Year Book*, Minister of Industry Trade and Commerce, various years

Table A.3

**Canadian official developmental assistance
(excluding multilateral) to Latin America
(thousands $Cdn.), 1970-90**

Country	1970-1	71-2	72-3	73-4	74-5	75-6	76-7
Argentina	567	212	10	28	–	62	14
Bolivia	129	170	93	708	1,111	559	410
Brazil	1,354	2,042	3,379	1,558	1,597	3,120	3,061
Costa Rica	–	4	1	61	212	165	142
Chile	2,357	819	2,174	2,179	371	123	144
Colombia	4,053	4,326	5,376	3,848	1,898	2,201	4,285
Cuba	–	57	427	452	3,757	4,283	4,522
Dom. Rep.	64	90	307	642	4,221	2,049	1,948
Ecuador	106	1,327	659	1,130	3,398	3,398	1,006
El Salvador	–	207	–	25	1,337	1,935	759
Guatemala	15	29	163	64	72	3,530	2,836
Haiti	143	292	452	451	1,669	3,269	5,118
Honduras	63	258	621	378	2,606	1,885	585
Nicaragua	–	33	98	1,503	1,100	177	816
Panama	–	8	17	6	–	13	63
Paraguay	–	53	9	109	50	128	157
Peru	380	204	369	966	2,016	2,747	3,270
Uruguay	–	50	20	32	48	86	63
Venezuela	–	–	112	40	–	89	38

Table A.3 (continued)

Canadian official developmental assistance (excluding multilateral) to Latin America (thousands $Cdn.), 1970-90

Country	1977-8	78-9	79-80	80-1	81-2	82-3	83-4
Argentina	26	259	–	126	191	720	1,047
Bolivia	695	2,582	1,824	1,723	5,263	5,704	15,193
Brazil	2,428	2,648	2,935	2,671	3,959	3,943	7,250
Costa Rica	298	357	205	386	1,010	4,446	7,685
Chile	131	69	18	247	574	2,782	3,347
Colombia	6,047	9,312	7,579	6,565	4,333	7,036	10,202
Cuba	4,522	1,057	–	–	–	–	71
Dom. Rep.	365	201	1,182	2,116	4,415	1,807	2,045
Ecuador	876	823	805	782	959	1,475	1,804
El Salvador	388	756	1,597	3,114	7,163	1,253	3,488
Guatemala	2,493	5,468	3,701	2,076	1,784	3,580	1,964
Haiti	7,885	11,757	9,229	10,108	8,014	13,927	13,853
Honduras	2,182	10,412	5,787	4,802	4,825	7,361	5,184
Nicaragua	862	348	1,292	2,344	7,333	3,866	11,744
Panama	113	139	81	514	609	732	783
Paraguay	73	98	539	267	196	213	463
Peru	9,348	5,084	5,162	4,096	6,901	6,278	17,457
Uruguay	62	37	50	132	119	275	326
Venezuela	3	–	–	–	75	71	165

Table A.3 (continued)

Canadian official developmental assistance (excluding multilateral) to Latin America (thousands $Cdn.), 1970-90

Country	1984-5	85-6	86-7	87-8	88-9	89-90
Argentina	1,805	2,066	3,656	2,631	3,523	2,839
Bolivia	3,277	2,933	11,072	6,507	10,191	13,121
Brazil	8,384	6,355	7,068	8,226	9,315	6,870
Costa Rica	8,072	8,702	15,364	21,557	13,856	15,019
Chile	4,717	4,332	6,703	5,745	5,966	5,752
Colombia	7,965	8,079	13,339	14,405	21,419	18,783
Cuba	56	137	193	90	75	260
Dom. Rep.	5,028	2,280	3,142	3,194	3,061	3,530
Ecuador	2,217	1,559	2,808	2,717	3,542	4,694
El Salvador	1,512	1,803	9,227	7,996	5052,505	
Guatemala	2,391	2,082	3,100	2,701	3,507	3,853
Haiti	8,801	7,742	17,470	15,492	15,492	17,535
Honduras	20,452	4,363	4,938	7,864	12,591	8,438
Nicaragua	8,518	8,104	8,511	15,274	16,013	8,365
Panama	771	639	1,525	1,015	1,063	823
Paraguay	219	239	298	738	805	735
Peru	16,902	18,869	20,460	27,930	29,981	28,236
Uruguay	461	839	624	2,385	2,373	2,187
Venezuela	109	59	170	148	1,172	827

Source: Canadian International Development Agency, Corporate Information Division, Hull, Quebec

Table A.4

**Yearly versus total percentage of
Canadian official development assistance
to Latin America, 1970-1990**

1970-1	3.850
1971-2	3.003
1972-3	2.798
1973-4	2.696
1974-5	2.219
1975-6	1.725
1976-7	1.754
1977-8	2.302
1978-9	2.586
1979-80	2.334
1980-1	1.953
1981-2	2.359
1982-3	2.249
1983-4	4.149
1984-5	2.939
1985-6	2.561
1987-8	3.659
1988-9	4.062
1989-90	4.399

Source: Statistics Canada, Corporate Information Division, Hull,
Quebec

Table A.5

Canadian foreign direct investment in Latin America, selected years (millions $Cdn.)

Country	1971	1975	1980	1984	1988	1990
Mexico	50	75	165	270	178	175
Brazil	711	1,039	691	952	1,356	1,566
Venezuela	12	19	59	54	88	67
Central America (including Nicaragua, Honduras, Guatemala, Costa Rica, Panama)	48	79	276	56	19	–
Cuba, Haiti, Dominican Republic	37	71	143	216	263	–
South America (including Colombia, Ecuador, Peru, Chile Bolivia, Paraguay, Argentina)	52	54	160	289	258	–

Source: Statistics Canada, *Canada's International Investment Position*, cat. 67-202, various years; F. Chow, Balance of Payments Division, Statistics Canada, Ottawa, 1991

Notes

Introduction

1 Robert W. Cox, *Production, Power and World Order: Social Forces in the Making of History* (New York: Columbia University Press 1987), 7.
2 See Robert Cox, 'Social Forces, States and World Orders: Beyond International Relations Theory,' in Robert Keohane, ed., *Neorealism and Its Critics* (New York: Columbia University Press 1986), 224.

Chapter 1: First Encounters

1 For a superb discussion of the history of Canada's economic interests in Latin America, see C. Armstrong and H. Nellis, *Southern Exposure* (Toronto: University of Toronto Press 1988).
2 Ibid, xi.
3 For a further discussion of this, see Eugene Miller, 'Canada and the Pan American Union,' *International Journal* 3 (1947):28; and D. Anglin, 'United States Opposition to Canadian Membership in the Pan American Union,' *International Organization* 15 (Winter 1961):2.
4 Records of Department of External Affairs, National Archives of Canada (NAC), 'Canada – The Pan American Union and the U.S. – a Memorandum to the Prime Minister,' RG 25-83-84-259, vol. 134, file 2226-40C.
5 Records of Department of External Affairs, NAC, 'The Attitude of the United States towards Canadian entry into the Pan American Union: A Memorandum to the Prime Minister,' RG 25, vol. 134, file 226-40C, sub. 4, chron. 4, 1 January 1943, 1.
6 Ibid.
7 Eugene Miller, 'Canada and the Pan American Union,' 29.
8 See J. Granatstein, *Canadian Foreign Policy: Historical Readings* (Toronto: Clark Copp Pitman 1986).
9 *Foreign Relations of the United States*, Washington, Government Printing Office, 1933, vol. 4, 127-8, cited in Anglin, 'United States Opposition to Canadian Membership in the Pan American Union,' 20.
10 Records of Department of External Affairs, NAC, 'Canada, the Pan American Union and the United States: A Memorandum for the Prime Minister,' RG 25-83-84-259, vol. 134, file 2226-40C, 13 April 1942, 4-5.

11 For a broader discussion of this, see Iris Podea, 'Pan American Sentiment in French Canada,' *International Journal* 3 (Autumn 1948):335.

12 Eugene Miller, 'Canada and the Pan American Union,' 30.

13 For a broader discussion of this, see D.R. Murray, 'Canada's First Diplomatic Missions in Latin America,' *Journal of Inter-American Studies and World Affairs* 16 (May 1974):154.

14 For a discussion of the Ogdensburg Agreement, see H.L. Keenleyside, 'The Canada-United States Permanent Joint Board on Defence, 1940- 1945,' *International Journal* 16 (Winter 1960-1):50-77.

15 See I. Podea, 'Pan American Sentiment in French Canada,' 334-5.

16 Records of Department of External Affairs, NAC, 'Memorandum for the Prime Minister,' RG 25, vol. 2728, file 261-40, 10 August 1940, 2. See also Records of Department of External Affairs, NAC, 'Letter from Assistant Secretary of State to Mr. Herbert, Canadian Ambassador to Mexico,' RG 25-Interim 106, vol. 348, file 10117-D-40, 5 April 1949, 2.

17 For an excellent discourse on the significance of this company, see Duncan McDowall, *The Light: Brazilian Traction, Light and Power Company Ltd., 1899-1945* (Toronto: University of Toronto Press 1988).

18 See D.R. Murray, 'Canada's First Diplomatic Missions in Latin America,' 160.

19 For a discussion of this, see P.E. Corbett, 'Canada in the Western Hemisphere,' *Foreign Affairs* 19 (1941):778-9.

20 See E. Miller, 'Canada and the Pan American Union,' 30-1.

21 For a discussion of the evolution of Canadian diplomatic relations with Latin America, see J.C.M. Ogelsby, *Gringos from the Far North: Essays in the History of Canadian-Latin American Relations, 1866-1968* (Toronto: Macmillan 1976). See especially Chapter 2 and, with regard to Brazil, 41-2.

22 See D.R. Murray, 'Canada's First Diplomatic Missions in Latin America,' 167.

23 Ibid., 17.

24 For a broader discussion of this theme see James Rochlin, 'The Evolution of Canada as an Actor in Inter-American Affairs,' *Millennium* 19 (Summer 1990): 229-48.

25 Records of Department of External Affairs, NAC, 'Canadian Entry into the Pan American Union: Appendix I, 31 October 1941,' RG 25, vol. 134, file 226-40-C, 15 December 1942, 17.

26 Records of Department of External Affairs, NAC, 'Canadian Entry into the Pan American Union: Appendix I,' 19.

27 This possibility has now become a reality. Ottawa's support for the U.S. invasion of Panama in 1989 alienated Latin America, since Canada was the only country besides El Salvador to side with Washington in that endeavour.

28 Records of Department of External Affairs, NAC, 'Canada, the Pan-American Union and the United States,' RG 25-83-84-259, vol. 134, file 2226-40C, 13 April 1942, 1.

29 Arguments for Canadian membership in the PAU, on both economic and strategic grounds, are found in J. Humphrey, *The Inter-American System: A Canadian View* (Toronto: Macmillan 1942). See especially 265-6 and Chapter 9.

30 For a further discussion of these and other arguments, see P.E. Corbett, 'Canada in the Western Hemisphere.'

31 Records of Department of External Affairs, NAC, 'Canada and the Pan American Union,' RG 25, vol. 134, file 2226-40C, 15 December 1942, 1.
32 NAC, 'Canada, the Pan American Union and the United States,' 1-2.
33 Ibid., 2.
34 NAC, 'Canada and the Pan American Union,' 7.
35 NAC, 'Canada, the Pan American Union and the United States,' 9.
36 NAC, 'Canada and the Pan American Union,' 7.
37 This view is also expressed by D.R. Murray, 'Canada's first Diplomatic Missions in Latin America.'
38 NAC, 'Canada, the Pan American Union and the United States,' 9.
39 From Canada, House of Commons Debates, 30 March 1939, 2,420, cited in E. Miller, 'Canada and the Pan American Union,' 33.
40 Records of Department of External Affairs, NAC, Dean Acheson, U.S. Secretary of State, 'Relations with Canadian Officials Abroad,' RG 25, vol. 3182, file 4889-40, 22 December 1942, 1.
41 Records of Department of External Affairs, NAC, 'Letter from Vincent Massey to Norman Robertson,' RG 25, file 4889-40C, 9 September 1942, 1-2.
42 Records of Department of External Affairs, NAC, 'Memorandum on Canadian Policy in Latin America,' RG 25, file 3671-40C, sub. 19, chron. 19, 8 October 1942, 2.
43 NAC, 'Letter from Vincent Massey to Norman Robertson,' 1.
44 Records of Department of External Affairs, NAC, quoted in 'Memorandum on Canadian Policy in Latin America,' RG 25, vol. 3081, file 4035-40, 8 October 1942, 1.
45 British Minister to Kin, 25 April 1942, EA 289-40, cited in Ogelsby, *Gringos from the Far North*, 57.
46 Records of Department of External Affairs, NAC, 'Report on Canadian Representation In and Relations With Latin American States,' RG 25, file 4035-40C, 31 March 1944, 9.
47 Ibid., 8.
48 Records of Department of External Affairs, NAC, 'Memorandum on U.S.-U.K. Rivalry in Brazil,' RG 25, file 3671-40, 13 May 1942.
49 Records of Department of External Affairs, NAC, 'Letter from Norman Robertson to Warwick Chipman, (the Canadian Ambassador, Chile),' RG 25, file 3671-40C, 17 October 1944, 1.
50 Records of Department of External Affairs, NAC, 'Letter from W. Turgeon of the Canadian Legation in Argentina, to the Secretary of State for External Affairs,' RG 25-Int-120, vol. 2855, file 1607-40, part 1, 2 May 1942, 2-3.
51 NAC, 'Memorandum on Canadian Policy in Latin America,' 1.
52 Ibid., 4.
53 Ibid., 3.
54 Ibid., 4-5.
55 Quoted in E. Miller, 'Canada and the Pan American Union,' 36.
56 Records of Department of External Affairs, NAC, 'Report on Canadian Representation In and Relations With Latin American States,' RG 25, file 3761-40C, 8 February 1943, 2.
57 Records of Department of External Affairs, NAC, 'Letter to Warwick Chipman,

Canadian Ambassador to Chile, from Canadian Under-Secretary of State for External Affairs,' RG 25, file 3671040C, 8 February 1943, 2.

58 Records of Department of External Affairs, NAC, 'Letter from Lester Glass, Canadian Commercial Attaché in Brazil, to C.H. Payne, Director, Commercial Intelligence Service,' RG 25-Int-15, vol. 301, file 3757-40, part 1, 6 April 1943, 1.

59 Ibid., 4-7.

60 Ibid., 5.

61 The caveat, of course, is that the U.S. dove from the world's leading capital exporter to the world's leading debtor nation in the 1980s.

62 NAC, 'Letter from Lester Glass,' 7.

63 For a broader discussion of this, see F. Soward and A. Macauley, *Canada and the Pan American System* (Toronto: Canadian Institute of International Affairs 1948), 27-8.

64 Records of Department of External Affairs, NAC, 'Letter from Warwick Chipman, Canadian Ambassador to Chile, to Norman Robertson, Under-Secretary of State for External Affairs,' RG 25, file 3671-40C, 3 October 1944, 1-2.

65 E. Miller, 'Canada and the Pan American Union,' 34.

66 D. Anglin, 'United States Opposition to Canadian Membership in the Pan American Union' 14.

67 Records of Department of External Affairs, NAC, 'The Development of Mexican-Canadian Relations,' RG 25, file 20-1-2-Mex-19, 2 January 1973, 1.

68 Ibid.

69 Ibid., 2.

70 Records of Department of External Affairs, NAC, 'Prime Minister's Statement in the House of Commons on Argentina,' RG 25, file 261-40, 9 March 1944, 1.

71 Ibid.

72 Records of Department of External Affairs, NAC, 'Letter from Warwick Chipman, Canadian Ambassador to Argentina, to Secretary of State for External Affairs,' RG 25, vol. 3182, file 261-40, 3 April 1946, 1.

73 For a discussion of this 'Great Contest,' see Fred Halliday, *The Making of the Second Cold War* (London: Verso 1986). For an excellent discussion of the Cold War's ideological dimensions, see Robert Cox, *Production, Power and World Order: Social Forces in the Making of History* (New York: Columbia University Press 1987).

74 Records of Department of External Affairs, NAC, 'Letter from Jules Leger, Canadian Chargé d'Affaires in Chile, to Secretary of State for External Affairs,' RG 25, vol. 3182, file 4875-40C, 28 May 1945, 1.

75 Quoted in Ibid., 1.

76 For a superb and balanced discussion of this issue see Walter LeFeber, *Inevitable Revolutions: The United States in Central America* (New York: Norton 1983) and *The American Age: United States Foreign Policy at Home and Abroad Since 1750* (New York: Norton 1989).

77 NAC, 'Letter from Jules Leger,' 3.

78 Records of Department of External Affairs, NAC, 'Letter from Mr. Robertson, Canadian High Commissioner in London, to Secretary of State for External Affairs,' RG 25, vol. 3182, file 4875-40C, 19 April 1947, 1.

79 Records of Department of External Affairs, NAC, 'Letter from H.L. Keenleyside, Canadian Ambassador to Mexico, to Secretary of State for External Affairs,' RG

25, vol. 3182, file 5682-40, 22 December 1945, 3.

80 Ibid.

81 Ibid., 1-6

82 'Canada Looks South,' *Inter-American* 5 (March 1946):42.

83 For a broader historical discussion of Canadian trade with Mexico, see J.C.M. Ogelsby, *Gringos from the Far North*, Chapter 3.

84 Ibid.

85 'Canada Moves for Trade Gains in Latin America,' *U.S. News and World Report*, 15 February 1946, 54.

86 Ibid.

87 Records of Department of External Affairs, NAC, 'Latest Developments on the Subject of Canadian Eventual Participation in the Pan American Union,' RG 25, vol. 3182, file 2226-40C, 21 March 1947, 1-8.

88 Ibid., 7.

89 See E. Miller, 'Canada and the Pan American Union,' 37.

90 Records of Department of External Affairs, NAC, 'Letter from Norman Robertson, High Commissioner for Canada in London, to the Secretary of State for External Affairs,' RG 25, vol. 3182, file 4875-40C, 19 April 1947, 1.

91 Records of Department of External Affairs, NAC, 'Letter from Felix Walter, Canadian Chargé d'Affaires in Argentina, to Secretary of State for External Affairs,' RG 25, vol. 3182, file 4875-40C, 28 February 1947, 1-2.

92 For a broader discussion of the OAS and its relation to Canadian interests, see K. McNaught, 'Canada's Pan-American Hot Seat,' *Saturday Night*, 5 August 1961, 15-17.

93 Records of Department of External Affairs, NAC, J.L. Delisle, 'Memorandum for Defence Liaison,' RG 25, file 4035-40, sub. 91, chron. 91, 3 October 1950, 3.

94 Records of Department of External Affairs, NAC, 'Letter from the Secretary of State for External Affairs to C.P. Herbert, Canadian Ambassador to Mexico,' RG 84-85-019, vol. 348, file 10117-D-40, 5 April 1949, 4.

95 Vincent Massey, 'Canada and the Inter-American System,' *Foreign Affairs* 26 (July 1948):694.

96 Ibid., 695.

97 Ibid., 697.

98 Ibid., 700.

99 Records of Department of External Affairs, NAC, 'Letter from Acting Secretary of State for External Affairs to the Canadian Ambassador to Mexico,' RG 25, 84-85-019, vol. 348, file 10117-D-40, 5 April 1949, 6.

Chapter 2: The Cold War

1 Prime Minister Louis St. Laurent, 'The Foundation of Canadian Foreign Policy in World Affairs,' (the Gray Lecture), University of Toronto, 13 January 1947, printed in J. Granatstein, ed., *Canadian Foreign Policy: Historical Readings* (Toronto: Clark Copp Pitman 1986), 28.

2 St. Laurent, Ibid., 32.

3 Ibid., 25-33.

4 Records of Department of External Affairs, NAC, J.L. Delisle, American and Far Eastern Division, 'Memorandum for Defence Liaison,' RG 25, file 4035-40, 3

October 1950, 6.

5 Experts on Colombia generally characterize Gaitan as a moderate social reformer, clearly a liberal. See, for example, Jenny Pearce, *Columbia: Inside the Labyrinth* (London: Latin American Bureau 1990), 5, 26, etc.

6 Records of Department of External Affairs, NAC, 'Letter from H. Richardson, Canadian Trade Commissioner in Bogotá, to Under Secretary of State for External Affairs,' RG 25, file 3456-33-6, 26 November 1949, 2.

7 Records of Department of External Affairs, NAC, Wiley Millyard, Canadian Trade Commissioner in Guatemala, 'A Record of Events Leading up to Present Tense Situation in Guatemala,' RG 25, vol. 3270, file 6397-40, part 1, 1 August 1950, 14.

8 See, for example, E. Burns, *Latin America: A Concise Interpretive History* (Englewood Cliffs, NJ: Prentice Hall 1986), 274-85; J. Booth, *Understanding Central America* (Boulder: Westview 1989), 38, 88; and T. Skidmore, *Modern Latin America* (Toronto: Oxford University Press 1984), 316-19.

9 Although there are a number of works on Central America, the role of the United Fruit Company is discussed in: Ralph Woodward, *Central America, a Nation Divided* (New York: Oxford 1985); Richard Fagen, *Forging Peace: the Challenge of Central America* (New York: Basil Blackwell 1987); N. Hamilton, ed., et al., *Crisis in Central America* (Boulder: Westview 1988); J. Booth, *Understanding Central America* (Boulder: Westview 1989); and other related books mentioned below.

10 Records of Department of External Affairs, NAC, Millyard, 'A Record of Events,' 12.

11 Records of Department of External Affairs, NAC, 'Communism in Latin America,' RG 25, file 50066-40, 30 December 1950, 1.

12 Ibid., 13.

13 Records of Department of External Affairs, NAC, 'Conference of Anti-Communist Labour Unions of the Western Hemisphere,' report from the Canadian Consul General, Caracas, to the Secretary of State for External Affairs, RG 25-Int-88, vol. 3214, file 5399-40, part 1, 25 November 1950, 2.

14 Records of Department of External Affairs, NAC, 'Communism in Latin America,' 13-14.

15 Ibid., 14.

16 Records of Department of External Affairs, NAC, Letter from the Canadian Ambassador to Peru to the Secretary of State for External Affairs, 'Haya de la Torre's Return to Peru,' RG 25, file 50066-40, 11 March 1961, 1-3.

17 Records of Department of External Affairs, NAC, 'Communism in Latin America,' 6.

18 Ibid., 2.

19 Ibid., 2.

20 Ibid., 9.

21 Ibid., 10.

22 Ibid., 5.

23 Records of Department of External Affairs, NAC, Letter from Secretary of State for External Affairs to the Canadian Ambassador to Argentina, 'Anti-United States Campaign in Argentina,' RG 25, file 5398-40, 27 August 1952, 2.

24 See C. Armstrong and H. Nelles, *Southern Exposure: Canadian Promoters in Latin*

America and the Caribbean 1896-1930 (Toronto: University of Toronto Press 1988).
25 Records of Department of External Affairs, NAC, 'Letter from Canadian Ambassador to the U.S. to the Secretary of State for External Affairs,' RG 25, file 6657-40-c, sub. 6, chron. 12, 23 September 1947, 1.
26 Records of Department of External Affairs, NAC, Letter from Under-Secretary of State for External Affairs to Canadian Ambassador in Washington, DC, 'Strike at La India Mines at El Limon, Nicaragua,' RG 25, file 6657-40, 31 May 1954, 1-2.
27 Canada, *Canada's Relations with the Caribbean and Central America*, Standing Committee on External Affairs and National Defence (Hull: Canadian Government Publishing Centre 1982), 21. For a broader discussion of this, see J. Rochlin, 'The Political Economy of Canadian Relations with Central America,' *North/South: Canadian Journal of Latin American and Caribbean Studies* 13 (1988):45-70; and J. Rochlin, 'Aspects of Canadian Foreign Policy Towards Central America, 1979-86,' *Journal of Canadian Studies* 22 (Winter 1988):5-26.
28 Interview, Deane Brown, Canadian Ambassador to Colombia, Bogotá, 20 May 1991.
29 Records of Department of External Affairs, NAC, Letter from Canadian Ambassador in Colombia to the Secretary of State for External Affairs, 'Some Aspects of the Economic Situation in Colombia,' RG 25, vol. 3184, file 4906-40, 19 February 1954, 1.
30 Records of Department of External Affairs, NAC, Letter from Jules Leger, Canadian Ambassador to Mexico, to the Secretary of State for External Affairs, 'Communism in the Caribbean,' RG Interim-9, vol. 3743, file 6660-40, part 2, 16 November 1953, 2.
31 Records of Department of External Affairs, NAC, Letter from H. Robinson, Office of the High Commissioner for Canada in London, to the Under-Secretary of State for External Affairs, 'Shipment of Arms to Guatemala,' RG 25, file 3671-40, 3 June 1954, 2.
32 Thomas Leonard, *Central America and the United States Policies, 1820s-1980s: A Guide to Issues and References* (Claremont: Regina Books 1985), 81.
33 John Foster Dulles, 'The Kremlin Out to Destroy the Inter-American System,' in J. Fried, ed., *Guatemala in Rebellion* (New York: Grove 1983), 78.
34 T. Leonard, *Central America and the United States Policies, 1820s-1980s: A Guide to Issues and References*, 57.
35 Walter LeFeber, *Inevitable Revolutions*, 118-19.
36 Records of Department of External Affairs, NAC, Letter from the Canadian Ambassador to Peru, B. Rogers, to the Secretary of State for External Affairs, 'First Interamerican Congress of Miners,' RG25, file 5399-40, 6 May 1957, 4.
37 Ibid., 1-2.
38 Ibid., 3.
39 Records of Department of External Affairs, NAC, Letter from R. Ford, Canadian Ambassador to Colombia, to the Secretary of State for External Affairs, 'The Place of Latin America in a World of New Power Relationships,' RG 25-Interim-9, vol. 3743, file 660-40, part 2, 29 October 1957, 2.
40 Ibid., 1.
41 Records of Department of External Affairs, NAC, Letter from the Canadian

Ambassador to Brazil to the Under-Secretary of State for External Affairs, 'Communist Diplomatic and Trade Drive in Brazil,' RG 25, file 50066-40, 14 November 1957, 2.

42 Records of Department of External Affairs, NAC, Letter from the Canadian Embassy in Brazil to the Under-Secretary of State for External Affairs, 'Suggestions by the Brazilian Embassy,' RG 25, file 37-16-1-BRA, 13 March 1964, 2.

43 Walter LeFeber, *The American Age: United States Foreign Policy at Home and Abroad Since 1750* (New York: Norton 1989), 538-9. See also Thomas Skidmore, *Modern Latin America* (New York: Oxford University Press 1989), for a further discussion of the Nixon trip and its implications.

44 Records of Department of External Affairs, NAC, Letter from American Division to Canadian Ambassador to Peru, A. Pick, RG 25, file 5399-40, 23 June 1958, 2.

45 Fred Halliday, 'International Relations: Is There a New Agenda?' *Millennium* 20 (Spring 1991):70. The same argument, although with differing implications, has been expressed in the celebrated piece by Francis Fukuyama, 'The End of History,' *The National Interest* 16 (Summer 1989):1-18.

46 Records of Department of External Affairs, NAC, Letter from Canada's Ambassador to Venezuela to the Secretary of State for External Affairs, 'Communism and Latin American Economic Ideology,' RG 25, file 50066-40, 13 June 1958, 1.

47 Ibid., 3.

48 The following is a list of major Canadian holdings in Latin America in 1958. (1) In Cuba: the Royal Bank, the Bank of Nova Scotia, Manufacturers' Life, and Sun Life. (2) In the Dominican Republic: Falconbridge, the Royal Bank, the Bank of Nova Scotia, Confederation Life, Sun Life, Crown Life, Manufacturers' Life, and the Foundation Company. (3) In Haiti: the Royal Bank, Crown Life, Manufacturers' Life, and Sun Life. (4) In Costa Rica: Western Assurance. (5) In El Salvador: Western Assurance. (6) In Guatemala: the Bank of London, the Bank of Montreal, and Western Assurance. (7) In Honduras: the Bank of London and Montreal and Western Assurance. (8) In Mexico: the Mexican Light and Power Company (this company was Canadian-registered, although Canadians controlled just 5 per cent of it), the International Power Company, Aluminum Ltd., Confederation Life, and Canadian House Insurance. (9) Nicaragua: Ventures Ltd. (10) Argentina: the Royal Bank, Sun Life, Massey-Ferguson, Hiram Walker, and Aluminum Ltd. (11) In Bolivia: the International Power Company. (12) In Brazil: Brazilian Traction, Light and Power, the Royal Bank, Massey-Ferguson, and Aluminum Ltd. (13) In Chile: Bata Shoes, Massey-Ferguson, and the Canadian Foreign Ore Development Corporation. (14) In Colombia: the Royal Bank, International Petroleum, Pato Consolidated, Confederation Life, and British American Assurance. (15) In Peru: the Royal Bank, International Petroleum, a Canadian-chartered subsidiary of Standard Oil of New Jersey, Seaoils Ltd., and a syndicate of Canadian investors who called themselves Peruvian Oils and Minerals Ltd. (16) In Uruguay: Massey-Ferguson and the Royal Bank. (17) In Venezuela: International Petroleum, the Royal Bank, Confederation Life, Sun Life, Western Assurance, Canadian Home Assurance, Aluminum Ltd., and the International Power Company. Source: Records of Department of External Affairs, NAC, 'Memorandum for the Minister,' file 2251-F-40, 14, 1-21.

49 Ibid., 4.

50 The Gordon Report, quoted in Michael Bliss, 'American Investment,' in N. Hillmer, ed., *Partners Nevertheless: Canadian-American Relations in the Twentieth Century* (Mississauga: Clark Copp Pitman 1989), 262.
51 For a discussion of this matter, see James Rochlin, 'The Evolution of Canada as an Actor in Inter-American Affairs,' *Millennium* 19 (Summer 1990):229-48.
52 Records of Department of External Affairs, NAC, 'Canada's Relations with the Inter-American System,' RG 25-Int-88, vol. 3183, file 4900-B-6-40, part 1, 6.
53 Ibid., 6.
54 Records of Department of External Affairs, NAC, R. Ford, Letter from Canadian Ambassador to Colombia to the Secretary of State for External Affairs, 'The Place of Latin America in a World of New Power Relationships,' RG Int-9, vol. 3743, file 660-40, part 2, 29 October 1957, 3.
55 See J. Ogelsby, 'Canada and the Pan American Union: Twenty Years On,' *International Journal* 14 (1969):572.
56 Walter Gordon, *A Choice for Canada: Independence or Colonial Status* (Toronto: McClelland and Stewart 1966), xix.

Chapter 3: Ideological Pluralism
1 Records of Department of External Affairs, NAC, Letter from A. Pick, Canadian Ambassador to Peru, to the Secretary of State for External Affairs, 'Meeting of U.S. Heads of Mission in Santiago, May 7-9,' RG 25, file 5670-40, 20 May 1959, 3.
2 See Ted Robert Gurr, *Why Men Rebel* (Princeton: Princeton University Press 1970).
3 Records of Department of External Affairs, NAC, Letter from the Canadian Ambassador in Peru to the Secretary of State for External Affairs, 'Race and Class in Peru,' RG Int-144, vol. 370, file 10492-40, part 1, 17 February 1959, 5.
4 See, for example, C. McClintock, 'The Prospects for Democratic Consolidation in a "Least Likely" Case: Peru,' *Comparative Politics* 21 (January 1989):127-48; R. Lee, 'Dimensions of the South American Cocaine Industry,' *Journal of Inter-American Studies and World Affairs* 30 (Summer 1988):87-103; and Alejandro Deustua, *El Narcotráfico y el Interés Nacional* (Lima: CEPEI 1987).
5 Records of Department of External Affairs, NAC, RG Int-120, vol. 2750, file 513-40, Letter from Canadian Ambassador to Cuba to the Secretary of State for External Affairs, 'Call on Cuban Permanent Representative to the United Nations,' 24 October 1957, 1.
6 Records of Department of External Affairs, NAC, Letter from the Canadian Chargé d'Affaires in Havana to the Secretary of State for External Affairs, 'Political Situation in Cuba,' RG 25, file 10224-40, 29 July 1957, 1.
7 Records of Department of External Affairs, NAC, Letter from the Canadian Ambassador in Havana to the Secretary of State for External Affairs, 'Cuban Internal Situation,' RG 25, file 10224-40, 31 March 1958, 2-3.
8 Ibid., 4.
9 Ibid., 2.
10 Records of Department of External Affairs, NAC, Letter from the Canadian Ambassador to Cuba to the Under-Secretary of State for External Affairs, 'Return of the Communist Party to Cuba,' RG 25-86-87-44, vol. 5-Int-139, file 10225-40, part 5, 19 March 1959, 4.

11 Ibid., 2.
12 Records of Department of External Affairs, NAC, Letter from the Canadian Ambassador to Cuba to the Secretary of State for External Affairs, 'Fidel Castro,' RG 86-87-414, vol. 5-Int-139, file 10224-40, part 6, 2 April 1959, 1-5.
13 Ibid., 6.
14 Ibid., 7.
15 Records of Department of External Affairs, NAC, Letter from the Canadian Ambassador to Cuba to the Secretary of State for External Affairs, 'Cuban Internal Situation to April 30,' RG 25-Int-88, vol. 3236, file 5620-40, part 1, 30 April 1959, 1-6.
16 Records of Department of External Affairs, NAC, 'Letter from H. Green, Department of External Affairs, to Canada's Ambassador to Cuba,' RG 25-Int-88, vol. 3236, file 5620-40, part 1, 25 September 1959, 1-6.
17 For a broader discussion of Canadian economic interests in Cuba, see J. Ogelsby, 'Continuing U.S. influence on Canada-Cuba Relations,' *International Perspectives*, September 1975, 35.
18 Records of Department of External Affairs, NAC, Letter from the Canadian Ambassador to Argentina to the Under-Secretary of State for External Affairs, 'Activities of Cuban Delegation during 150th Anniversary Celebrations,' RG 25, file 513-40, 3 June 1960, 2.
19 Ibid.
20 Records of Department of External Affairs, NAC, Letter from Canadian Ambassador to Argentina to the Secretary of State for External Affairs, 'Latin American Reaction to Events in Cuba,' RG 25, file 2251-F-40, 6 July 1960, 1-2.
21 Records of Department of External Affairs, NAC, Letter from C. Small, Canadian Government Trade Commissioner, to the Under-Secretary of State for External Affairs, 'China and Cuba,' RG Int-139, vol. 3122, file 4678-40, part 1, 2 August 1960, 1-2.
22 Ibid., 2.
23 Records of Department of External Affairs, NAC, 'Letter from C. Small, Canadian Government Trade Commissioner in Hong Kong, to the Under-Secretary of State for External Affairs,' RG 25, file 4678-40, 4 October 1960, 3.
24 Records of Department of External Affairs, NAC, Letter from the Canadian Ambassador to Venezuela to the Under-Secretary of State for External Affairs, 'Visit of Soviet Ambassador to Mexico,' RG 25, file 50066-40, 28 March 1961, 1.
25 Records of Department of External Affairs, NAC, Letter from the Canadian Ambassador to Brazil, 'Canada and the OAS,' RG 25, file 50066-40, 3 May 1961, 1.
26 Records of Department of External Affairs, NAC, Letter from the Canadian Ambassador to Peru to the Secretary of State for External Affairs, 'Repression of Communism and Fidelismo,' RG 25, file 50066-40, 4 February 1961, 1.
27 Records of Department of External Affairs, NAC, 'Department of External Affairs Communiqué,' RG 25, file 4889-40, 18 May 1961, 1.
28 Records of Department of External Affairs, NAC, Letter from the Canadian Ambassador to Venezuela to the Secretary of State for External Affairs, 'Venezuela, Cuba and the United States,' RG 25, file 3132-40, 9 May 1961, 3.
29 See John Saywell, *Canadian Annual Review For 1961* (Toronto: University of

Toronto Press 1961), 125.

30 Canada, Parliament, House of Commons, *Debates, 24th Parliament, 4th Session* (Ottawa: Queen's Printer 1961), 3795.

31 Ibid.

32 Ibid., 3827.

33 See J. Granatstein, *Canada 1957-67: The Years of Uncertainty and Innovation* (Toronto: McClelland and Stewart 1986), 113-16. See also David Dewitt and John Kirton, *Canada as a Principal Power* (Toronto: Wiley and Sons 1983), 61.

34 A very good summary of Canada's role in the crisis is presented by Don Munton, 'Ottawa and the Great Missile Showdown,' *Globe and Mail*, 23 October 1992.

35 Records of Department of External Affairs, NAC, Letter from the Canadian Chargé d'Affaires to Peru to the Secretary of State for External Affairs, 'Second Punta del Esta Conference,' RG-Interim-15, File 6811-40-part 1, 26 February 1962, 3.

36 Records of Department of External Affairs, NAC, Letter from the Canadian Chargé d'Affaires in Costa Rica to the Under-Secretary of State for External Affairs, 'Costa Rican Reaction to Cuban Developments,' RG 25, file 3412-40, 30 October 1962, 2.

37 John Holmes, 'Is Canada's Foreign Policy Made in Washington?' *Canadian Business*, July 1961, 56.

38 Kenneth McNaught, 'Castro's Cuba, Ottawa and Washington,' *Saturday Night*, 21 January 1961, 10.

39 Ibid.

40 Records of Department of External Affairs, NAC, A. Pick, Latin American Division, Department of External Affairs, 'Cuba,' RG 25-80-81-22, vol. 3, file 20-1-2-Cuba, part 2, 13 January 1964, 1-2.

41 Ibid., 3.

42 Ibid., 8.

43 Ibid., 8.

44 Ibid., 9-10.

45 Ibid., 10.

46 Records of Department of External Affairs, NAC, J.W. Graham, Latin American Division, Department of External Affairs, 'Canadian Policy in Cuba,' RG 25, file 20-1-2-LatAm-81, 1 March 1966, 1.

47 Ibid., 4.

48 Ibid., 4.

49 See, for example, Michael Bliss, 'American Investment,' in N. Hillmer, ed., *Partners Nevertheless: Canadian-American Relations in the Twentieth Century* (Toronto: Clark Copp Pitman 1989), 259-70.

50 Records of Department of External Affairs, NAC, External Affairs analysis, Latin American Division, J. Graham, 'Canadian Policy on the Dominican Republic,' RG 25, file 50066-44, 25 February 1966, 1.

51 Ibid., 2.

52 Ibid., 1.

53 Ibid., 2.

54 Records of Department of External Affairs, NAC, J. Graham, Latin American Division, Department of External Affairs, 'The Emergence of British and/or

American Policies which might Conflict Significantly with Canadian Policy or Interests in the Area,' RG 25, file 20-1-2-Latam-81, 3 July 1967, 1.

55 Records of Department of External Affairs, NAC, Letter from Canadian Ambassador to Colombia to the Department of External Affairs, 'Some Thoughts Regarding the Colombian Proposal re Cuba before the OAS,' RG 25, file 3062-40, 28 November 1961, 2.

56 See John Harbron, 'Canada and Latin America: Ending a Historic Isolation,' *International Perspectives* (May 1972):28.

57 Peter Plow, 'Canada and Cuba,' *Canadian Commentator*, 5, 5.

58 *Canadian Business*, 34 (May 1961):32.

59 See J. Midwinter, 'Canada Joins ECLA,' *Foreign Trade*, 18 November 1961, 28-9.

60 Records of Department of External Affairs, NAC, Department of External Affairs document, 'OAS,' RG 25, file 20-4-OAS-1, 22 June 1964, 1.

61 Ibid., 2.

62 Records of Department of External Affairs, NAC, Letter from the Canadian Ambassador to the Dominican Republic, 'OAS and Winds of Change,' RG 25, file 20-4-OAS-1, 2 December 1965, 2.

63 Quoted in James Goodsell, 'Canada Welcome in the OAS,' *Commentator* 9 (December 1965):9.

64 Ibid.

65 Ibid., 8.

66 For a further discussion of the Dominican crisis and the issue of Canada and the OAS, see D. Smith, 'Should Canada Join the Organization of American States?' *Queen's Quarterly* 73 (Spring 1966):101-14.

67 John Holmes, 'Canada and Pan America,' *Journal of Inter-American Studies and World Affairs* (April 1968):173.

68 See I. Brecher and R. Brecher, 'Canada and Latin America: The Case for Canadian Involvement,' *Queen's Quarterly* 74 (Autumn 1967):462-71.

Chapter 4: New Approaches

1 See J. Granatstein and R. Bothwell, *Pirouette: Pierre Trudeau and Canadian Foreign Policy* (Toronto: University of Toronto Press 1990), 18.

2 Mitchell Sharp, 'The Third Option,' in Hillmer, ed., *Partners Nevertheless*, 128.

3 See Peter Dobell, *Canada's Search for New Roles* (London: Royal Institute of International Affairs 1972), 115.

4 For a further discussion of this, see J. Ogelsby, 'Canada and Latin America,' in P. Lyon and T. Ismael, eds., *Canada and the Third World* (Toronto: Macmillan 1976), 181-2.

5 Granatstein and Bothwell, *Pirouette*, 34.

6 Government of Canada, *Foreign Policy for Canadians* (FPC) (Ottawa: Queen's Printer 1970), 6.

7 *FPC*, 22.

8 *FPC*, 8.

9 *FPC*, 7.

10 *FPC*, 7.

11 *FPC*, 10.

12 *FPC*, 29, 24.

13 *FPC*, 23.
14 A short list of those engaged in the mainstream debate regarding the decline of U.S. hegemony includes: Robert Gilpin, *War and Change in World Politics* (Cambridge: Cambridge University Press 1981); William Avery and David Rapkin, *America in a Changing World Political Economy* (London: Longman 1982); Robert Keohane, *After Hegemony: Cooperation and Discord in the World Political Economy* (Princeton: Princeton University Press 1984); Stephen Gill, *The Global Political Economy* (Baltimore: Johns Hopkins University Press 1988); Bruce Russet, 'America's Continuing Strengths,' *International Organization* 39 (1985); Robert Cox, *Production, Power and World Order: Social Forces in the Making of History* (New York: Columbia University Press 1987); and Fred Halliday, *The Making of the Second Cold War* (London: Verso 1986).
15 *FPC*, 9.
16 Granatstein and Bothwell, *Pirouette*, 23.
17 Ibid., 26.
18 *FPC*, 14.
19 *FPC*, 25.
20 *FPC*, 16.
21 *FPC*. See, for example, the discussion of the significance of multinational corporations on page 24.
22 *FPC*, 28.
23 Peyton Lyon, 'A Review of the Review,' *Journal of Canadian Studies* 5 (May 1970):34.
24 Peyton Lyon, 'The Trudeau Doctrine,' *International Journal* 16 (Winter 1970-1):20.
25 Quoted in Granatstein and Bothwell, *Pirouette*, 34.
26 *Latin America: Foreign Policy for Canadians* (*LA:FPC*) (Ottawa: Queen's Printer 1970), 5.
27 Ibid., 6.
28 Quoted in Granatstein and Bothwell, *Piroutte*, 51.
29 *LA:FPC*, 6.
30 Ibid.
31 Ibid., 29.
32 Ibid., 16.
33 Ibid., 17-18.
34 Ibid., 32.
35 Harald von Riekhoff, 'The Impact of Trudeau on Foreign Policy,' in J. Granatstein, *Canadian Foreign Policy: Historical Readings* (Toronto: Clark Copp Pitman 1986), 253.
36 Harald von Riekhoff, 'The Third Option in Canadian Foreign Policy,' in B. Tomlin, ed., *Canada's Foreign Policy: Analysis and Trends* (Toronto: Methuen 1978), 87.
37 For a broader discussion of this, see Dewitt and Kirton, *Canada as a Principal Power*, 71.
38 Mitchell Sharp, 'Canada-U.S. Relations: Options for the Future,' reprinted in Norman Hillmer, ed., *Partner's Nevertheless*, 126-7.
39 Ibid., 127.
40 Ibid., 128.

41 Ibid., 131.
42 Ibid.
43 Ibid., 135.
44 Ibid., 131.
45 Ibid., 137.
46 Granatstein and Bothwell, *Pirouette*, 175.
47 Ibid., 176.

Chapter 5: 1968-73
1 The countries included Venezuela, Colombia, Peru, Chile, Argentina, Brazil, Mexico, Guatemala, and Costa Rica.
2 Canada, Department of External Affairs, 'Preliminary Report of the Ministerial Mission to Latin America,' 27 October to 27 November 1968 (Ottawa: Queen's Printer 1968), 3.
3 Ibid., 26.
4 Records of Department of External Affairs, NAC, Report by P. Thibault, Latin American Division, 'Brief for the Ministerial Mission to Latin America: Views of the Canadian Embassies Concerned,' RG 25, file 20-1-2-Latam-1, 17 September 1968, 2.
5 Canada, Department of External Affairs, 'Preliminary Report of the Ministerial Mission to Latin America,' 2.
6 Canada, Department of External Affairs, 'Preliminary Report of the Ministerial Mission to Latin America,' 19.
7 Records of Department of External Affairs, NAC, 'Joint Mexico/Canada Committee,' RG 25, file 37-16-1 Mexico, 20 November 1968, 1.
8 Canada, 'Preliminary Report of the Ministerial Mission to Latin America,' 11.
9 James John Guy, 'Trudeau's Foreign Policy and Latin America,' *Revista/Review Interamericana* 7 (Spring 1977):103.
10 See, for example, Records of Department of External Affairs, NAC, 'Brief for the Ministerial Mission to Latin America: Views of the Canadian Embassies Concerned,' RG 25/80-81/022, vol. 20, file 20-1-2-Latam-1, part 2, 17 September 1968; 'Ministerial Mission to Latin America,' RG 25/80-81/022, vol. 28, file 20-1-2-Latam-1, 15 August 1968; and 'Ministerial Mission to Latin America,' RG 25-80-81/022, vol. 20, file 20-1-2-Latam-1, part 1, 6 August 1968.
11 Guy, 1977, 103.
12 Records of Department of External Affairs, NAC, 'Brief for the Ministerial Mission to Latin America,' RG 25-80-81-022, vol. 20, file 20-1-2-Int-1, part 2, 17 September 1968, 2.
13 Canada, 'Preliminary Report of the Ministerial Mission to Latin America,' 17.
14 Ibid.
15 Ibid., 11.
16 Records of Department of External Affairs, NAC, 'Ministerial Mission to Latin America,' RG 25, 20-1-2-Latam-1, vol. 34, file 28-7-3, 20 August 1968, 1.
17 Ibid., 1.
18 Ibid., 2.

19 Records of Department of External Affairs, NAC, 'Brief for the Ministerial Mission to Latin America: Views of the Canadian Embassies Concerned,' RG 25/80-81-022, vol. 20, file 20-1-2-Int-1, part 2, 17 September 1968, 2-3.

20 Records of Department of External Affairs, NAC, RG 25, file 37-16-1-Argentina, 26 September 1968, 3.

21 Ibid.

22 Canada, 'Preliminary Report of the Ministerial Mission to Latin America,' 17.

23 Records of Department of External Affairs, NAC, 'Conversations with Foreign Minister of Mexico, May 18-19 (1968),' RG 25, file 37-16-1-Mexico, Latin American Division, 4 June 1968, 1.

24 Records of Department of External Affairs, NAC, RG 25, file 20-2-2-Latam, 26 September 1969, 1-9.

25 Ibid.

26 Ibid.

27 See J. Ogelsby, 'A Trudeau Decade: Canadian-Latin American Relations 1968-78,' *Journal of Inter-American Studies and World Affairs* 21 (May 1979):198.

28 Ibid., 189.

29 John Sokol, 'Hope Lies with Economic Integration,' *Commentator* 14 (September 1970):9.

30 Records of Department of External Affairs, NAC, Latin American Division, 'Country Policy Objectives,' RG 25, file 20-1-2-Latam-17, 26 October 1970, 1-2.

31 Ibid., 1.

32 Ibid., 2.

33 Records of Department of External Affairs, NAC, 'Canada-Mexico Ministerial Committee Meeting, Ottawa, 21-22 October 1971,' RG 25, file 37-16-1-Mexico.

34 Ibid.

35 Records of Department of External Affairs, NAC, 'Invitation to PM to Visit Chile,' RG 25, file 37-16-1-Chile, 23 July 1971, 1.

36 Records of Department of External Affairs, NAC, RG 25, file 37-16-1-Chile, 15 January 1971, 1.

37 Records of Department of External Affairs, NAC, Bureau of Western Hemisphere Affairs, 'Relations with Latin America,' RG 25, file 20-1-2-Latam-17, 20 April 1971, 2.

38 Records of Department of External Affairs, NAC, Latin American Division, 'Report on the March 8, 1972 meeting of the Interdepartmental Committee on Latin America,' RG 25, file 20-1-2-Latam, 13 March 1972, 2.

39 Canada, Department of External Affairs, Monthly Bulletin, *Canada and the Organization of American States*, 13 (June 1971):200.

40 Records of Department of External Affairs, NAC, Latin American Division, 'OAS: Review of Our Association,' RG 25, file 20-4-OAS-1-10, 1 October 1973, 1.

41 Records of Department of External Affairs, NAC, Latin American Division, 'Canadian Relations with Latin America,' RG 25, file 20-1-2-Latam, 1 May 1973.

42 Galo Plaza, 'The New Latin American Nationalism,' *Toward Latin American Development* (Washington, DC: Organization of American States 1972), S9-S10.

43 Michael Lubbock, 'CALA: Catalyst in a $17 Billion Market,' *Canadian Business* 138 (May 1972):4.

44 Ibid.

45 See J. Ogelsby, 'A Trudeau Decade,' *Journal of Inter-American Studies and World Affairs* 21 (May 1979):192-3.

46 See J. Guy, 'Trudeau's Foreign Policy and Latin America,' *Revista/Review Interamericana* 7 (Spring 1977):103.

47 Records of Department of External Affairs, NAC, 'Canadian Relations with Latin America,' RG 25, file 20-1-2-Latam, 1 May 1973, 1.

48 Records of Department of External Affairs, NAC, 'Report of the March 8, 1972 meeting of the Interdepartmental Committee on Latin America,' RG 25, file 20-1-2-Latam, 13 March 1972, 2.

49 Ibid.

50 Records of Department of External Affairs, NAC, Bureau of Western Hemisphere Affairs, 'Brazil,' RG 25, file 20-1-2-Bra-19, 22 September 1972, 2.

51 Records of Department of External Affairs, NAC, 'Country Planning and Programming System Statement of Country Objectives: Mexico,' RG 25, file 20-2-1-Latam-19-10, 14 January 1973, 1.

52 Records of Department of External Affairs, NAC, Latin American Division, 'OAS: Review of Our Association,' RG 25, file 20-4-OAS-1-10, 1 October 1973.

53 Records of Department of External Affairs, NAC, 'Country Planning and Programming System Statement of Country Objectives: Argentina,' RG 25, file 20-1-2-Latam-19-10, 14 January 1973, 1.

54 Ibid., 5.

55 Records of Department of External Affairs, NAC, Latin American Division, Western Hemisphere Affairs Branch, RG 25, file 37-16-1-Chile-19, 'Chile-Situation Report,' 27 October 1972, 2.

56 Ibid., 5.

57 Records of Department of External Affairs, NAC, 'Chile,' RG 25, file 37-16-1-Chile-13, 12 January 1972, 1.

58 Records of Department of External Affairs, NAC, 'Chilean Situation Report,' 2.

59 Quoted in Graeme Mount, 'Aspects of Canadian Economic Activity in the Spanish-Speaking Caribbean,' *Laurentian University Review* 5 (November 1972):96.

60 Records of Department of External Affairs, NAC, 'Visit to Canada of President Luis Echeverría, World Power Relationships,' RG 25, file 20-1-2-Mex-28, 16 March 1973, 1.

61 Ibid., 2.

62 Records of Department of External Affairs, NAC, Latin American Division, 'Visit to Canada of President Echeverría of Mexico,' RG 25, file 20-1-2-Mex-19, 12 January 1973, 1-4.

63 Records of Department of External Affairs, NAC, 'Annual Review of the Department, Canada in Latin America and the Caribbean,' RG 25, file 20-1-2-Latam-19, 18 June 1973, 1-2.

64 Records of Department of External Affairs, NAC, Latin American Division, 'Canadian Objectives in Latin America,' RG 25, file 20-1-2-Latam, 14 June 1973, 1-6.
65 Records of Department of External Affairs, NAC, Canada's Mission at the OAS, 'OAS Background Briefing,' RG 25, file 20-1-2-Latam, 29 March 1973, 5.
66 Quoted in J. Ogelsby, 'A Trudeau Decade,' 193.
67 Records of Department of External Affairs, NAC, Canada's Mission at the OAS, 'OAS Background Briefing,' RG 25, file 20-4-OAS, 29 March 1973, 5.
68 Quoted in George Hanff, 'Decision-Making Under Pressure: A Study of the Admittance of Chilean Refugees by Canada,' *North/South: Canadian Journal of Latin American and Caribbean Studies* 4 (1979):120.
69 For a broader discussion of these issues, see G. Hanff, 'Decision-Making Under Pressure,' 120.

Chapter 6: 1974-9

1 Canadian Imperial Bank of Commerce, 'Canada and Latin America,' Toronto, issue 1, 1976.
2 Records of Department of External Affairs, NAC, Department of External Affairs, 'Canada and Latin America,' RG 25, File 20-1-2-Latam-10, 12 November 1975, 4.
3 Canadian Imperial Bank of Commerce, 'Canada and Latin America,' issue 1.
4 Records of Department of External Affairs, NAC, Canadian Ambassador to Cuba, 'Canada and Latin America,' RG 25, file 20-1-2-Latam-10-28, 31 October 1974, 1.
5 Records of Department of External Affairs, NAC, 'Prospects for Stability in Chile,' RG 25, file 37-16-1-Chile-19, 4 February 1974, 3-4.
6 For a broader discussion of the issue, see 'Cuba,' *Canadian Commerce* 136 (May 1972):7-31; J. Pearson, 'Sovereignty vs. the Multinationals: Cuba Trading With Whose Enemy?' *Business Week* 47 (6):7.
7 Records of Department of External Affairs, NAC, K.R. Higson, Latin American Division, OAS Mission, 'OAS Conference of Plenipotentiaries for the Reform of the Tiar – July 1975, San Jose, Costa Rica – Report of the Observer,' RG 25, file 20-3-OAS-1-10, 11 August 1975, 3.
8 Ibid., 4.
9 Ibid.
10 Ibid., 5.
11 Ibid.
12 Ibid., 6.
13 Ibid.
14 See also the article by Canada's ambassador to the OAS, A.Pick, in *International Perspectives*, July/August 1975.
15 See James Guy, 'Trudeau's Foreign Policy and Latin America,' *Revista/Review Interamericana* 7 (Spring 1977):104.
16 See J. Guy, 'Trudeau's Foreign Policy and Latin America,' 103.
17 Records of Department of External Affairs, NAC, Latin American Division, 'Canada and Latin America,' RG 25, file 20-1-2-Latam-19, 25 August 1975, 3.
18 Tim Draimin and Jamie Swift, 'What's Canada Doing in Brazil,' *This Magazine* 8

(January 1975):3.

19 Ibid., 5.

20 CIDA, *Annual Review*, 1974-5, 19.

21 See James Eayrs, 'Defining a New Place for Canada in the Hierarchy of World Power,' *International Perspectives*, May/June 1975, 15-24.

22 Ibid.

23 See David Dewitt and John Kirton, *Canada as a Principal Power* (Toronto: Wiley and Sons 1983).

24 CIDA, *Annual Aid Review* (Ottawa: Queen's Printer 1977), 9.

25 J. Ogelsby, 'Latin America,' *International Journal* 33 (Spring 1978):404.

26 For a wider assessment of the visit, see George Radwanski, 'Trudeau in Latin America Set Stage for Closer Relations,' *International Perspectives*, May/June 1976, 6-10.

27 Records of Department of External Affairs, NAC, 'Canada's Foreign Policy Interests in Latin America: Prime Minister's Visit to Cuba,' RG 25, file 20-1-2-Latam, March 1977, 2.

28 Radwanski, 'Trudeau in Latin America,' 9.

29 Ibid., 10.

30 See Roger Megelas, 'A New Kind of Dialogue Between Canada and Cuba,' *International Perspectives*, July/August 1976, 21.

31 Records of Department of External Affairs, NAC, 'Canadian Relations with Latin America,' RG 25, file 20-1-2-Latam-10, 1 April 1976, 1.

32 See James Guy, 'Canada and Latin America,' *World Today* 33 (October 1976):376-81.

33 Radwanski, 'Trudeau in Latin America,' 8.

34 Records of Department of External Affairs, NAC, Letter from Canadian Embassy in Brasilia to External Affairs, RG 25, file 37-16-1-Bra, 3 April 1976, 4.

35 Records of Department of External Affairs, NAC, 'Canadian Relations with Latin America,' RG 25, file 20-1-2-Latam-10, 1 April 1976, 2.

36 Records of Department of External Affairs, Latin American Division, NAC, 'Meeting to Review Canadian-Brazilian Relations,' RG 25, file 20-1-2-Bra-10, 11 May 1976, 1.

37 J. Ogelsby, 'A Trudeau Decade,' *Journal of Inter-American Studies and World Affairs* 21 (May 1979):204.

38 Records of Department of External Affairs, NAC, Canadian Delegation Report from the General Assembly Meeting of the OAS, Chile, 'Memorandum for the Minister, Canada and the Organization of American States,' RG 25, file 20-3-OAS-4-1-15, 11 August 1976, 2.

39 Ibid., 2.

40 Records of Department of External Affairs, NAC, 'Canada's Foreign Policy Interests in Latin America,' RG 25, file 20-1-2-Latam, March 1977, 5.

41 See Dewitt and Kirton, *Canada as a Principal Power*, 220-1.

42 Records of Department of External Affairs, NAC, 'Canada's Foreign Policy Interests in Latin America, Similarity of Canadian and American Interests,' RG 25, file 20-1-2-Latam-10, March 1977, 1.

43 Records of Department of External Affairs, NAC, 'Canada's Foreign Policy Interests in Latin America,' RG 25, file 20-1-2-Latam, 30 November 1977, 2-3.

44 Ibid., 7.
45 Records of Department of External Affairs, NAC, 'Canadian-Mexican Relations,' RG 25, 20-1-2-Mexico-10, 25 January 1978, 1.
46 Records of Department of External Affairs, NAC, RG 25, file 20-1-2-Mexico-17, 9 March 1978, 2.
47 Ibid.
48 *Globe and Mail*, 18 April 1978.
49 Records of Department of External Affairs, NAC, 'Canada's Foreign Policy Interests in Latin America,' 4, 17.
50 Jim Guy, 'Brazil's Pursuit of Greatness Affects Relations with Canada,' *International Perspectives*, May/June 1978, 20.
51 Records of Department of External Affairs, NAC, 'Canada Argentina Relations,' RG 25, file 20-1-2-Argen, 1 November 1978, 1.
52 Records of Department of External Affairs, NAC, 'Canada-Argentina Trade and Economic Relations,' RG 25, file 37-16-1-Arg-32, 4 August 1977, 4.
53 Ibid.
54 Ibid., 1.
55 Ibid.
56 Amnesty International estimated the number of disappeared in Argentina to range from 15,000 to 30,000. See Records of Department of External Affairs, 'Call by Argentine Ambassador,' RG 25, file 20-1-2-Argen, 2 May 1979, 2.
57 No CANDU for Argentina Committee, 'Concerns of the No CANDU for Argentina Committee,' Toronto, 14 February 1979, 1.
58 Records of Department of External Affairs, NAC, 'Memorandum for the Minister,' RG 25, file 45-Argen-13, 7 July 1979, 2.
59 NAC, 'Call by Argentine Ambassador,' 2-3.
60 See J. Granatstein and R. Bothwell, *Pirouette: Pierre Trudeau and Canadian Foreign Policy* (Toronto: University of Toronto Press 1990), 209-10.
61 See George Hanff, 'Decision-Making Under Pressure: a Study of the Admittance of Chilean Refugees by Canada,' *North/South: Canadian Journal of Latin American and Caribbean Studies* 4 (1979):123.
62 See Reg Whitaker, *Double Standard: The Secret History of Canadian Immigration* (Toronto: Lester and Orpen Dennys 1987), 254-61.
63 Hanff, 'Decision-Making Under Pressure,' 123.
64 See Granatstein and Bothwell, *Pirouette*, 271.
65 Ibid., 123.
66 *Toronto Star*, 29 November 1973.
67 *Toronto Star*, 21 January 1974.
68 Whitaker, *Double Standard*, 254-5.
69 Patricia Tomic and Ricardo Trumper, 'Canada and the Streaming of Immigrants: A Personal Account of the Chilean Case,' unpublished article, 1991, 6.
70 Records of Department of External Affairs, NAC, 'Canadian Relations with Latin America,' RG 25, file 20-1-2-Latam-10, 1 April 1976, 4.
71 Patricia Tomic and Ricardo Trumper, 'Canada and the Streaming of Immigrants,' 8.
72 Records of Department of External Affairs, NAC, 'Canada's Foreign Policy Interests in Latin America,' RG 25, file 20-1-2-Latam, 30 November 1977, 5.

73 Records of Department of External Affairs, NAC, 'Chile,' RG 25, file 20-1-2-Chile-47, 31 March 1978, 2.
74 Regarding other criticisms of Canadian policy vis-à-vis the Chilean refugees, see: *Globe and Mail*, 5 March 1974; *Ottawa Citizen*, 10 October 1974; *Montreal Star*, 22 December 1976; and *Toronto Star*, 17 December 1976.
75 Canada and Mexico cooperated, for example, in their efforts to discourage nuclear proliferation in Latin America.

Chapter 7: 1980-4

1 From the perspective of the New Right, see Jeane Kirkpatrick, 'Dictatorships and Double Standards,' *Commentary*, no. 68, November 1979; and for a critical view, see Fred Halliday, *The Making of the Second Cold War*, (London: Verso 1983).
2 Robert Cox, *Production, Power and World Order: Social Forces in the Making of History* (New York: Columbia University Press 1987), 289.
3 See Dewitt and Kirton, *Canada as a Principal Power* (Toronto: Wiley and Sons 1983), 80.
4 Canada, Standing Committee on External Affairs and National Defence, *Canada's Relations with Latin America and the Caribbean* (Ottawa: Queen's Printer 1982), 6.
5 Ibid., 7.
6 Ibid.
7 Ibid., 9.
8 Ibid., 13-14.
9 Much of the discussion in this section has been derived from J. Rochlin's works: 'Aspects of Canadian Foreign Policy Towards Central America, 1979-1986,' *Journal of Canadian Studies* 22 (Winter 1987-8):5-26; 'The Political Economy of Canadian Relations with Central America,' *North/South: Canadian Journal of Latin American and Caribbean Studies* 13 (1988):5-26; 'The Evolution of Canada as an Actor in Inter-American Affairs,' *Millennium* 19 (Summer 1990):229-48; and 'The Political Economy of Canadian Foreign Policy Towards Central America, 1979-1986,' PhD Thesis, University of Alberta, 1987.
10 Interview, Emile Martel, Director, Caribbean and Central American Relations Division, Department of External Affairs, Ottawa, 28 May 1985.
11 Canadian exports to the Caribbean were worth $954 million in 1984, almost twice as much as those to Central America. See Joe Clark, *Competitiveness and Security: Directions for Canada's International Relations* (Ottawa: Supply and Services 1985), 16.
12 See David Haglund, 'Canada and the International Politics of Oil: Latin American Source of Supply and Import Vulnerability in the 1980s,' *Canadian Journal of Political Science* 15 (June 1982):259-98.
13 For a discussion of the strategic threats from Central America to U.S. national security, see: H. Kissinger et al., U.S. National Bipartisan Commission on Central America, *Report of the President's National Bipartisan Commission on Central America* (New York: Macmillan 1984); Jeane J. Kirkpatrick, 'Dictatorships and Double Standards,' *Commentary*, no. 68, November 1979, 36; and Robert Tucker, *The Purposes of American Power: An Essay on National Security* (New York: Praeger 1981). For a critique of some of these perspectives, see Lars Schoultz, *National*

Security and United States Foreign Policy Towards Latin America (Princeton, NJ: Princeton University Press 1987).

14 Records of Department of External Affairs, NAC, 'El Salvador, Nicaragua, Cuba,' RG 25, file 20-4-OAS-1, 9 February 1982, 3.

15 Interview, Robert Miller, Director of Research of the Canadian House of Commons Standing Committee and Associate, Parliamentary Centre for Foreign Affairs and Foreign Trade, Ottawa, 31 May 1985. The Standing Committee's report is entitled *Canada's Relations with the Caribbean and Central America* (Hull: Government Publishing Centre 1982).

16 Interview, David Bickford, Department of External Affairs, Caribbean and Central American Bureau, Nicaraguan Desk, Ottawa, 29 May 1985.

17 Secretary of State for External Affairs Howard Green, 'Letter of Instructions to J.L. Delisle,' 17 June 1961, Department of External Affairs Archives, PARC 2B98-A-40, 5.

18 Ibid., 1.

19 This issue is also discussed in James Rochlin's 'Aspects of Canadian Foreign Policy Towards Central America, 1979-1986,' *Journal of Canadian Studies* 22 (Winter 1987-8):5-26.

20 *Report of the President's National Bipartisan Commission on Central America* (New York: Macmillan 1984), 5, 104.

21 Canada, *Canada's Relations with the Caribbean and Central America*, Report to the House of Commons (Ottawa: Queen's Printer 1983), 10-11.

22 Ibid., 23-4, 37.

23 *Report of the President's National Bipartisan Commission on Central America*, 109, 135, 111.

24 *Canada's Relations with the Caribbean and Central America*, 6.

25 *Report of the President's National Bipartisan Commission on Central America*, 127.

26 Ibid., 137.

27 *Canada's Relations with the Caribbean and Central America*, 34, and *Report of the President's National Bipartisan Commission on Central America*, 105.

28 *Canada's Relations with the Caribbean and Central America*, 34.

29 *Report of the President's National Bipartisan Commission on Central America*, 147-8, and *Canada's Relations with the Caribbean and Central America*, 38.

30 *Canada's Relations with the Caribbean and Central America*, 6; Interview, Meyer Brownstone, Director, OXFAM-Canada, Toronto, 21 May 1985.

31 Canada, Department of External Affairs Bulletin, *Canada and Central America*, 6 December 1985.

32 Reg Whitaker, 'The Cold War and the Myth of Liberal Internationalism: Canadian Foreign Policy Reconsidered, 1945-1953,' paper presented at the Canadian Political Science Association Annual Meeting, 8 June 1986.

33 Peter Prongos, 'Canada and the Sandinistas,' *Connexions*, September 1986.

34 *San Jose News*, 23 May 1980.

35 Quoted in Timothy Draimin, *Canada and Central America: Whither Canadian Foreign Policy?*, Toronto, CAPA, August 1983, 10.

36 *Barricada* (Nicaragua), 16 February 1983.

37 See, for example, the *Globe and Mail*, 19 October 1983 and the *Toronto Star*, 29

July 1983 and 30 July 1983.

38 A superb account of the U.S. government's alleged role in drug trafficking as part of its effort to support the Contras during the 1980s is found in Peter Scott and Jonathan Marshall, *Cocaine Politics: Drugs, Armies, and the CIA in Central America* (Berkeley, Los Angeles: University of California Press 1991).

39 Quote from speech by Hon. Allan J. MacEachen, Deputy Prime Minister and Secretary of State for External Affairs, University of Ottawa, 3 June 1983.

40 See J. Petras and P. Morley, *The United States and Canada: State Policy and Strategic Perspectives on Capital in Central America* (Kingston: Queen's University Studies in National and International Development 1984), 32-3.

41 Quote from remarks made by Prime Minister Trudeau at the Heads of Government Meeting of the Commonwealth Caribbean and Canada, St. Lucia, 20 February 1983.

42 See Edgar Dosman's 'Points of Departure: The Security Equation in Canadian-Commonwealth Relations,' *International Journal* 42 (1987): 821-47.

43 For a broader discussion, see Stephen Clarkson, *Canada and the Reagan Challenge* (Toronto: Lorimer 1985), 350.

44 Quote from remarks made by Secretary of State for External Affairs Allen J. MacEachen at a press conference in San José, Costa Rica, 3 April 1984. Text made available by the Department of External Affairs.

45 Quote from remarks made by Secretary of State for External Affairs Allan J. MacEachen at a press conference in Tegucigalpa, Honduras, 12 April 1984. Text made available by the Department of External Affairs.

46 CBC Radio, 'Morningside,' 16 April 1984.

47 CBC Radio, 'Morningside,' 13 April 1984.

48 Quote from letter by Brian Mulroney, Leader of the Opposition, 6 April 1984.

49 Interview, Ambassador Francis Filleul, Canadian Embassy in San José, Costa Rica, 30 July 1984.

50 Ibid.

51 Ibid.

52 *Globe and Mail*, 5 February 1981. MacGuigan would later claim he was misquoted, and that he had said 'quiescence' not 'acquiescence.'

53 See J. Lemco, *Canada and the Crisis in Central America* (New York: Praeger 1991), 22.

54 See Petras and Morley, *The United States and Canada.*

55 *Edmonton Journal*, 3 April 1984.

56 Claude T. Charland, 'A Canadian View of Latin America and the Caribbean,' *Canada, the United States, and Latin America: A Conference Report* (Washington, DC: The Woodrow Wilson International Center for Scholars 1984), 15.

57 *La Tribuna* (Honduras), 14 April 1984.

58 Ibid.

59 Interview, Ambassador Filleul, 30 July 1984.

60 Ibid.

61 For a discussion of the history of Central America, and Costa Rica's distinct position within it, consult Murdo J. MacLeod, *Spanish Central America: A Socio-economic History, 1520-1720* (Berkeley: University of California Press 1973); and Ralph Lee Woodward, Jr., *Central America, a Nation Divided* (New York: Oxford

University Press 1976).

62 *Globe and Mail*, 8 May 1984.
63 Maurice Dupras, 'Canada's Political and Security Interests in Latin America and the Caribbean,' *Canada, the United States and Latin America: A Conference Report*, 24.
64 *Globe and Mail*, 27 March 1984.
65 *Globe and Mail*, 25 October 1984.
66 *Globe and Mail*, 20 October 1984.
67 *Globe and Mail*, 2 November 1984.
68 For a discussion of this, see T. Draimin, 'Canadian Foreign Policy in El Salvador,' in L. North, *Bitter Grounds: Roots of Revolt in El Salvador* (Toronto: Between the Lines 1981), 99-100.
69 Canadian International Development Agency Bulletin, *Aid Disbursements to Central America* (Hull: CIDA various years).
70 Canada, Department of External Affairs Bulletin, *Canada and Central America*, 6 December 1985.
71 Julie Leonard, *Canadian Links to the Militarization of the Caribbean and Central America*, CAPA, Toronto, May 1985, 7.
72 Maurice Dupras, *The Case for the OAS* (Ottawa: Queen's Printer 1983), 1.
73 Interview, Pat Doyle, Senior Political Risk Analyst, Export Development Corporation, Ottawa, 30 May 1985; Interview, B. Khan, Manager, Special Services, International Trade and Correspondent Banking, Royal Bank, Toronto, Main Branch, 23 May 1985.
74 Interview, Pat Doyle, 23 May 1985.
75 Interview, Leslie Borbas, Canadian Association for Latin America and the Caribbean, Toronto, 23 May 1985.
76 See, for example, Cranford Pratt, 'Dominant Class Theory and Canadian Foreign Policy: The Case of the Counter-Consensus,' *International Journal* 39 (Winter 1983-4):99-135; and J. Rochlin, 'The Political Economy of Canadian Relations with Central America,' *North/South: Canadian Journal of Latin American and Caribbean Studies* 13 (1988):45-70.
77 See Latin American Working Group, 'INCO in Guatemala,' LAWG Letter, vol. 5, no. 7/8, 1979, 9-10; and *Central America Update*, 9 November 1979, 79.
78 See, for example, Latin American Working Group, 'INCO in Guatemala,' 1979, 10.
79 See, for example, Tim Draimin and M. Czerny, *Canadian Policy Toward Central America*, CAPA, Toronto, January 1985.
80 Although this has been the case throughout the 1980s, it is expressed eloquently in Liisa North, ed., *Negotiations for Peace in Central America* (Ottawa: Canadian Institute for International Peace and Security 1985), 9.
81 See, for example, Taskforce on the Churches and Corporate Responsibility, *Annual Report 1982-83*, Toronto.
82 Taskforce on the Churches and Corporate Responsibility, *Annual Report 1982-83*; *Toronto Star*, 22 July 1982; and *Financial Post*, 19 March 1983.
83 *Le Devoir*, 3 September 1986.
84 Records of Department of External Affairs, NAC, 'Record of Discussion between the Deputy Prime Minister and Secretary of State for External Affairs and the Foreign Minister of Mexico, March 16, 1983,' RG 25, file 20-1-2-Mexico, 17

March 1983, 10.
85 Cranford Pratt, 'Dominant Class Theory and Canadian Foreign Policy,' *International Journal* 39 (Winter 1983-4):133.
86 See David Haglund, 'Canada and the International Politics of Oil: Latin American Source of Supply and Import Vulnerability in the 1980s,' *Canadian Journal of Political Science* 15 (June 1982):259-98.
87 For an elaboration of this point, see Sheldon E. Gordon, 'The Canadian Government and Human Rights Abroad,' *International Perspectives*, November/December 1983, 81-90.
88 Interview, Robert Miller, Parliamentary Centre for Foreign Affairs and Foreign Trade, Ottawa, 31 May 1985.
89 Riordan Roett, for example, provides an excellent summary of the evolution of the Latin American debt crisis in 'Latin America's Debt: Problems and Prospects,' *International Journal* 43 (Summer 1988):428-45.
90 Canada, Standing Senate Committee on Foreign Affairs, *Canada, the International Financial Institutions and the Debt Problem of Developing Countries* (Ottawa: Supply and Services 1987), 11.
91 Ibid., 9.
92 Ibid., 13.
93 Ibid., 12.
94 Ibid., 26.
95 Ibid., 37.
96 Michael Kaufman, 'The Internationalization of Canadian Bank Capital,' *Journal of Canadian Studies* 19 (Winter 1984/5):70.
97 Ibid., 69.
98 Canada, Standing Committee on Foreign Affairs, *Canada, the International Financial Institutions and the Debt Problem*, 46.
99 Ibid.
100 Quoted in D.R. Murray, 'The Bilateral Road: Canada and Latin America in the 1980s,' *International Journal* 37 (Winter 1981-2):112.
101 Ibid.
102 Ibid.
103 Stephen Banker, 'The Changing OAS,' *International Perspectives*, May/June 1982, 23-6.
104 Canada, Standing Committee on Foreign Affairs, *Canada, the International Financial Institutions and the Debt Problem*, 18.
105 Ibid., 19.
106 See Sheldon Gordon, 'The Canadian Government and Human Rights Abroad,' *International Perspectives*, November/December 1983, 10.
107 Records of Department of External Affairs, NAC, 'OAS Role in Falklands Conflict,' RG 25, file 20-4-OAS-1, 29 July 1982, 6.
108 Ibid., 4.
109 Ibid., 9. Other Canadian officials appreciated the damage to the OAS incurred as a result of the Falklands conflict. See, for example, Records of Department of External Affairs, NAC, Canadian Embassy in Venezuela, 'Falklands and the OAS: Venezuelan Position,' RG 25, file 20-Venz-1-3, 30 June 1982.
110 Records of Department of External Affairs, NAC, Canadian Embassy in Brazil,

'Current Negotiations in the OAS – Brazilian Views,' RG 25, file 20-4-OAS-1, 1-4.
111 Ibid., 3.
112 Canada, Standing Committee on Foreign Affairs, *Canada*, 17-22.
113 Ibid., 17-19.
114 Ibid., 21.
115 Ibid., 27-9.
116 Charles Davies, 'Why Mexico Matters,' *Canadian Business*, November 1982, 25.
117 See D. Murray, 'The Bilateral Road,' 118.
118 Ibid., 115-16.
119 Ibid., 114.
120 Records of Department of External Affairs, NAC, 'An Overview of Canada-Mexico Relations,' RG 25, file 20-1-2-Mexico, December 1982.
121 Records of Department of External Affairs, NAC, 'Record of Discussion between the Deputy Prime Minister and Secretary of State for External Affairs and the Foreign Minister of Mexico, 16 March 1983,' RG 25, file 20-1-2-Mexico, 17 March 1983.
122 Records of Department of External Affairs, NAC, 'Canada-Mexico Bilateral Relations,' RG 25, file 20-1-2-Mexico, 11 April 1983.
123 Records of External Affairs, NAC, 'Record of a Conversation between Prime Minister Trudeau and Prime Minister Miguel de la Madrid of Mexico on Monday, May 7, 1984, at 11:30 am at 24 Sussex Drive,' RG 25, file 20-1-2 Mexico, 8 May 1984, 3.
124 Statistics Canada, 'Imports: Merchandise Trade,' cat. 65-203; and 'Exports: Merchandise Trade,' cat. 65-202, various years.
125 Ibid.
126 Data supplied by Frank Chow, Statistics Canada.
127 See G.K. Helleiner, 'Canada, the Developing Countries and the International Economy: What Next?,' *Journal of Canadian Studies* 19 (1984):16-27.
128 See Peter Wyse, *Canadian Foreign Aid in the 1970s: An Organizational Audit* (Montreal: Centre for Developing-Area Studies 1983).
129 See Fred Halliday, *The Making of the Second Cold War*.

Chapter 8: 1984-8
1 See Stephen Clarkson, *Canada and the Reagan Challenge: Crisis and Adjustment, 1981-85* (Toronto: Lorimer 1985), 336.
2 Canada, *Canadian Trade Policy for the 1980s: A Discussion Paper* (Ottawa: Department of External Affairs 1983).
3 For an excellent discussion of this matter and of CUSFTA generally, see G. Bruce Doern and Brian Tomlin, *Faith and Fear: The Free Trade Story* (Toronto: Stoddart 1991), 21.
4 See, for example, Rae Murphy, Robert Chodos, and Nick Aug der Maur, *Brian Mulroney: The Boy from Baie-Comeau* (Toronto: Lorimer 1984).
5 See D. Pollock and G. Manuge, 'The Mulroney Doctrine,' *International Perspectives*, January/February 1985, 5.
6 Canada, SSEA Joe Clark, *Competitiveness and Security: Directions for Canada's International Relations* (Ottawa: Supply and Services 1985), 1.
7 Ibid., 5.

8 Ibid., 7.

9 Ibid., 8.

10 For a discussion of this, see Gerald Epstein, 'Mortgaging America,' *World Policy Journal* 8 (Winter 1990-1):27-59; and Robert Gilpin, *The Political Economy of International Relations* (Princeton: Princeton University Press 1987).

11 Canada, *Competitiveness and Security*, 6a, 29.

12 The discussion appears on page 16a.

13 Ibid.

14 *Globe and Mail*, 26 September 1984.

15 Canada, *Competitiveness and Security*, 42.

16 Ibid., 23.

17 See Mel Hurtig, *The Betrayal of Canada* (Toronto: Stoddart 1991), 217.

18 Canada, *Competitiveness and Security*, 36.

19 Ibid., 38.

20 Ibid., 41.

21 See, for example, A. Dorscht, T. Keating, G. Legare, and J. Rious, 'Canada's International Role and Realism,' in *International Perspectives*, September/October 1986, 6-8.

22 See David Dewitt and John Kirton, *Canada as a Principal Power* (Toronto: Wiley and Sons 1983).

23 Canada, *Interdependence and Internationalism*, Report of the Special Joint Committee on Canada's International Relations (Ottawa: Queen's Printer 1986), 24.

24 Ibid.

25 Ibid., 12.

26 It is important to emphasize that the purpose here is not to provide an in-depth account of trade negotiations but to outline some of the forces behind the formation of CUSFTA – forces which were also responsible for the slide towards North American and hemispheric free trade arrangements.

27 See Pollock and Manuge, 'The Mulroney Doctrine,' *International Perspectives*, January/February 1985, 6.

28 See Doern and Tomlin, *Faith and Fear*, 67.

29 Quoted in Doern and Tomlin, *Faith and Fear*, 33.

30 See Robert Cox, *Production, Power, and World Order: Social Forces in the Making of History* (New York: Columbia University Press 1987); and S. Gill and D. Law, *The Global Political Economy* (Baltimore: Johns Hopkins University Press 1989).

31 Ibid., 22.

32 A great deal of the discussion on Central America is taken from J. Rochlin's works, cited in the bibliography.

33 For a broader discussion of this, see North, *Negotiations for Peace in Central America*, 37.

34 Canada, Department of External Affairs, Canadian Aid to Central America, May 1988.

35 See the *Toronto Star*, 28 December 1988. For an additional discussion of human rights violations in Guatemala, see the *New York Times*, 4 September 1988.

36 Although this incident is outside the scope of the period under study here, it indicates that the trend towards human rights abuses was not improving.

37 *Ottawa Citizen*, 14 December 1989.

38 Interview, Stanley Gooch, Canadian Ambassador to Central America, Canadian Embassy, San José, Costa Rica, 1 December 1987.
39 Although this comment was made in 1990, it is pertinent to the period under study here. Joe Clark, 'Notes for a Speech by the Secretary of State for External Affairs, the Right Honourable Joe Clark, to the University of Calgary on Canadian Policy to Latin America,' February 1990, 4.
40 Joe Clark, 'Statement in the House of Commons on his Central American Trip, 21-29 November 1987,' 7.
41 *Toronto Star*, 5 October 1989.
42 Canada, Department of External Affairs Bulletin, *Briefing Notes on Specific Countries in Central America*, 14 January 1986.
43 Canada, Department of External Affairs Bulletin, *Contadora*, June 1985, 12.
44 Canada, Department of External Affairs, Speech, John Graham, 14 January 1986.
45 Canadian Broadcasting Corporation, Radio, 'As it Happens,' 28 January 1985.
46 John Graham, Director General of the Department of External Affairs' Caribbean and Central American Division, Speech, Centre for International Studies, Toronto, 23 May 1986.
47 John Ferch, Former U.S. Ambassador to Honduras, quoted in *Central America Update* 6 (September/October 1986):9.
48 Prime Minister Brian Mulroney, letter to Mr. Eric Salmond, 26 September 1986, reprinted by Canada-Caribbean-Central America Policy Alternatives, November 1986.
49 'The Heeney-Merchant Report – Canada and the United States: Principles for Partnership,' reprinted in J. Granatstein, ed., *Canadian Foreign Policy: Historical Readings* (Toronto: Copp Clark Pitman 1986), 47.
50 See L. North, *Between War and Peace in Central America* (Toronto: Between the Lines 1990), 48.
51 Interview, Francis Filleul, Canadian Ambassador to Nicaragua, Costa Rica and El Salvador, San José, Costa Rica, 30 July 1984; and *Ottawa Citizen*, 6 June 1986.
52 *Globe and Mail*, 4 November 1986.
53 Quoted in *Central America Update* 8 (July/August 1986):1.
54 See L. North, *Between War and Peace in Central America*, 179.
55 Quoted in L. North, *Between War and Peace in Central America*, 165.
56 Interview, Deane Brown, Director General, South America Bureau, Department of External Affairs, 2 August 1988, Ottawa; and with Richard Gorham, Roving Ambassador for Latin America, and Permanent Observer for Canada at the Organization of American States, Ottawa, 2 August 1988.
57 Canadians for Self-Determination, *Non-intervention in Central America: Canadians for Self-Determination, Mission for Peace: A Report* (Toronto: March 1986), 9.
58 *Globe and Mail*, 12 February 1987.
59 *Toronto Star*, 31 December 1988. These figures indicate persons seeking refugee status in Canada between 1 January 1988 and 18 December 1988.
60 *Globe and Mail*, 12 February 1987.
61 *Globe and Mail*, 8 September 1988; and the *Toronto Star*, 4 December 1988.
62 Canada, Standing Committee on Foreign Affairs, *Canada, the International Financial Institutions and the Debt Problem of Developing Countries* (Ottawa: Supply and Services 1987), 39.

63 *Globe and Mail*, 17 October 1989 and 25 October 1989.
64 Roy Culpepper, *The Debt Matrix* (Ottawa: North/South Institute 1988), 3.
65 *Toronto Star*, 25 April 1989.
66 *Globe and Mail*, 19 September 1988.
67 Ibid.
68 See *Globe and Mail*, 21 May 1988.
69 *Globe and Mail*, 7 December 1987.
70 *Globe and Mail*, 4 January 1989.
71 Canada, Department of External Affairs, Latin American Division, 'Canada's Vital Interests in Latin America and How We Are Pursuing Them,' 1988.
72 Comments made by Richard Gorham, Canada's Roving Ambassador to Latin America, during a speech on 'Canada's New Policy Initiatives in Latin America,' Kelowna, 21 March 1990 (notes, 17).
73 Government of Canada, 'Canada's Vital Interests in Latin America,' 1.
74 These are figures for Canadian exports to ALADI, the Latin American Integration Association, which includes Argentina, Bolivia, Brazil, Chile, Colombia, Ecuador, Mexico, Paraguay, Peru, Uruguay, and Venezuela. From Statistics Canada, Summary of Canadian International Trade, cat. 65-001, various years.
75 Ibid.
76 William Ruiz, *A View from the South: Canadian/Latin American Links* (Ottawa: North/South Institute 1988), 3.
77 From Statistics Canada, *Canada's International Investment Position*, cat. 67-202, various years. The aggregate figure includes investments for Mexico, Jamaica, Cuba, the Dominican Republic, Haiti, Nicaragua, Guatemala, Honduras, Costa Rica, Panama, Colombia, Ecuador, Peru, Chile, Bolivia, Paraguay, Argentina, Venezuela, and Brazil.
78 Ibid.
79 Statistics Canada, *Canada's Direct Investment Abroad*, cat. 67-202, various years.
80 Ruiz, 'A View from the South,' 8.
81 Statistics Canada, *Canada's Direct Investment Abroad*.
82 For a broader discussion of this, see E. Stephens, 'Capitalist Development and Democracy in South America,' *Politics and Society* 17 (1989):281-344.
83 See P. Mirowski and S. Helper, 'Maquiladoras: Mexico's Tiger by the Tail?' *Challenge: Magazine of Economic Affairs*, May/June 1989, 24-30.

Chapter 9: NAFTA

1 See *Globe and Mail*, 11 November 1991.
2 See G. Bruce Doern and Brian Tomlin, *Faith and Fear: The Free Trade Story* (Toronto: Stoddart 1991), 67.
3 Policy Planning Staff, Department of External Affairs, *From a Trading Nation to a Nation of Traders: Towards a Second Century of Canadian Trade Development* (Ottawa: Department of External Affairs 1992), Policy Planning Staff Paper, no. 92/5, 13 March 1992, 9.
4 For a broader discussion of this, see M. Delal Baer, 'North American Free Trade,' *Foreign Affairs* 70 (Fall 1991):132-49.
5 Policy Planning Staff, Department of External Affairs, *From a Trading Nation to a*

Nation of Traders, 61.

6 Noted American economist Lester Thurow observed recently: 'You can repudiate the deal, but it wouldn't make any difference if you did.' See *Globe and Mail*, 15 January 1993.

7 *Globe and Mail*, 23 October 1991.

8 *Globe and Mail*, 30 January 1993.

9 See Ann Weston, 'From FTA to NAFTA: Whither Canadian Trade Policy towards the South?' paper presented at the Annual Conference of the Canadian Association for Latin American and Caribbean Studies, October 1992, 5.

10 *Globe and Mail*, 26 August 1992.

11 See G. Hufbauer and J. Schott, *North American Free Trade* (Washington, DC: Institute for International Economics 1992), 4.

12 For a broader discussion of this, see Michael Hart, *A North American Free Trade Agreement* (Halifax: Institute for Research on Public Policy 1990), 20; and *Globe and Mail*, 19 February 1993.

13 See Peter H. Smith, 'The Political Impact of Free Trade on Mexico,' *Journal of Inter-American Studies and World Affairs* 34 (Spring 1992):5.

14 See *North American Free Trade Agreement, Part One* (Ottawa: Supply and Services 1992), 4-8.

15 For an elaboration of this point, see G. Hufbauer and J. Schott, *North American Free Trade*, 166.

16 Standard and Poor report that General Motors posted a loss of $23 billion in 1992, with Ford posting a loss of $7.4 billion that year. These are the two greatest corporate annual losses in history. See the *Daily Courier* (Kelowna), 11 February 1993.

17 Jorge Calderon, 'The Free Trade Agreement and Mexican Agriculture,' paper presented at Migration, Human Rights and Economic Integration Conference, York University, 19 November 1992, 2.

18 See Sidney Weintraub, 'U.S.-Mexico Free Trade: Implications for the United States,' *Journal of Inter-American Studies and World Affairs* 34 (Summer 1992):35.

19 See J. Calderon, 'The Free Trade Agreement,' 1.

20 See Chapter 7, *North American Free Trade Agreement*.

21 See Chapter 3, Annex 300-B, *North American Free Trade Agreement*.

22 See Hufbauer and Schott, *North American Free Trade*, 273.

23 See, for example, Mel Hurtig, *The Betrayal of Canada* (Toronto: Stoddart 1991), Chapter 15.

24 See Chapter 6, *North American Free Trade Agreement*, especially 6-9.

25 See 'North American Free Trade Agreement,' *Backgrounder*, January 1993, 5. For a fuller discussion of financial services, see Chapter 14 of the agreement.

26 See 'North American Free Trade Agreement,' *Backgrounder*, January 1993, 6.

27 See Chapter 17, *North American Free Trade Agreement*.

28 See Sylvia Ostry, *Governments and Corporations in a Shrinking World* (New York: Council on Foreign Relations 1990).

29 See Hufbauer and Schott, *North American Free Trade*, 173.

30 *North American Free Trade Agreement*, 11-10.

31 See *Globe and Mail*, 4 November 1992.

32 See Edgar Dosman, 'Canada and Latin America: The New Look,' *International*

Journal 62 (Summer 1992):541.

33 See Patricio Meller, 'A Latin American Perspective of NAFTA,' paper presented at the Annual Conference of the Canadian Association of Latin American and Caribbean Studies, Ottawa, October 1992, 4.

34 *Globe and Mail*, 6 March 1992.

35 Statistics Canada, *Exports by Commodity*, cat. 65-004, various years.

36 *Globe and Mail*, 26 February 1993.

37 Unofficial Department of External Affairs figure, provided by William Pound, Mexican Desk, March 1993.

38 *Globe and Mail*, 16 February 1993 and 18 February 1993.

39 Canadian Labour Congress, 'Critical Notes on the Economics of the Proposed North American Free Trade Agreement,' 27 February 1992, 4.

40 *Globe and Mail*, 17 April 1992.

41 Canadian auto parts manufacturers in Mexico include Bendix Safety Restraints, Fleck, Custom Trim, the Woodbridge Group, and Sheller Globe. Recently, two Canadian companies have returned their operations to Canada, including Fleck (electronics wire harness operation) and Westinghouse Canada. See Ann Walmsley, 'Turning the Tide,' *Report on Business Magazine*, June 1992, 29. Some Canadian corporations have returned from Mexico to Canada due to the high turnover rate among employees, low productivity in Mexican plants, and so on.

42 Policy Planning Staff, Department of External Affairs, 61.

43 Ibid.

44 See *Globe and Mail*, 28 February 1992.

45 'A New Hope for the Hemisphere,' *New Perspectives Quarterly* 8 (Winter 1991):6.

46 See Michael Porter, *Canada at the Crossroads: The Reality of a New Competitive Environment* (Ottawa: Business Council on National Issues and Supply and Services 1991).

47 Canada, Department of External Affairs, 'North American Free Trade Negotiations: A Situation Report,' no. 4, April 1992, 7.

48 See Ricardo Grinspun, 'North American Free Trade Area: A Critical Economic Perspective,' Ottawa, Canadian Centre for Policy Alternatives, September 1991, 10.

49 *Globe and Mail*, 30 January 1992.

50 See Jim Stanford, *Going South: Cheap Labour as an Unfair Subsidy in North American Free Trade* (Ottawa: Canadian Centre for Policy Alternatives 1991), 1.

51 It should be emphasized, however, that Canadian exports to the U.S. have risen 28 per cent between the period 1987 and 1991, and that a record level of exports was destined for the U.S. in 1992. See *Globe and Mail*, 18 December 1992.

52 See Hufbauer and Schott, *North American Free Trade*, 60.

53 See *Globe and Mail*, 22 January 1993.

54 Maxwell Cameron and Laura Macdonald, Rapporteurs' Report, 'Consultative Session on a North American Free Trade Agreement,' FOCAL, North-South Institute, Ottawa, 28 September 1990, 7.

55 Sidney Weintraub, 'The Canadian Stake in U.S.-Mexico Free Trade Negotiations,' *Business in the Contemporary World*, Autumn 1990, 128.

56 See Ann Weston and Ada Piazze-McMahon, 'Free Trade with a Human Face? The Social Dimensions of CUSFTA and the Proposed NAFTA,' unpublished article,

May 1992, 15.

57 Statistics Canada, 'Canada's and Mexico's Trade Position in the United States Market,' *Summary of Canadian International Trade*, cat. 65-001, December 1991, xiii.

58 *Globe and Mail*, 15 January 1992.

59 Canadian Centre for Policy Alternatives, 'North American Free Trade Agreement, Draft Text February 21, 1992, Preliminary Briefing Notes,' Ottawa, 6 April 1992, 47.

60 See *Globe and Mail*, 25 November 1992.

61 Statistics Canada, 'Canada's and Mexico's Trade Position in the United States Market,' xiii.

62 See *Globe and Mail*, 26 October 1991, 27 October 1991, and 28 February 1992.

63 For an in-depth discussion of this, see Albert Berry, 'Small and Medium Business Under Trade Liberalization: Canadian and Latin American Experiences and Concerns,' paper presented at the Colloquium for Trade Liberalization Arrangements in the Western Hemisphere: CUSFTA, NAFTA, and Other Sub-Regional Integration Schemes, University of Toronto, 31 May to 2 June 1992.

64 *Globe and Mail*, 16 June 1992.

65 See *North American Free Trade Agreement*, 10-24.

66 Obviously, the level of the Canadian dollar is a related concern.

67 See 'A New Hope for the Hemisphere?' *New Perspectives Quarterly* 8 (Winter 1991):4-9.

68 Canada, House of Commons Standing Committee on External Affairs and International Trade, *North American Free Trade* (Ottawa: Supply and Services 1991), 24.

69 See *Globe and Mail*, 19 February 1993.

70 *Globe and Mail*, 2 March 1993.

71 Quote by Robert Zoelick, Under-Secretary for Economic and Agricultural Affairs, quoted in E. Dosman, 'Canada and Latin America: The New Look,' *International Journal* 62 (Summer 1992):541.

72 *Globe and Mail*, 7 January 1993.

73 Gerald Epstein, 'Mortgaging America,' *World Policy Journal* 8 (Winter 1990-1):33.

74 See also Canadian Labour Congress, 'Critical Notes on the Economics of the Proposed North American Free Trade Agreement,' 27 February 1992, 7.

75 See International Development Bank, 'Support to the Process of Hemispheric Trade Liberalization: Summary of the Second Colloquium on Global Issues,' Washington, DC, 30 April to 1 May 1992.

76 Social polarization may occur as a result of declining real wages for unskilled labour and a loss of manufacturing jobs as opposed to the retention of relatively high wages, especially by those in the knowledge-intensive sector. See Hufbauer and Schott, *North American Free Trade*, 107-12.

77 See M. Hart, *A North American Free Trade Agreement*, 40.

78 See J. Teichman, 'The Political Economy of Trade Liberalization and Export Promotion in Mexico,' paper presented at the Annual Meeting of the Canadian Association for Latin American and Caribbean Studies, Laval University, 31 October to 3 November 1991, 15.

79 *Globe and Mail*, 30 January 1993.

80 Statistics Canada, 'Trade With Mexico,' *Summary of Canadian International Trade,* cat. 65-001, January 1991, xi-xxi.
81 The report from *El Financiero* was carried in the *Globe and Mail,* 8 May 1992.
82 *Globe and Mail,* 28 February 1992.
83 Ibid.
84 See, for example, Tony Clarke, 'Alternative Proposals for Development and Trade,' *Action Canada Network Dossier,* November 1991, no. 34, 9-15; Ricardo Grinspun, 'North American Free Trade: A Critical Economic Perspective,' 10; Canadian Labour Congress, 'Critical Notes on the Economics of the Proposed North American Free Trade Agreement,' 7; Max Cameron and Ricardo Grinspun, eds., *Critical Perspectives on North American Integration* (New York: St. Martin's 1992).
85 See John Stopford and Susan Strange, *Rival States, Rival Firms: Competition for World Market Shares* (New York: University of Cambridge Press 1992).
86 See B. Wilkinson, 'Trade Liberalization, the Market Ideology, and Morality: Have We a Sustainable System?' in Cameron and Grinspun, eds., *Critical Perspectives on North American Integration.*
87 Tony Clarke, 'Alternative Proposals for Development and Trade,' 13.
88 Wilkinson, 'Trade Liberalization, the Market Ideology, and Morality.'
89 M. Hurtig, *The Betrayal of Canada.*
90 See Tony Clarke, 'Alternative Proposals for Development and Trade.'
91 See, for example, Ostry, *Governments and Corporations in a Shrinking World*; and Stopford and Strange, *Rival States, Rival Firms.*
92 The Department of External Affairs has already received advice to work for stronger state promotion of trade relations with Latin America. See R. Gorham, 'Long Term Strategy for Latin America,' DEA, Latin American Division, 24 April 1989. See Sylvia Ostry, *Governments and Corporations in a Shrinking World,* for an excellent discussion of state-business relations.
93 For an excellent and broader discussion of this, see Ann Weston, 'Free Trade with a Human Face? The Social Dimensions of CUSFTA and the Proposed NAFTA,' paper presented at the Colloquium for Trade Liberalization Arrangements in the Western Hemisphere: CUSFTA, NAFTA, and other Sub-Regional Integration Schemes, University of Toronto, 31 May to 2 June 1992, 5.
94 Robert Reich, *The Work of Nations: Preparing Ourselves for 21st-Century Capitalism* (New York: Knopf 1991), 154.
95 See Reich, *The Work of Nations,* 163.
96 The shape of the parallel accords was unclear at the time of this writing.
97 See Edward Broadbent, 'Human Rights and the North American Free Trade Agreement,' speech given to the B'nai B'rith Hillel Foundation, 23 March 1992. Text provided by the International Centre for Human Rights and Democratic Development, 7-11.
98 Interview, Jorge Alvarez, Counsellor, Embassy of Mexico, Ottawa, 19 June 1992.
99 *Globe and Mail,* 16 June 1992.
100 President Carlos Salinas de Gortari, 'Social Liberalism: Our Path,' *Mexico: On the Record* 1:2.

101 President Carlos Salinas de Gortari, 'Social Liberalism,' 3.
102 Interview with Michael Wilson by John Harbron, *North-South: The Magazine of the Americas* 1 (October-November 1991):32.
103 A good discussion of the Enterprise for the Americas Initiative is provided by Joel Paul, 'The New Inter-American Development Policy,' paper presented at the annual conference of the Canadian Association for Latin American and Caribbean Studies, 23 October 1993.
104 U.S. Government, Washington, DC, Press Release, 'President George Bush, Remarks Announcing the EAI,' 27 June 1990.
105 These statistics are from Richard Harris, 'Free Trade in the Americas: Some New Estimates of the Economic Impact,' paper presented at the Colloquium for Trade Liberalization Arrangements in the Western Hemisphere: CUSFTA, NAFTA, and other Sub-Regional Schemes, University of Toronto, 31 May to 2 June 1992, 12.
106 A. Berry, L. Waverman, and A. Weston, 'Canada and the Enterprise for the Americas Initiative: A Case of Reluctant Regionalism,' *Business Economics* 27 (April 1992):31.
107 See Abraham Lowenthal, 'Latin America: Ready for Partnership?' *Foreign Affairs* 72 (1993):90.
108 *Globe and Mail*, 16 May 1992.
109 Stanley Gooch, Assistant Deputy Minister, Latin American Division, Department of External Affairs, 'Canada and Latin American Integration,' paper presented at the Colloquium for Trade Liberalization Arrangements in the Western Hemisphere, University of Toronto, 31 May to 2 June 1992, 2.
110 See Robert Cox, *Production, Power, and World Order: Social Forces in the Making of History* (New York: Columbia University Press 1987); and S. Gill and D. Law, *The Global Political Economy* (Baltimore: Johns Hopkins University Press 1989).
111 See Fred Bergsten, 'The Primacy of Economics,' *Foreign Policy*, no. 87 (Summer 1992):3-24.

Chapter 10: Canada and the OAS

1 Quoted in Richard Gorham, former Canadian Ambassador to the Organization of American States, Department of External Affairs, Discussion Paper, 'Some Preliminary Thoughts About Latin America and the Organization of American States,' 11 May 1988, 6.
2 See Richard Gorham, 'Canada and the OAS: A commentary,' in M. Dickerson and S. Randall, eds., *Canada and Latin America: Issues to the Year 200 and Beyond* (Calgary: University of Calgary Press 1991), 165.
3 See Edgar Dosman, 'Canada and Latin America: The New Look,' *International Journal* 47 (Summer 1992):529-54.
4 Department of External Affairs, 'Notes for Remarks by the Right Honourable Joe Clark, SSEA, at the Meeting of the General Assembly of the Organization of American States,' Washington, DC, 13 November 1989, 1.
5 Ibid., 3.
6 See Liberal party of Canada, 'Government Receives Failing Grade on Liberal Report Card on Canada and the OAS 1st Anniversary,' *Communiqué,* 8 January 1991. In a number of publications, the Canada-Caribbean-Central America Policy Alternatives group also criticized the Canadian position on Panama.

7 Alfred Pick, Letter to the Editor, *Globe and Mail*, 3 November 1989.

8 See Richard Gorham, Canada's Roving Ambassador to Latin America and former Permanent Observer at the OAS, Notes for Remarks by Ambassador R.V. Gorham at a Luncheon Meeting of the Rotary Club of Woodstock, Ontario, 23 April 1990, 'The Organization of American States: What is It and Why did Canada Join?,' 15.

9 Department of External Affairs, *Canada's First Year in the Organization of American States: Implementing the Strategy for Latin America* (Ottawa: Department of External Affairs 1991).

10 See David Mackenzie, 'The World's Greatest Joiner: Canada and the Organization of American States,' *British Journal of Canadian Studies* 6 (1991):215.

11 See *Toronto Star*, 26 July 1991, and, for a broader discussion, Canada-Caribbean-Central America Policy Alternatives (CAPA), 'Report on Canada's Second Year in the OAS,' Toronto, April 1992, 2.

12 CAPA, 'Report on Canada's Second Year,' 6.

13 Ibid., 3-4.

14 Secretary of State for External Affairs Barbara McDougall, Department of External Affairs News Release, no. 216, 'McDougall Attends OAS Meeting on Haiti,' 1 October 1992.

15 Secretary of State for External Affairs Barbara McDougall, Department of External Affairs News Release, 'Notes for a Statement by the Honourable Barbara McDougall, Secretary of State for External Affairs, at OAS Headquarters: Crisis in Peru,' Washington, DC, 13 April 1992, 1.

16 Department of External Affairs, Press Release on Peruvian situation, received by author 12 March 1993.

17 See Abraham Lowenthal, 'Latin America: Ready for Partnership?' *Foreign Affairs* 72 (1993):84.

18 CAPA, 'Report on Canada's Second Year,' 18.

19 Ibid., 20.

20 See Department of External Affairs, *Canada's First Year in the Organization of American States*, 2-3.

21 Permanent Mission of Canada to the Organization of American States, 'Notes for an Address by H.E. Jean-Paul Hubert, Ambassador, Permanent Representative of Canada to the Organization of American States, to the Annual Conference of the Canadian Council on International Law,' 18 October 1991, 12.

22 See Abraham Lowenthal, 'Latin America,' 83 for a discussion of low intensity democracy.

23 See Robert W. Cox, 'Social Forces, States and World Orders: Beyond International Relations Theory,' in Robert Keohane, ed., *Neorealism and Its Critics* (New York: Columbia University Press 1986), 219.

24 Ibid.

25 Cox, 'Social Forces, States and World Orders,' 219. He was referring to hegemony in general, not to hegemony in the inter-American context specifically.

Chapter 11: Security and Conflict Resolution

1 See Robert Pastor, 'The Latin American Option,' *Foreign Policy*, no. 88 (Fall 1992):112.

2 See Robert Pastor, 'The Latin American Option,' 114.

3 See Hal Kelpak, *Canada and Latin America: Strategic Issues for the 1990s* (Ottawa: Department of National Defence 1990).
4 For an excellent discussion regarding the philosophical underpinnings of redefining gender and international relations, see V. Spike Peterson, 'Transgressing Boundaries: Theories of Knowledge, Gender and International Relations,' *Millennium* 21 (Summer 1992):183-208.
5 See, for example, R. Grant and K. Newland, eds., *Gender and International Relations* (Bloomington: Indiana University Press 1991); and C. Enloe, *Bananas, Beaches and Bases: Making Feminist Sense of International Politics* (London: Pandora 1989).
6 Canada, House of Commons Special Committee on the Peace Process in Central America, *Supporting the Five: Canada and the Central American Peace Process* (Ottawa: Supply and Services 1988).
7 H.P. Klepak, *Canada and Latin America: Strategic Issues for the 1990s* (Ottawa: Department of National Defence 1990), Extra Mural Paper no. 54, 183.
8 For a broader discussion of this, see L. North, ed., *Between War and Peace in Central America: Choices for Canada* (Toronto: Between the Lines 1990), 186-7.
9 See, for example, North, *Between War and Peace in Central America*, 217.
10 Secretary of State for External Affairs Joe Clark, 'Notes for a Speech by Secretary of State for External Affairs, the Right Honourable Joe Clark, to the University of Calgary on Canadian Policy to Latin America,' February 1990, 4.
11 See J. Rochlin, 'The Evolution of Canada as an Actor in Inter-American Affairs,' *Millennium* 19 (Summer 1990):239.
12 Pastor, 'The Latin American Option,' 115.
13 Much of this discussion is extracted from J. Rochlin, 'Canada and the Andean Drug Wars: Issues for the 1990s,' in J. Haar and E. Dosman, eds., *Canada's New Role in the Americas* (Miami: Transaction 1992).
14 See P. Andreas, et al., 'Dead-End Drug Wars,' *Foreign Affairs*, no. 85 (Winter 1991-2):106-28.
15 See W. Morales, 'Militarizing the Drug War in Bolivia,' *Third World Quarterly* 13, (1992):363.
16 See P. Andreas and K. Sharpe, 'Cocaine Politics in the Andes,' *Current History*, February 1992, 79.
17 See C. McClintock, 'The War on Drugs: The Peruvian Case,' *Journal of Inter-American Studies and World Affairs* 30 (Summer 1988):128.
18 Ibid.
19 Interviews with peasants who grow coca in Peru's Huallaga Valley, June 1993.
20 Canada, Royal Canadian Mounted Police, *National Drug Intelligence Estimate: With Trend Indicators Through 1992* (Ottawa: Supply and Services 1991), 29.
21 The price of Peruvian coffee has dropped from $153.43 (U.S.) for 100 kg in 1989 to $65.17 in 1992. Similarly, production costs for other legitimate crops, such as corn, have risen dramatically, thereby rendering them less economically viable. See Andean Commission of Jurists, *Drug Trafficking Update*, no. 29 and no. 30, 7 September 1992 and 13 October 1992.
22 Guillermo Rochabrun Silva, 'Crisis, Democracy and the Left in Peru,' *Latin American Perspectives* 15 (1988):88.
23 R.B. Craig, 'Illicit Drug Traffick,' *Journal of Inter-American Studies and World Affairs*

29 (Summer 1987):11.
24 *Globe and Mail*, 12 September 1990.
25 *Latin American Weekly Report*, 28 February 1991.
26 *Latin American Weekly Report*, 27 February 1992.
27 Carlos Paredes and Jeffrey Sachs, *Estabilizatión y Crecimiento en El Peru* (Lima: Grade/Brookings Institution 1990), 3.
28 'Cifras de la Pobreza,' in *La Razón*, La Paz, Bolivia, 20 June 1993.
29 *Globe and Mail*, 12 September 1990.
30 For a broader discussion of the safety valve component, see *El Impacto del Capital Financiero del Narcotráfico en Desarrollo in America Latina* (La Paz, Bolivia: Centro para el Estudio de las Relaciones Internacionales y el Desarrollo 1991).
31 See Andreas and Sharpe, 'Cocaine Politics in the Andes,' 113.
32 Alejandro Deustua, *El Narcotráfico y el Interés Nacional* (Lima: CEPEI 1987), 38.
33 Andreas and Sharpe, 'Cocaine Politics in the Andes,' 113.
34 *Latin American Weekly Report*, 24 January 1991.
35 *El Comercio*, Lima, 28 July 1990.
36 Interview with peasants who grow coca in Peru's Huallaga Valley, June 1993. The U.S. continues to insist upon the ability of Spike to eradicate coca production. A spokesperson at the U.S. military base in the Huallaga Valley indicated to me that 'only radicals like Greenpeace' oppose Spike for environmental reasons (Interview, Huallaga Valley, 19 July 1990). Environmental damage caused by Spike appears to be a real possibility. In 1988, the Eli Lilly Company, a producer of Spike, refused to accept any liability for damages to the people or ecology of the Huallaga Valley region if the defoliant was used. There have also been reports of U.S. biological weapons being used against coca production. See *Latin American Weekly Report*, 5 March 1992.
37 Andean Commission of Jurists, *Andean Newsletter*, no. 70, Lima, 21 September 1992.
38 See *Latin American Weekly Report*, WR-92-43, 5 November 1992.
39 Abraham Lowenthal, 'Latin America: Ready for Partnership?' *Foreign Affairs* 72 (1993):83.
40 *Página Libre*, Lima, 14 July 1990.
41 Washington Office on Latin America, 'Going to the Source: Results and Prospects for the War on Drugs in the Andes,' 7 June 1991.
42 *Página Libre*, 13 July 1990.
43 See *Latin American Weekly Report*, 27 February 1992.
44 See A. Labrousse, 'Dependence on Drugs: Unemployment, Migration and an Alternative Path,' *International Labour Review* 129 (1990):346-8; and Craig, 'Illicit Drug Traffick.'
45 See United Nations Drug Control Program (UNDCP), La Paz, Bolivia, 'Money Laundering in Bolivia: A First Analysis,' internal document no. 7/93, June 1993.
46 See Andreas and Sharpe, 'Cocaine Politics in the Andes,' 113; and Hernando José Gomez, 'El Impacto del Narcotráfico en el Desarrollo de America Latina: Aspectos Económicos,' in *El Impacto de Capital Financiero del Narcotráfico de America Latina*, 292. 1993 estimates from UNDCP, La Paz, 'Money Laundering in Bolivia.'
47 See Andreas and Sharpe, 'Cocaine Politics in the Andes,' 113; and Hernando José Gomez, 'El Impacto del Narcotráfico en el Desarrollo de America Latina: Aspectos

Económicos,' in *El Impacto de Capital Financiero del Narcotráfico de America Latina*, 292.

48 W. Morales, 'Militarizing the Drug War in Bolivia,' *Third World Quarterly* 13 (1992):354.

49 See Morales, 'Militarizing the Drug War in Bolivia,' 363.

50 See Andean Commission of Jurists, *Drug Traficking Update*, no. 29, Lima, 7 September 1992.

51 See Andreas and Sharpe, 'Cocaine Politics in the Andes.'

52 Bruce Bagley, 'Colombia y La Guerra Contra Las Drogas,' in J. Tokatlian and B. Bagley, eds., *Economía y Política del Narcotráfico*, 177.

53 Washington Office on Latin America, *Colombia Besieged: Political Violence and State Responsibility* (Washington: Washington Office on Latin America 1989), 10.

54 *Colombia Estadística: 1988*, vol. 2 (Bogotá: Departamento Administrativa Nacional de Estadísticas 1988), 797-812.

55 Americas Watch, *The Central-Americanization of Colombia? Human Rights and the Peace Process* (New York: Americas Watch 1986), 10-11.

56 J. Tokatlian, 'National Security and Dugs: Their Impact on Colombian-U.S. Relations,' *Journal of Interamerican Studies and World Affairs* 30 (Spring 1988):149; and Marc Chernick, 'The Drug War,' *NACLA Report on the Americas* 23 (April 1990):33.

57 See *Seizing Opportunities*, University of San Diego, Latin American Politics Department, 1992, 29.

58 Interview, Alfonso Cuellar Araujo, Editor, Páginas Internacional, *El Tiempo* (Bogotá), 24 July 1990.

59 Interview, General Miquel Maza, Jefe, Departamento Administrativo de Seguridad (DAS), Bogotá, 25 July 1990.

60 The conservative view of narcotraffickers is well known, and there is much literature on this point. A recent discussion appears in *Universal* (Venezuela), 11 August 1990.

61 See Jenny Pearce, 'The People's War,' *NACLA Report on the Americas* 23 (April 1990):13.

62 Bruce Bagley, 'Colombia y La Guerra Contra Las Drogas,' 177.

63 The U.N. has issued reports linking the Colombian armed forces with assassinations of adversaries and with other human rights abuses. See *New York Times*, 3 March 1991.

64 Americas Watch, *Informe Sobre Derechos Humanos En Colombia* (Bogotá: Universidad de Los Andes 1989), 50-5.

65 Andean Commission of Jurists, *Colombia: El Derecho a la Justicia* (Lima: Andean Commission of Jurists 1988), 84-5.

66 See *Latin American Weekly Report*, 5 December 1991 and 12 December 1991.

67 'Heroin is Colombia's New Export,' *Miami Herald*, 21 June 1993.

68 *Latin American Weekly Report*, 5 March 1992.

69 *Latin American Weekly Report*, WR-93-11, 18 March 1993.

70 *Latin American Weekly Report*, 5 November 1992.

71 See *Globe and Mail*, 9 November 1992.

72 Ibid.

73 Article by Daniel Bland, for the Andean Commission of Jurists (Toronto), *Globe*

and Mail, 16 March 1993. About 28,000 Colombians were murdered in 1992.

74 See Andreas and Sharpe, 'Cocaine Politics in the Andes,' 107.

75 See Morales, 'Militarizing the Drug War in Bolivia,' 365.

76 Nobel prize winner Milton Friedman, among others, has suggested such an approach. See *Drug Trafficking Update*, 6 July 1992.

77 Health and Welfare Canada, *National Alcohol and other Drugs Survey* (Ottawa: Supply and Services 1990), ix. For an excellent discussion of domestic drug issues in Canada, see 'Drug Issues: A Canadian Perspective,' *Journal of Drug Issues* 21 (Winter 1991):1-197.

78 This figure is from Ian Head, Chair of the Metro Toronto Drug Action Committee, *Globe and Mail*, 19 February 1992.

79 Canada, Royal Canadian Mounted Police, *National Drug Intelligence Estimate 1990: With Trend Indicators Through 1992* (Ottawa: Supply and Services 1991), 128.

80 Ibid., 134.

81 Ibid., 26-8.

82 Canada, RCMP, 'Drugs Seized in Canada, 1986-91'; and Addiction Research Foundation, Toronto, 'Canadian Profile, Alcohol and Other Drugs 1992: Annual Sourcebook,' 167.

83 Canada, RCMP, *National Drug Intelligence Estimate*, 34.

84 See H.P. Klepak, *Canada and Latin America*, 219.

85 Interview, General Miguel Maza, Jefe, Departamento Administrativo de Seguridad (DAS), Bogotá, 25 July 1990; and Department of External Affairs, Latin American Division, official, 13 March 1992.

86 'Showing Their Teeth: Concern in South America regarding Increased U.S. Intervention,' *Semana*, no. 425, 26 June 1990, 36-53.

87 Interview, confidential source, Department of External Affairs, Latin American Division, 13 March 1992.

88 Interview, various officials, Canadian Embassy, Bogotá, 31 July 1990.

89 Interview, Anne Charles, Canadian Ambassador to Peru, Lima, 13 July 1990.

90 Interview, Department of External Affairs, Latin American Division, confidential, 13 March 1992.

91 Interview, Ambassador Deane Brown, Bogotá, Colombia, 20 May 1991.

92 Department of External Affairs, 'Fact Sheet Peru,' 1990.

93 Ibid.

94 Organization of American States, CICAD Information Document, Washington, DC, 23 May 1990, 3.

95 Interview, confidential, Department of External Affairs, Latin American Division, 13 March 1992.

96 *Latin American Weekly Report*, 11 March 1993, WR-93-10.

97 For a cursory discussion of the role of NORAD in drug interdiction, see the *Daily Courier* (Kelowna), 12 September 1990.

98 Statistics Canada, International Trade Division, 'Domestic Exports by Commodity and Country of Destination,' 1989.

99 Departamento Administrativo de Seguridad (DAS), Bogotá, Colombia, Press Release (Communicada de Prensa), 7 June 1990, 2-3.

100 Interview, Irving Tragen, Executive Secretary of CICAD, OAS, 6 September 1990.
101 Interview, Ambassador Anne Charles, Canadian Embassy, Lima, Peru, 13 July 1990.
102 Employment and Immigration Canada, *Immigration 1990* and *Immigration 1991*, Ottawa.
103 The January-September statistics present annual comparisons and are the latest data available at the time of writing.
104 Employment and Immigration Canada, *Immigration 1990* and *Immigration 1991*.
105 See Department of External Affairs, *Canada's First Year in the Organization of American States Implementing the Strategy for Latin America* (Ottawa: Department of External Affairs 1991).

Conclusion

1 See Robert Cox, *Production, Power and World Order: Social Forces and the Making of History* (New York: Columbia University Press 1987), 7.
2 Abraham Lowenthal, 'Latin America: Ready for Partnership?' *Foreign Affairs* 72 (1993):84.
3 For an excellent discussion of Canadian NGOs and their effect on Canadian foreign policy, see Laura Macdonald, 'Further Directions for Canadian NGOs in Latin America,' in J. Haar and E. Dosman, eds., *Canada's New Role in the Hemisphere* (Miami: Transaction 1993).

Bibliography

Armstrong, C. and H. Nelles. *Southern Exposure: Canadian Promoters in Latin America and the Caribbean 1896-1930*. Toronto: University of Toronto Press 1988

Brecher, I. and R. Brecher. 'Canada and Latin America: The Case for Canadian Involvement,' *Queen's Quarterly* 74 (Autumn 1967):462-71

Burns, E. Bradford. *Latin America: A Concise Interpretive History*. Englewood Cliffs, NJ: Prentice-Hall 1986

Canada. Standing Committee on External Affairs and National Defence. *Canada's Relations with the Caribbean and Central America*. Hull: Canadian Government Publishing Centre 1982

Canada. Standing Committee on Foreign Affairs. *Canada, the International Financial Institutions and the Debt Problem of Developing Countries*. Ottawa: Supply and Services 1987

–. *Foreign Policy for Canadians*. Ottawa: Queen's Printer 1970

–. *Report of the Special Joint Committee on Canada's International Relations*. Ottawa: Queen's Printer 1986

Canada. House of Commons Special Committee on the Peace Process in Canada-Caribbean-Central American Policy Alternatives (CAPA). *Report on Canada's Second Year in the OAS*. Toronto: CAPA 1992

Canada. House of Commons Special Committee on the Peace Process in Central America. *Supporting the Five: Canada and the Central American Peace Process*. Ottawa: Supply and Services 1988

Clark, Joe. *Competitiveness and Security: Directions for Canada's International Relations*. Ottawa: Supply and Services 1985

Clarkson, Stephen. *Canada and the Reagan Challenge: Crisis and Adjustment, 1981-85*. Toronto: Lorimer 1985

Cox, Robert. *Production, Power and World Order: Social Forces in the Making of History*. New York: Columbia University Press 1987

Dewitt, David and John Kirton. *Canada as a Principal Power*. Toronto: Wiley and Sons 1983

Dickerson, Mark and Stephen Randall. *Canada and Latin America: Issues to the Year 2000 and Beyond*. Calgary: University of Calgary Press 1991

Dobell, Peter. *Canada's Search for New Roles*. London: Royal Institute of International Affairs 1992

Doern, Bruce and Brian Tomlin. *Faith and Fear: The Free Trade Story*. Toronto: Stoddart 1991

Dupras, Maurice. *The Case for the OAS*. Ottawa: Queen's Printer 1983

Eayrs, James. 'Defining a New Place for Canada in the Hierarchy of World Power,' *International Perspectives*, May/June 1975, 15-24

Fukuyama, Francis. 'The End of History,' *The National Interest* 16 (Summer 1989):1-18

Gill, Stephen and D. Law. *The Global Political Economy*. Baltimore: Johns Hopkins University Press 1989

Gordon, Walter. *A Choice for Canada: Independence or Colonial Status*. Toronto: McClelland and Stewart 1966

Granatstein, J.L. *Canada 1957-1967: The Years of Uncertainty and Innovation*. Toronto: McClelland and Stewart 1986

–. *Canadian Foreign Policy: Historical Readings*. Toronto: Clark Copp Pitman 1986

Granatstein, J.L., and Robert Bothwell. *Pirouette: Pierre Trudeau and Canadian Foreign Policy*. Toronto: University of Toronto Press 1990

Gurr, Ted Robert. *Why Men Rebel*. Princeton: Princeton University Press 1970

Haglund, David. 'Canada and the International Politics of Oil: Latin American Source of Supply and Import Vulnerability in the 1980s,' *Canadian Journal of Political Science* 15 (June 1982):259-98

Halliday, Fred. *The Making of the Second Cold War*. Halifax: Institute for Research on Public Policy 1990

Hart, Michael. *A North American Free Trade Agreement*. Halifax: Institute for Research on Public Policy 1990

Helleiner, G.K. 'Canada, the Developing Countries and the International Economy: What Next?' *Journal of Canadian Studies* 19:4(1984):16-27

Hillmer, Norman, ed. *Partners Nevertheless: Canadian-American Relations in the Twentieth Century*. Toronto: Clark Copp Pitman 1989

Hufbauer, G. and J. Schott. *North American Free Trade*. Washington, DC: Institute for International Economics 1992

Humphrey, John. *The Inter-American System: A Canadian View*. Toronto: Macmillan 1942

Hurtig, Mel. *The Betrayal of Canada*. Toronto: Stoddart 1991

Keenleyside, H.L. 'The Canada-United States Permanent Joint Board on Defence, 1940-45,' *International Journal* 16 (Winter 1960-1):50-77

Keohane, Robert. *Neorealism and Its Critics*. New York: Columbia University Press 1986

Kissinger, Henry et al. *Report of the President's National Bipartisan Commission on Central America*. New York: Macmillan 1984

Klepak, Hal. *Canada and Latin America: Strategic Issues for the 1990s*. Ottawa: Canadian Department of National Defence 1990

LeFeber, Walter. *Inevitable Revolutions: The United States in Central America*. New York: Norton 1983

–. *The American Age: United States Foreign Policy at Home and Abroad Since 1750*.

New York: Norton 1989

Lemco, Jonathan. *Canada and the Crisis in Central America.* New York: Praeger 1991

Lowenthal, Abraham. 'Latin America: Ready for Partnership?' *Foreign Affairs* 72 (1993):81-103

Lyon, Peyton, and T. Ismael, eds. *Canada and the Third World.* Toronto: Macmillan 1976.

McDowall, Duncan. *The Light: Brazilian Traction, Light and Power Company Ltd., 1899-1945.* Toronto: University of Toronto Press 1988

MacLeod, Murdo. *Spanish Central America: A Socioeconomic History, 1520-1720.* Los Angeles: University of California Press 1973

Miller, Eugene. 'Canada and the Pan American Union,' *International Journal* 3 (1947):66-82

Murray, D.R. 'Canada's First Diplomatic Missions in Latin America,' *Journal of Inter-American Studies and World Affairs* 16 (May 1974):12-31

North, Liisa. *Bitter Grounds: Roots of Revolt in El Salvador.* Toronto: Between The Lines 1981

–. *Negotiations for Peace in Central America.* Ottawa: Canadian Institute for International Peace and Security 1985

– and CAPA, eds. *Between War and Peace in Central America.* Toronto: Between The Lines 1990

Ogelsby, J.C.M. *Gringos from the Far North: Essays in the History of Canadian-Latin American Relations, 1866-1968.* Toronto: Macmillan 1976

Ostry, Sylvia. *Governments and Corporations in a Shrinking World.* New York: Council on Foreign Relations 1990

Podea, Iris. 'Pan-American Sentiment in French Canada,' *International Journal* 3 (Autumn 1948):21-36

Porter, Michael. *Canada at the Crossroads: The Reality of a New Competitive Environment.* Ottawa: Business Council on National Issues and Supply and Services Canada 1991

Reich, Robert. *The Work of Nations: Preparing Ourselves for 21st-century Capitalism.* New York: Knopf 1991

Rochlin, James. 'Aspects of Canadian Foreign Policy Towards Central America, 1974-86,' *Journal of Canadian Studies* 22 (Winter 1988):5-26

–. 'The Evolution of Canada as an Actor in Inter-American Affairs,' *Millennium* 19 (Summer 1990):229-48

–. 'The Political Economy of Canadian Relations With Central America,' *North/South: Canadian Journal of Latin American and Caribbean Studies* 13 (1988):45-70

Schoultz, Lars. *National Security and United States Foreign Policy Towards Latin America.* Princeton, NJ: Princeton University Press 1987

Scott, Peter and Jonathan Marshall. *Cocaine Politics: Drugs, Armies and the CIA in Central America.* Los Angeles: University of California Press 1991

Skidmore, Thomas. *Modern Latin America.* Toronto: Oxford University Press 1984

Soward, Frank and A. Macauley. *Canada and The Pan American System.* Toronto: Canadian Institute of International Affairs 1948

Whitaker, Reg. *Double Standards: The Secret History of Canadian Immigration.* Toronto: Lester and Orpen Dennys 1987

Woodward, Ralph. *Central America, a Nation Divided.* New York: Oxford University Press 1985

Wyse, Peter. *Canadian Foreign Aid in the 1970s: An Organizational Audit.* Montreal: Centre for Developing Area Studies 1983

Index